The Civilization of the American Indian Series

THE AUTHOR

W. David Baird received the Ph.D. degree from the University of Oklahoma. He is presently Chairman of the Department of History in Oklahoma State University. Baird is the author of several books, among them *Peter Pitchlynn: Chief of the Choctaws,* also published by the University of Oklahoma Press.

THE QUAPAW INDIANS
A HISTORY OF THE
DOWNSTREAM PEOPLE

W. DAVID BAIRD

THE QUAPAW INDIANS

A HISTORY OF THE DOWNSTREAM PEOPLE

University of Oklahoma Press: Norman

BOOKS BY W. DAVID BAIRD

Peter Pitchlynn: Chief of the Choctaws (Norman, 1972)

The Quapaw Indians: A History of the Downstream People (Norman, 1980)

Library of Congress Cataloging in Publication Data

Baird, W. David.
    The Quapaw Indians.

(The Civilization of the American Indian series;
v. 152)
    Bibliography: p. 269
    Includes index.
    1.   Quapaw Indians—History.   I.   Title.
II.   Series: Civilization of the American Indian
series; v. 152.
E99.Q2B33   970'.004'97   79-4731

The Quapaw Indians: A History of the Downstream People is Volume 152 in *The
Civilization of the American Indian Series.*

For Jane, Angela, and Anthony

PREFACE

Living in northeastern Oklahoma are the remnants of a people whose place in American history has never been fully recognized. The Quapaw Indians deserve a better fate. During the eighteenth century both France and Spain looked to them to uphold their imperial ambitions west of the Mississippi River. Originally natives of Arkansas, the Quapaws were initially a valuable ally to the United States as well, but were later judged as impediments to the agricultural exploitation of the Arkansas River valley and in time were removed to Indian Territory. Reservation life was traumatic and stimulated major transformations of traditional lifeways, resulting in profound accommodations to alien cultural patterns. As a consequence, in 1893 the Quapaws unilaterally allotted their reservation and all but abandoned their tribal life in common. The process of assimilation was accelerated by the great wealth that accrued to individual members of the tribe following the discovery of lead and zinc ore on the reservation. Indeed, the mining boom of the 1920's made some of the Quapaws among the richest people in the world. Today gigantic piles of chat give mute testimony to those glory years, for the mines are abandoned and the money is gone. The assimilation of the Quapaw people, however, continued uninterrupted until the late 1950's, when the tribe determined to reclaim and preserve some of the traditions that once had made it distinctive.

After 300 years of accommodation to the so-called white man's way, the Quapaws would seem to merit a study of their history. In the pages that follow, the story of the tribe appears in the general context of Indian-white relations. Yet at the same time I have attempted to focus on how the Quapaws coped with both internal and external forces affecting them. Accommodation is viewed as a creative response by the tribe rather than as the end result of dispossession and oppression. In addition to emphasizing the "Indian side," I have carried the present work through 1975. Studies of other tribes generally end with allotment, but to close the Quapaw story with 1893 would leave much of it untold. I have attempted to be discreet when dealing with some facets of the twentieth century, particularly the impact of wealth upon specific families.

If this work has merit it is, in part, because others have provided notable assistance. Research began in 1971 with the aid of a generous grant from the American Philosophical Society. Robert Kvasnicka at the National Archives in Washington, D.C., shepherded me through the voluminous records in his custody. Equally helpful were George Younkin at the Federal Records Center in Fort Worth, Texas, Mrs. Rella Looney at the Oklahoma Historical Society in Oklahoma City, Russell Baker at the Arkansas History Commission in Little Rock, and Mrs. Harold Hantz at the University of Arkansas Library in Fayetteville. Special thanks go also to Professor James Chase, whose support of this project was monumental, and to Professor James A. Wisman for assistance in duplicating photographs. And I am indebted to Professor Orland Maxfield of the University of Arkansas for his kindness in preparing the maps for this volume.

I would be remiss not to extend special appreciation also to Robert Whitebird, Jess McKibben, Mrs. Odie McWatters, and Mrs. Charles Banks Wilson, respectively the spiritual leader, chairman, and historians of the Quapaw Tribe. Their assistance was invaluable and to work with them was an honor. Research for this study would have been especially difficult had it not been for the hospitality of my brother, Marvin Baird, and his family in McLean, Virginia. And completion of the project would have been impossible without the understanding of my children, Angela and Anthony. Only six and four when the manuscript was in preparation, they asked no more than that their father eat breakfast and play "just a little bit" with them. That they are what they are, of course, is due to their mother, Jane, who not only has done double duty at home but continues to type my manuscripts in her spare time. Because she is incomparable and her children remarkable, this book is dedicated to them.

W. DAVID BAIRD

Stillwater, Oklahoma

CONTENTS

ILLUSTRATIONS

MAPS

THE QUAPAW INDIANS
A HISTORY OF THE
DOWNSTREAM PEOPLE

CHAPTER I
THE
DOWNSTREAM
PEOPLE

When ethnologists Alice C. Fletcher and Francis La Flesche were assembling material for their widely acclaimed study, *The Omaha Tribe*, they encountered difficulty in securing relevant information on a cognate tribe, the Quapaw Indians. "All is gone; gone long ago," their informants sadly reported.[1] Unfortunately, the passage of nearly seventy-five additional years has not made any easier the task of reconstructing Quapaw society as it existed when first encountered by Europeans. Yet by drawing upon archeological studies, tribal traditions, and documentary evidence, a reasonably adequate though not always precise picture of tribal lifeways does emerge.

Unlike other Indian peoples, the Quapaws have not preserved elaborate traditions explaining the genesis of their ancestors. Indeed, they remember only that their Ancient Ones issued forth from the water. Beyond that, their traditions assert that at one time they and their Dhegiha Sioux kinsmen—the Omahas, Osages, Kansas, and Poncas—lived in the Ohio Valley and that sometime before 1673 they migrated west and southwest to the locations where they were first observed by Europeans. Although sketchy and imprecise, similar accounts have also been preserved by the other components of the Dhegiha Sioux family, all of whom, though widely dispersed, speak the same language.[2]

Because they imply that the Quapaws and their kinsmen would have participated in the splendid Hopewellian culture that flourished in the Ohio Valley, these traditions are generally rejected by professional archeologists.[3] Such a conclusion, though, seems to ignore a rather impressive array of documentary as well as archeological evidence, not to mention the well-established tradition itself. One of the earliest identifiable cultures of the Ohio Valley was that of the Indian Knoll people. Centering in northern Kentucky, these folk of the Archaic period sustained themselves by hunting and fishing, especially mussels or clams. The empty shells and other camp refuse soon accumulated into large mounds on the top of which villages were later established. In time the tribe moved across the Ohio into southern Indiana and Illinois. Because the Omaha Indians during historic times had a large clam shell in the sacred bundles of the tribe, and the Quapaws traced their origin to water and had subdivisions named for the fish and turtle, it seems possible that the Dhegiha Sioux were associated with this Indian Knoll complex.[4]

In Early Woodland times a peaceful immigration of southern Indians altered the established culture patterns of the Ohio Valley. Bringing with them elaborate funeral ceremonies and the practice of burying the dead in large mounds, the new arrivals are known as Adena folk, after the estate near Chillicothe, Ohio, where their mounds were first excavated. The Adenas introduced their new religion as the more numerous Indian Knoll people began making pottery, planting crops, and using tobacco. A social revolution resulted, embracing both newcomers and older inhabitants, manifesting itself in large population concentrations, multiple family houses, a highly organized social order, ceremonial centers, and a faith that venerated gods in the sky as opposed to earth-bound animal gods. The Adena culture reached its apex in what has been called the Hopewellian era, which was renowned for its great wealth and splendor. Conical burial mounds were filled with skillfully fashioned grave offerings made of exotic minerals, metals, rare stones, and organic materials that were imported from as far away as the Rocky Mountains and the Gulf of Mexico. Equally impressive were the long earthen embankments that were frequently constructed into effigy figures, the most notable being the Great Serpent Mound of Ohio.[5]

Although archeologists may take exception to the idea, what is known about the Adena-Hopewellian Indians does not contradict the Dhegiha Sioux tradition that their ancestors were residents of the Ohio Valley in prehistoric times. Indeed, there is much to suggest that the post-contact Quapaws and their kinsmen were the remnants of the Mound Builders, although it is a conclusion not always measurable by artifacts. In historic times, for example, the Dhegihas had a form of religion that corresponded to that of the Hopewellians, featuring a pantheon of sky spirits and earth-bound gods. Both, moreover, venerated the serpent. Further, the highly developed ceremonial life of the historic Dhegiha Sioux was, unlike other tribes identified with the Mound Builders, similar to that which must have existed among the Hopewellians. Finally, hair styles of the two groups were one and the same.[6]

In addition to archeology, a considerable amount of documentary evidence can be marshalled in support of the tradition of an early Quapaw residence in the Ohio Valley. When the French came into the Mississippi River valley the tribes they first encountered still had a clear recollection of when the Dhegiha Sioux lived along the Ohio. In 1673 an Illinois Indian, for example, identified the Quapaws for Father Marquette as the "Akansea," an Algonquin word. Father Douay, who was with LaSalle in 1686–87, noted that the Akansea once lived in the Ohio Valley but were driven out by the Iroquois "some years ago." In 1700, Father Gravier wrote that the Illinois Indians called the Ohio River the Akansea, "because the Akansea [the Quapaw group] formerly dwelt upon it." Moreover, a Dutch map dated 1720 placed the Akansea tribe on the south bank of the lower Ohio, while the so-called Popple Map, 1733, designated the Cumberland River of Kentucky as the "Akanseapi." Thus, the earliest records available not only confirm the Quapaw traditions but suggest that the Dhegiha Sioux were in the Ohio Valley as recently as late prehistoric or early historic times.[7]

With our knowledge of the Indian Knoll-Adena-Hopewellian complexes not contradicting tribal traditions, and with documentary evidence supporting it, why then did the French first encounter the Quapaws on the lower Mississippi River near its confluence with the Arkansas? In other words, what circumstances prompted the Ohio Valley exodus? Far to the east in what is now upper New York State the Iroquoian people by 1570 had organized their renowned confederation. Supplied with guns by the Dutch after 1614, they warred in earnest upon the French allied Hurons and destroyed them in 1648. Next they turned to the Neutrals (1650–51) and then to the Eries (1653–56), the reduction of whom placed the Iroquois in the Ohio Valley watershed. If we are to believe the Delaware Indian tradition recorded in the Walam Olum, a similar invasion of Algonquin people occurred simultaneously. And somewhat earlier, from the south other peoples with a temple mound culture pushed northward, establishing themselves at such centers as Cahokia near present St. Louis, Illinois. These militant invaders provided the *coup de grace* for the Hopewellian complex that had begun to fade even before 1450. For the Dhegiha Sioux, of course, the alien penetration necessitated an abandonment of their prehistoric homeland and a migration to more distant lands.[8]

The Quapaws and their kinsmen, though, did not flee all at once or in disarray. The process was a lengthy one, perhaps encompassing a century or more. According to the various tribal traditions, when the Dhegihas in their westward movement reached the Mississippi, they attempted to cross the river in skin boats. After the Osages had reached the western shore, a heavy mist arose, preventing the rest of the migrants from crossing. The Omahas went north up the river and crossed in the vicinity of present Des Moines. The Quapaws, however, went downstream, later to appear on the Arkansas River. To their kindred tribes they were thereafter known as Ugaxpa, or "drifted-downstream."[9]

Although there are minor variations of the emigration tradition,[10] one essential fact is clear. As the Dhegiha Sioux migrated westward, its member tribes separated and went different ways, with the Quapaws moving south along the eastern shore of the Mississippi, eventually establishing themselves on the west bank above and on the Arkansas River. Indeed, this migration was still in process when the French entered the region in 1673, for one of the tribal villages was still on the east bank of the Mississippi.[11] Theirs, moreover, was undoubtedly a militant penetration. French visitors, for example, recorded an ancient animosity that existed between the Quapaws and Chickasaws, their immediate neighbors to the east. An 1827 account preserved by George Izard, governor of Arkansas Territory, also asserted that the Downstream People led by Chief Paheka had forcibly displaced the Tonnika (Tunica) and Illinois Indians.[12] Interestingly, the Izard document corresponds with what the Europeans first observed. In 1682 the Tunicas were situated below the Quapaws near the mouth of the Yazoo River, and nine years earlier Marquette set down on his map a Michigamea (Illinois) village just west of them.[13]

The Quapaws not only forced their way into their historic domain, but they also apparently occupied the village sites of previous inhabitants. In 1698, Father St. Cosme observed that New Kappa, centered around an artificial mound about forty feet high, was located on the Mississippi River where no previous settlement had

Quapaw pottery, Mainard site. Courtesy Arkansas Archaeological Survey.

existed twelve years before. Given the recent occupation of the site, the mound must have been the legacy of earlier residents.[14] Moreover, recent excavations at Osotouy, the only site identified as a Quapaw village that has thus far been given careful attention by archeologists, have revealed a form of pottery known as Wallace Incised. Strikingly similar to the pottery usually identified with the Oneota complex which flourished between 1600 and 1640 among the Sioux in the upper Mississippi Valley and among the Osages of the Ozark Mountains, it has been dismissed as a superficial addition to a culture that was basically of the local Mississippian pattern.[15] Yet these "superficial additions" may have marked the arrival of new occupants who brought with them a style of pottery adopted earlier. If that was the case, then at Osotouy the Quapaws not only settled a previously inhabited site but fashioned and decorated their pottery according to the custom adopted when the Dhegiha Sioux shared a common residence farther up the river during the Oneota period.

The Downstream People, therefore, were recent arrivals in the Arkansas and Mississippi River region when they were first encountered by the French in 1673. Pushed out of their Ohio Valley settlements after 1600 by well-armed Iroquoian and Algonquin invaders, they and their Dhegiha Sioux kinsmen moved slowly westward toward the Mississippi. In those villages established during the course of their migration, they retained many of the religious and social characteristics that identified them as Hopewellians, but they also acquired some of the traits common to the prevailing Oneota culture. For some reason that is not historically discernible, the Dhegihas separated. By the mid-seventeenth century the Quapaws turned down the Mississippi, pushing before them previous occupants of the region and not hesitating to establish their own communities on the ruins of the dispossessed. The lateness of the migration explains why, in the 1680's and 1690's, Illinois Indians could easily recall that the Akansea or Quapaws once dwelled in the Ohio Valley and, in 1827, that Governor Izard's informant would assert that the grandfather of the then principal chief of the Downstream People led the tribe in its southward trek.[16]

The view that the Quapaws arrived in the lower Mississippi and Arkansas River valleys in the mid-seventeenth century contradicts the once widely held view that they were the people DeSoto encountered in 1541.[17] Based largely upon the fact that the sixteenth-century Pacahas and the Quapaws occupied the same region, the latter position has now been rejected by historians, most ethnologists, and some archeologists. Several factors account for the new conclusion. For one thing, the Pacahas ruled over a small-scale empire, whereas the seventeenth-century Quapaws were associated on terms of comparative equality. For another, the people whom DeSoto met maintained a temple mound, a feature unknown to the Downstream People. Moreover, the Pacaha villages were enclosed by stockades, structures that were not in evidence when the French arrived in the valley. Thus, in 1938 the DeSoto Commission, charged with the responsibility of determining the route of the Spanish explorer, concluded that the Pacahas were a branch of the Tunica and not Quapaws.[18] Laboriously made, the conclusion was not without precedent. A century earlier Governor Izard's informant had specified the Tunica as that tribe displaced by the invading Downstream People.

When first encountered by Europeans, therefore, the Quapaws had just established hegemony in a new homeland. Having previously supported a dense population and nurtured an impressive Indian civilization, the domain offered limitless opportunities to its new occupants. Dominating the region, of course, were the Mississippi and Arkansas rivers. Other streams of significance included the St.

Francis and the White, both of which emptied separately into the Mississippi from the west just above the mouth of the Arkansas. These rivers linked the Quapaws with tribes both north and south and gave easy access to the forested Ozark Mountains, the vast expanse of the Great Plains, and even the distant Rocky Mountains. Over the centuries, due to periodic floods, they had also laid down a sheet of alluvial soil rich in organic matter that sustained a forest cover of cypress, elm, pine, cottonwood, willow, oak, walnut, hickory, and maple. Upland prairies, some of considerable extent, dotted the landscape as well. With a gentle, humid subtropical climate that provided as many as fifty inches of rain and two hundred frost-free days each year, the habitat of the Downstream People was rich indeed.

As they had done during their residence in the Ohio Valley, the Quapaws developed a culture carefully tuned to this natural environment. This fact was particularly apparent in the way they sustained themselves. Using spears and nets they took from the rivers different species of fish and turtles. The forest provided an abundance of roots, nuts, and fruits, particularly paw paws, haws, grapes, persimmons, hackberries, plums, mulberries, hickory nuts, walnuts, pecans, and acorns. Still more important was the meat furnished by geese, bustards, ducks, turkeys, marshhens, swans, hazels, grouse, pheasants, partridges, rabbits, bears, wildcats, deer, and bison.

Of all the forest creatures upon which the Downstream People subsisted, probably none was as important as the buffalo. So significant was it to their lifeway that tribal hunters periodically ranged as far west as the Wichita Mountains in southwestern Oklahoma and were especially alert upon approaching salt springs. Moreover, they engaged in elaborate rituals immediately before and just after the animal was killed. On the day of the actual hunt they fasted and painted their bodies black. After the kill, the head of the buffalo was dyed red and covered with the down of the swan and bustard; the clefts of its hoofs and nostrils were stuffed with tobacco; its tongue was excised and the mouth was also filled with tobacco; and pieces of its flesh were placed on a horizontal bar held above the ground by two small forked sticks. The gods having been properly approached and thanked, the butchering process was completed and the meat dried preparatory to the return trip to the tribal settlements.[19]

Although the food resulting from fishing, gathering, and hunting provided a substantial part of the tribe's diet, an even greater portion was supplied by agriculture. The first European visitors all noted the abundance of vegetables, specifically gourds, pumpkins, sunflowers, beans, squash, and corn. Of the annual crops, corn was most important, leading one Jesuit missionary to observe that the Quapaws lived on nothing "scarcely" but it. If the Jesuit calculated correctly, then cultivation of this crop was extensive. With an estimated population of 15,000 to 20,000 in 1682, hundreds of acres of corn would have been necessary to sustain the Downstream People from year to year. Indeed, in 1687 Henri Joutel observed one field on the Mississippi that was a league in width and a league and a half in length, or about eight and a half square miles, and a host of smaller fields south of the Arkansas River.

In addition to vegetables, the Quapaws also seemingly cultivated different varieties of fruits. Two of the earliest French visitors recorded seeing watermelons, while two others observed peaches. Since both species are Old World in origin, they must have been transported to the lower Arkansas valley via Spanish settlements in Florida or Mexico before the penetration of the Downstream People. No less curious was the presence of what Europeans took to be domesticated animals, namely "cocks and hens," turkeys, and bustards. Whatever the status of these flocks, they, along with a surprising fruit and intensive vegetable culture, showed that the Quapaws were agriculturalists of remarkable ability.[20]

The abundance of the field and the forest provided the Downstream People with a harvest that had to be stored and then prepared for individual consumption. They kept their corn in large baskets made of cane or in gourds as large as half-barrels. Later it was made into hominy (sagamity) or ground into meal preparatory to being cooked by wrapping a mixture of meal and beans in corn leaves and boiling the whole. The Quapaws also produced a tasty beverage by crushing grapes in water. When not used immediately, both meat and fruit were dried and stored for later use. Once prepared for consumption, meals were served on oval wooden platters or in clay pots and eaten by means of a spoon made of a buffalo horn.[21]

The focus of Quapaw life was the permanent village. The French counted four of these: Tourima and Osotouy on the north side of the Arkansas River, the former near the river's mouth and the latter sixteen miles west; Tongigua on the east bank of the Mississippi, eleven miles above the Arkansas; and Kappa on the west side, ten miles farther north. The towns were in reality clusters of multiple family dwellings, each of which was of rectangular design and constructed of long poles driven into the ground, arched together at the top, and covered with cypress bark and cane mats. Inside the house the Quapaws built elevated sleeping platforms along the outer edges as well as fireplaces for each individual family unit. As refuse from household activities gathered outside the structure, the resultant depression inside was filled with clay to prevent water from draining inward and to provide a hard-surfaced floor more easily kept clean. In the summer they raised sleeping platforms fifteen to twenty feet high outside the dwelling to take advantage of better air circulation and to gain some protection from mosquitoes.[22]

Each community also contained at least two structures not directly related to family activities. One, of the same design as the house but considerably larger, was centrally located and served as a focal point for tribal ceremonies and public gatherings. Several hundred Quapaws could assemble in this public facility. The other, which had a flat roof supported by four corner poles and a carpet of fine rush mats, headquartered the local chief when the weather permitted. It was to this place that guests were first escorted when they visited the village. Although not elaborate, these structures and the individual domiciles were functional and adequately served the needs of the tribe.[23]

In their personal appearance, the Downstream People were impressive. One Frenchman judged them "the best formed Savages we have seen," while another described them as "better made" than northern Indians, while still another reckoned them "as the largest and handsomest of all the Indians of this continent" and worthy of the characterization, les beaux hommes, or "the handsome men."[24] For the most part their complexions were dark, their eyes elongated, and their features aquiline. Because of the gentle climate, dress was not a matter of great concern for the Quapaws. The men were observed as "stark naked," donning buffalo robes only during the winter months. European influence later encouraged more traditional Indian attire, such as moccasins, leggings, breech-cloth, and a hunting shirt that was seamed up and slipped over the head.[25] Wrapping themselves only in a deer skin that reached from the waist to the knees, Quapaw women were adjudged "half-naked." Thus, wrote an American traveler in 1791, they "very innocently displayed their Navals, [although] the curious eye might have explored other parts which civilized Nations industriously conceal."[26] Men plucked their body hair and fashioned the hair on their head into a scalplock. Women, on the other hand, braided their hair into two plaits which they brought around to either ear in a cylindric form. After marriage the braids were unfolded and the hair brought together behind their heads in a single lock. To adorn themselves, men intertwined rings, feathers, and beads in their scalplocks and hung pendants of beads on their ears and nose. Women ornamented their hair similarly prior to marriage. Habits of bodily cleanliness and characteristics of honesty, fidelity, constraint, and lightheartedness added still other dimensions to the general attractiveness of the Quapaws.[27]

The social organization of the Downstream People had its basis in the family unit. Marriage between non-relatives occurred only after parental approval and was announced publicly by a simple and frugal ceremony. The groom presented his bride with a leg of deer, and she in turn extended to him an ear of corn. The rite usually occurred about sunrise, but the couple generally remained separated till sunset. Only then was the marriage physically consummated. Although it might happen that the groom would later take another wife, polygamy was not common among the Quapaws. At the same time, divorce was as frequent as it was simple. The father could recall his daughter from her husband's household if his son-in-law became obnoxious to her, while the husband could abandon his wife if she became odious to his family.[28] Or, in the words of a twentieth-century chief: "No courts or attorney fee—just quit."[29] Easy divorces did not mean, however, that children were not cherished. Upon the birth of a child, during a sunrise ritual, he received a personal name from a tribal elder. Not only did this identify him with a specific social unit, but it insured him of a full and lengthy life. In due course, he imitated his parents and established still another family fireside.[30]

Among the Quapaws, individual family units were grouped together into a myriad of clans and subclans and took for their name a member of the animal kingdom or some cosmic phenomenon. These names included Deer, Elk, Black Bear, Grizzly Bear, Buffalo, Beaver, Dog, Panther, Fish, Turtle, Serpent, Eagle, Small Bird, Crane, Star, Thunder, and Sun clans. Identification with a particular clan or subclan was determined by heredity, the line of descent on the father's side. Thus both male and female children were reckoned as members of the paternal social unit. The clan system gave individual Quapaws a spiritual identity and morally obligated each to help and shield one another in times of personal crisis. More important was its regulation of marriage. Because fellow clan members were related by blood or were considered relatives, they were not permitted to marry one another; that is, the tribe was exogamous.[31]

The Downstream People grouped the clans into two major divisions, or moieties. One of these was the *Hānka*; the name of the other was not preserved, although it may have been *Tīju*. As among their Dhegiha Sioux kinsmen, one of these groups was doubtlessly associated with the land and the other with the sky. Membership descended through the male line, and exogamy was practiced, but because the Quapaws were a Woodland people, they did not express the complementary nature of their grand divisions in spatial terms when camping on a hunting expedition.[32] On the whole, however, the social organization of the Quapaws does not seem to have been as fully developed as that of their Dhegiha relatives. This may have been because the early seventeenth-century separation from their kinsmen was so wrenching that the tribal social structure never recovered. More probably, the traumatic experiences following European contact so obliterated tribal ties and traditions that late nineteenth-century Quapaws were unable to convey a different impression.

The governmental organization of the Quapaws reflected the four-part physical division of the tribe. Each of the towns had a single, hereditary chief who was responsible for making decisions affecting his community. On critical matters involving the whole tribe, the four chiefs apparently consulted with each other. Decisions made on those occasions were generally honored but never blindly accepted by each political unit. Although their authority was paramount, the chiefs were by no means autocrats. All major determinations were made in light of deliberations by the tribal elders. In addition to respected counselors, a contingent of younger men selected on the basis of their wartime conquests waited upon the chief, responding to his personal directions and needs. On ceremonial occasions, these younger men and the elders stationed themselves immediately posterior to the chief, while the other men of the tribe gathered farther behind and in front of the women and children. Slaves, Indians taken in battle and representing the lowest level of tribal political and social life, were not included in the deliberations of the Downstream People.[33]

The presence of slaves in the different settlements reflected the significance of war in tribal lifeways. Indeed, for the Quapaws it was a matter of central importance. Having violently expelled the previous inhabitants of their homeland, they were subject to frequent retaliatory raids from tribes farther south and to attacks from the warlike Chickasaws east of the Mississippi. Moreover, by 1673 they had not yet consolidated their control of the immediate region and were required to make expeditions against Illinois Indians farther west. Although small parties might have taken independent actions, the Downstream People acting in concert made the decision for war. On such an occasion the Quapaws gathered in the council house, where they were addressed by a chief or an orator who proclaimed the necessity for combat. At the conclusion of the speech, the chief held out a bundle of twigs, and all the men who wanted to fight enlisted by taking one. Assembling the next morning, the warriors watched one of their number paint red a club which would be carried to the edge of enemy territory and placed by a tree upon which they would also carve and paint red two crossed arrows. Red denoted that the Quapaws wanted revenge and would not be satisfied until enemy blood was shed.[34]

Before actually setting forth to the contest, the chief held another council to which he invited any allied tribe. A feast of dog flesh, as well as singing and dancing, followed. All the young men were painted red for the war dance, during which the participants acted out the imminent attack and the taking of scalps. In the wake of the pulsating event, the warriors consulted their guardian spirit, or manitou, painted their bodies red, and prepared their weapons. In the meantime the chief or leader of the war party had purged his body, painted it black, and fasted. Later he washed and also painted himself red, exhorted his followers, and set out with them to encounter the enemy.[35] After the battle, some of the younger warriors left immediately to carry the news of victory to their villages. Through a system of cries they announced how many of the enemy had been killed, the number of prisoners taken, and how many scalps had been taken. Whether the captives, who were bound and painted black, lived or died was determined by the women. Those who had lost a husband or a son in the battle had the right to make one of the prisoners a slave to replace the deceased. The captives not adopted were then burned to death over a slow fire.[36]

Yet intercourse with different Indian groups did not always involve warfare. As often as not, relations with other tribes were peaceful, including nothing more than commerce. The Quapaws, for example, exchanged earthen vessels, wooden platters, and canoes with the Caddoes on Red River for bows and arrows and salt. So significant was this trade that a well-established trace or route existed between the settlements of the two tribes. After the arrival of the Europeans but before they had reached the Mississippi Valley, the Downstream People also sought a mutual commerce with Indians who had already obtained manufactured items from the white man. In quest of knives, hatchets, and beads, they traded with eastern tribes who had connections with the Spanish in Florida and with "California" Indians who carried goods over the plains from New Mexico. By 1679, perhaps in an effort to by-pass middlemen, the Quapaws were pushing north into Illinois in an attempt to establish commercial relations directly with the French.[37]

That the Quapaws were able to sustain an extensive trade suggested the quality of their workmanship. Their pottery, for example, was in appearance symmetrically pleasing, delicately designed, and tastefully painted. The type of ceramics ranged from bowls to teapots and from platters to effigies. Their canoes were just as remarkable. Called "bateaux" by the French, these vessels were basically dugouts fashioned from large cypress logs and capable of carrying at least twenty persons. The artistic proclivities of the Downstream People also found expression through painting designs on deer and buffalo skins. Using different colors extracted from clay, they depicted pipes, birds, and animals on the dried hides that were then used as table or bed coverings.[38] Although it was not related to their commerce, another skillful expression of their culture was music. Gourd rattles and drums constructed of dried skins stretched over either end of a ceramic cylinder provided accompaniment for songs and rhythmic dances. Considered no more than a "roar" and as "monotonous and fatiguing to the Ear" by some observers, such music when combined with a dance seemed to others as comparing favorably with the opening of a ballet in Paris.[39]

No manifestation of the Quapaw culture, however, was as sublime as that of their religion. To be sure their faith was not as

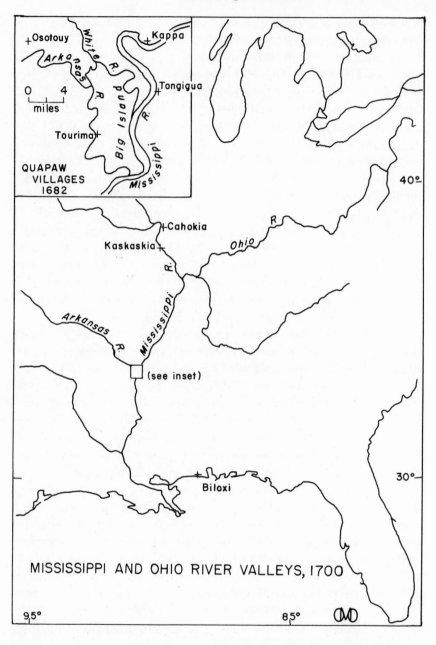

Mississippi and Ohio river valleys, showing location of Quapaw villages.

institutionalized as that of some of their neighbors, especially the Natchez, but it underlay every aspect of tribal life. The central force of the universe was *Wah-kon-tah*, "the mysterious life power permeating all natural forms and forces and all phases of man's conscious life." Thus, in some indefinable way each Quapaw was related to such diverse natural phenomena as clouds, rocks, and animals. Because *Wah-kon-tah* was all and in all, the Downstream People revered the animate and the inanimate, the seen and the unseen, and the known and the unknown. In the celestial world the sun and the moon were held in particular esteem, while in the terrestrial world the serpent, or *We-sa-pa-ktean-ka-han*, was of special importance.[40]

The pantheon of Quapaw gods also included lesser spirits. The *Ke-jan-qa* was a small species of water tortoise, the tail of which no one lifted lest there be a deluge. Infrequently seen but still important were two types of dwarfs, the *Pahi-zka-jika*, small ones with white hair, and the *Wakantake-jika*, small mysterious ones. The *Tannan*, or thunder people, made their abode in the upper world, as did special folk who walked the Milky Way, or the Road of the Ghosts. In addition to these and other deities that accounted for the frequent inexplicable happenings of everyday life, individual Quapaws usually selected some sacred object as their guardian spirit, or manitou. To this they attributed both their good and bad fortune. And the tribe as a whole revered a collection of similar objects which were carefully wrapped in skins and concealed in the house of the chief. This sacred bundle was never put on display and was moved only when the entire community changed residences.[41]

The eschatology of the Downstream People included a belief in an existence after death and implied a judgment that consigned one to a life of joy or to perpetual torment. When death occurred, loved ones buried the body in or just outside the family dwelling or adjacent to the tombs of those previously deceased. Grave offerings were interred with the remains or placed upon and above the burial mounds. The practice of hanging offerings and the personal effects of the dead on upright stakes led one observer to characterize a Quapaw cemetery as "a forest of poles and posts. . . ." These offerings, of course, were to supply the needs of the departed on his long journey into eternity. After a reasonable length of time, the fact that the provisions remained unused was calculated as a sure sign that the dead had arrived at a bountiful hunting ground. In addition to leaving grave offerings, relatives also mourned for the deceased. Men and women together wept and wailed each sunrise and sunset. Small fires were frequently built near the burial site if the dead had been interred beyond the family dwelling. If the grave was within or just outside the living unit, apparently the whole structure was set aflame. The fire presumably warmed the body of the dead during its final journey.[42]

In consulting the deities, the Quapaws relied upon the intercessions of worldly intermediaries. This group of Holy Men was called the *Wapinan*. Although they belonged to different societies, as a class they plumbed the mysteries of *Wah-kon-tah* and sought to interpret the Life Force to their people. They presided at tribal ceremonies, supervised the performance of religious rituals and advised tribal leaders on issues of great moment. They also performed feats of magic, probably in an effort to confirm their own authority. One Holy Man pushed a seventeen-inch deer rib down through his throat into his stomach and then extracted it by pulling the exposed part of the bone out through his mouth. But the most important prerogative of the *Wapinan* was the bestowing of personal names. Because these names contributed to the success or failure of one's life, the Holy Men thus exercised an enormous influence upon individual members of the tribe. Perhaps of more significance, they were able to perpetuate some of the timeless traditions of the Downstream People.[43]

In addition to the intercessions of *Wapinan*, the Quapaws sought divine blessing by means of elaborate ritual and ceremony. Foremost of these was the sacred dance of the calumet. A special kind of pipe, the calumet was made of polished red stone pierced so that one end received the tobacco and the other end was attached to a hollow reed some two feet long. To the stone bowl were attached different colored feathers. In significance the pipe itself seemed to be the "god of peace and war, the arbiter of life and death." Moreover, it had some relationship to the sun, to which it was offered if calm, rain, or fair weather was desired.[44]

The Quapaws also used the calumet to cement friendly relations with other Indians or distinguished guests. On such occasions the pipe became the central focus of a dance that extended through the night. The one to be favored with the ceremony was escorted to the center of the council house, where his face was washed and he was given a seat of honor. Before him two red painted, forked sticks were stuck ritualistically into the ground; another was laid horizontally upon the two; buffalo and goat skins were draped over all; and the calumet was placed upon the hides. The Indians sang, rattled gourds, drummed and swayed, with those nearest the guest clasping his shoulders and rocking him to the tempo of the music. Later a feather was added to his hair. As the ceremony progressed, dancers would strike poles erected for the occasion and recount brave deeds accomplished during warfare. At the proper moment, usually the next morning, the tobacco in the pipe was lighted and ceremoniously presented to the visitor. After all had smoked, the dance concluded, and the pipe was wrapped in the skins and given to the feted one. He in turn was expected to reciprocate with presents of his own. This latter feature led some Europeans to conclude cynically that the Quapaws danced the calumet for the purpose of extracting gifts only.[45]

The Downstream People also importuned the deities in an effort to insure the success of their agricultural endeavors. Before planting, the women selected a lean dog and, as an act of sacrifice, devoured it alive. After the harvest, the Quapaws did not fail to thank *Wah-kon-tah* for the bounty. When the maize was in its milk, they danced the Green Corn Dance, a celebration both of joy and renewal.[46]

Ceremonialism and ritual even surrounded the serving of meals, especially when guests were present. On such occasions the host served the food in two to four dishes, placing them first before the honored visitor. After he had eaten, the plates were pushed to the person nearest the guest, who then ate his fill. The process continued until all had been served. The host replenished the dishes when necessary, taking care not to eat the food he served. Moreover, to mark his celebrated position he painted himself red or black.[47]

Body paint represented only one type of ceremonial attire. Distinguished warriors in the personal service of the chief also attached to their waists gourds filled with pebbles and to their backsides the tails of horses or wildcats. Thus, "when they ran, the Gourds made a rattling Noise, and the Tail being borne up by the Wind stood out at its full Length." As the men were also "stark naked and besmear'd," European observers were certain that "Nothing could be seen more ridiculous." On other special occasions, the Downstream People added to body paints head gear of different colored feathers, buffalo horns, or "conic pelt caps." Dancers might also hold gigantic

wooden masks before their faces or masquerade under a female fig-
ure with a head of wood and a hollow leather body.[48]

In one way or another the rituals and ceremonies of the
Downstream People were petitions to the spirit world. Generally all,
furthermore, were articulated or accompanied by some kind of a
dance. Thus there were dances dealing with religion, war and peace,
marriage and death, medicine, hunting, joy and even sensuality. The
latter were held secretly at night by light of a large fire. Both men
and women danced completely nude, synchronizing their poses and
gestures with songs that expressed their sexual desires. Although
the French considered the dance lewd and obscene, it simply
achieved a oneness with another facet of the Life Force of the universe.[49]

On the whole, Quapaw culture as observed by the French in the
late seventeenth century was an expression of a people once situated
in the Ohio Valley whose civilization had been modified by foreign
intrusions, by dislocations, and by adaptations of cultural characteristics common to other peoples. Thus it was heterogeneous in
nature, not strong in traditions, and more flexible than rigid. Had
the Downstream People been located in their Arkansas homeland
well before the arrival of the French, the cultural continuum would
obviously have been different. As it was, the Quapaws were no more
than emigrants and, like all aliens, were in a state of transition
because their social institutions were in partial disarray. It was a
condition that others, more certain of themselves and of their mission, could easily exploit.

CHAPTER II
A CENTURY OF
FRIENDSHIP, 1673-1763

From the outset of European settlement the various colonial powers waged a vigorous contest for control of North America. Initially focused on the Atlantic coast, the struggle in the late seventeenth century expanded into the interior of the continent, where the competitors for empire hinged the success of their colonial ambitions upon political and economic alliances with the native population. Given their number and the strategic location of their settlements, the Quapaws were reckoned as one of the tribes whose allegiance was critical to any European power aspiring to dominate the Mississippi River valley. Although the Downstream People had other options, they early elected to make common cause with France, a commitment from which they seldom wavered and for which they won the lasting admiration of friends and foes alike. In 1758, for example, Louisiana Governor Louis Kerlerec wrote that they were not only the "bravest" of those nations associated with the French but "the only one which [had] never soaked their hands in French blood."[1] Reflecting the importance of the tribe's role in the international contest, such an accolade came only at the expense of much of the cultural integrity of the Downstream People and fearful quantities of their own blood and treasure.

The first Europeans to encounter the Quapaws were the French explorers, Jacques Marquette and Louis Joliet. Mid-seventeenth-century rumors of a mighty river that coursed through the continent and spilled into the Pacific had stirred the imaginations of the sons of France situated in the St. Lawrence River valley. To confirm the existence of the fabled waterway, Father Marquette and Joliet pushed to Lake Michigan, portaged to the Wisconsin River, and reached the Mississippi in June, 1673. Turning their canoes south and armed only with an Illinois calumet, the two reached Kappa, the northernmost Quapaw village, in mid-July. The welcome they received was less than friendly. Brandishing bows, arrows, axes, war-clubs, and shields, the Downstream People prepared to attack, for a time ignoring the calumet that Marquette held high above his head. Ultimately the Indians recognized the pipe of peace and invited the Frenchmen ashore where they were ushered to the chief's scaffold and informed by an Algonquin-speaking captive that they were the guests of the "Akamsea." Marquette explained the nature of his mission and delivered a discourse "about God and the mysteries of our holy faith," after which the Quapaws feasted the Frenchmen with sagamity and dog flesh and danced the calumet ritual. During the course of these events, the explorers were able to establish that the Mississippi flowed into the Gulf of Mexico rather than the Pacific and that the tribes farther downriver were warlike. Disappointed by this information, Marquette and Joliet determined to go no farther and, following another day's rest with the hospitable Quapaws, turned back up the Father of Waters to Lake Michigan.[2]

The news that south and west of the Great Lakes there existed a vast and "unclaimed" land drained by mighty streams and occupied by a large native population stimulated a vital French expansion into the interior of North America. Still, nearly a decade elapsed before anyone retraced the route of Father Marquette. In 1682 an expedition commanded by Robert Cavelier Sieur de la Salle eventually pushed to the Mississippi by way of the Illinois River. Turning south, it continued downstream until March 13, when war cries and drumbeats penetrated a heavy mist to announce that Kappa lay obscured on the western shore. Turning quickly to the opposite bank, the French took refuge behind hastily constructed breastworks. In due time, Henri de Tonti, La Salle's lieutenant, returned to the riverbank where, in Algonquin, he hailed the Indians, parties of whom were already at mid-stream, and asked their identity. An Illinois captive among the Quapaws, perhaps the same one who had replied to a similar question by Marquette, answered "Akansa." Upon coming closer, one warrior shot an arrow toward Tonti to determine whether the Frenchman's mission was of peace or war. When he did not respond in kind, the Indians beached their canoes, confidently approached the redoubt, and with La Salle smoked the calumet. Thereafter Jean du Lignor, another member of the French party, and two Quapaws crossed back to the village and returned with six of the tribal elders, who, after also smoking the calumet and receiving presents, invited the entire French party to make Kappa their headquarters.[3]

Once they removed to the settlement La Salle and his men were treated with the greatest of hospitality. Not only were they ceremoniously received by the chief but the Quapaws built them a cabin, brought wood to burn, and supplied an abundance of food. La Salle was even honored with the calumet dance. But the Downstream People were not altogether selfless in their liberality. As early as 1680 they had gone in search of French weapons with which they could achieve dominance over their enemies. Although they were unsuccessful then, La Salle represented another opportunity to realize their goal. With rising expectations they watched as the Frenchmen on March 14 erected first a cross and then a large column on which had been painted the coat of arms of Louis XIV. They listened with approval as Father Membré explained some of the mysteries of God and were delighted when the French raised their muskets, fired a volley, and in unison shouted "Vive le Roi." For the Quapaws such a ceremony seemed a virtual guarantee that His Majesty would fight those who attacked them. In their joy they danced through the night, pausing at times to rub the column with their hands which they then passed over their own bodies. Later they even built a palisade around the pole and cross.[4]

Provided with supplies and interpreters by the chief, La Salle and his party left Kappa several days later. Some fourteen miles downstream on the east bank they paused at Tongigua and then stopped seven miles farther on the west bank again at Tourima. These villages received the French just as hospitably and also acknowledged their fealty to "His Majesty." After learning of a fourth settlement (Osotouy) up the Arkansas River, Father Membré calculated the Quapaw population as 15,000 to 20,000 souls. His estimate was probably an exaggeration, for Tonti later estimated the warriors as numbering no more than 1,500. Whatever the count, the Downstream People had been liberal hosts to La Salle and his men, who by March 17 continued their descent of the Mississippi. On April 9, 1682, they arrived at the Gulf of Mexico, raised a cross and the Arms of France, chanted the "Vexilla Regis" and "Te Deum," fired a volley of muskets, and in the name of Louis XIV took possession of "Louisiana."[5]

La Salle knew, however, that there was a vast difference between claiming Louisiana and actually controlling it. As he and his party turned back toward Canada, he conceived of a plan whereby France might derive full benefit of his "discovery." His king needed only to establish along the Mississippi a series of posts at strategic locations such as that occupied by the Arkansas people. By virtue of these facilities France could exploit the commercial potential of the natives and also provide a base from which she could challenge other colonial powers, particularly the Spanish in Mexico and Florida. That such plans were feasible, at least locally, seemed certain as La Salle interrupted his upstream voyage by brief visits with the Indians. Among the Quapaws, for example, he was again welcomed warmly and was especially impressed by the fact that they had enclosed the cross and arms he had erected with a palisade. Indeed, so anxious was the tribe to be the single beneficiary of French largess that its leaders imposed upon him to leave with them two Taensa Indians whom he had included in his party. The Downstream People no doubt feared that the more southern tribe might work to divert the trade that had been promised to them.[6]

Convinced that the Indians earnestly sought French alliances, La Salle hastened upriver. Pausing only briefly in Quebec, he carried his vision of empire and commercial exploitation directly to Louis XIV at Versailles. The king, too, was infected with the explorer's enthusiasm and, in time, gave his blessing to a project aimed at establishing French control of the interior of North America. On July 24, 1684, La Salle sailed from La Rochelle, France, with four vessels and several hundred troops and colonists. His destination was the mouth of the Mississippi, where he anticipated building the first of the posts that would link the Gulf of Mexico with the Great Lakes.

Conceived in the depths of a pristine wilderness and among an unspoiled people, the expedition at birth was mortally crippled and doomed to an early death. By-passing the Mississippi, it reached land at Matagorda Bay on the Texas coast. Shipwreck and mutiny followed. Despite the travail, La Salle did not immediately push overland toward the river that had inspired his dreams but led a party into the interior of Texas, probably in search of the fabled Gran Quivira, the Mountain of Silver. In the meantime, either from anxiety or poor instructions, Henri de Tonti in February, 1686, set out from his Illinois post with twenty-five Frenchmen and nine Indians to learn the fate of the expedition. Arriving at the Gulf in April, he found no evidence of the settlement planned by his old associate. He reluctantly abandoned the search and returned upriver to the Quapaw villages, where some of his men requested permission to remain. Since La Salle had given him a seigniory, or a landed estate, on the Arkansas in 1682, Tonti consented that Jean Couture and five others should establish a post on the river from which they should continue the vigil for La Salle and initiate commerce with the Downstream People.[7]

While the Arkansas Indians rejoiced at the prospects of European trade, La Salle continued his futile wanderings in Texas. By late 1686, however, he determined to lead a relief expedition northeast toward the Mississippi in the hope of making connections with Tonti. After one abortive effort, La Salle and seventeen of his men reached the Brazos River the following March, where an even greater tragedy occurred. La Salle was slain by a mutinous faction of his own group. After burying their leader, six of the party, led by La Salle's brother, Abbe Jean, and his nephew, Henri Joutel, pushed on and reached the Arkansas River in July, 1687. To their great joy, they sighted on the opposite bank in the Quapaw village of Osotouy a cabin of European construction and a cross, the latter promising an immediate if not an eternal deliverance. In a moment, Jean Couture and Jacques Cardinal, who for the past year had continued Tonti's vigil while trading with the Arkansas people, emerged from the cabin to fire shots of welcome.[8]

For their part, the residents of Osotouy received the Frenchmen with their usual hospitality. Kept ignorant of La Salle's death, they regaled their guests with food and the calumet dance. When they learned that the white men desired supplies, a canoe, and guides to take them on up the Mississippi River, they summoned the chiefs of the other three villages to discuss the request. After a lengthy council, the tribal elders agreed to furnish one guide from each community, provisions, and transportation. The remnants of the relief party were then escorted to Tourima, Tongigua, and Kappa. At each village they were treated as honored guests, receiving frequent invitations to take meals with individual Quapaw families. But as before, the hospitality showered upon the French was not without purpose. The Downstream People were anxious that La Salle's brethren remember the alliance that had been made with them five years earlier. Only after Joutel emphasized that the French would return with guns and help fight the tribe's enemies did the Downstream People speed the Europeans on their way. Leaving their horses, most of their ammunition, some knives, axes, beads, and one member of their party to remain with Tonti's men, the expedition laboriously made its way up the Mississippi and reached the Illinois country in mid-September, 1687.[9]

Because of property considerations, Joutel and his colleagues kept secret the fact of La Salle's death. Thus it was not until April, 1688, that Tonti learned from Jean Couture about the disaster on the Brazos. Concerned about the fate of those Frenchmen La Salle had left in Texas, he and a small party set off down the Mississippi and in January, 1689, reached the Quapaw villages. There they "were received with demonstrations of joy, . . . dancing, feasting, and mascarading," all of which he wrote, "confirmed the last alliance." Tonti took the opportunity to visit his "commercial house" on the Arkansas River at Osotouy, for the first time inspecting those facilities that had succored the remnants of La Salle's relief expedition. Later that month he pushed on to the southwest only to learn from the Caddo Indians that no one in the French settlement in Texas had survived. By late July, Tonti was back among the Quapaws, where, ill with fever, he remained for some two weeks before returning to his headquarters in Illinois.[10]

This third trip to the domain of the Downstream People gave Tonti an opportunity to reassess the value of the region. The prospects of commerce with the Quapaws were bright indeed. The Indians had buffalo and deer hides in abundance, and they could be taught to trap beaver. To get the furs to market, though, presented a problem. Quebec was distant and at times inaccessible. Moreover, authorities there were anxious to restrict the extent of the North American trade, for they feared that the French population would disperse too widely across the continent and weaken the St. Lawrence settlements. Given these considerations, Tonti sought in 1689 to win some official sanction for his Quapaw venture. Accordingly, he granted two tracts of land near his Arkansas Post to the Jesuit fathers provided that they would send missionaries to the Indians, build two chapels, raise a cross, and say an annual mass for him. Four years later he also requested permission to construct a seaworthy vessel at the Arkansas that would pioneer a route to France via the Gulf.[11]

Although Tonti's commercial interests were never officially recognized, he continued to send his men among the Downstream People. The Quapaws treated them with as much favor as if they had been Tonti himself, exchanging their peltries for trinkets and a limited number of weapons. But on the whole the trade worked to their great disadvantage. In 1699, Fathers Montignay, St. Cosme, and Davion, missionaries of the Seminary of Quebec on a tour of the lower Mississippi Valley, noted that smallpox had so ravaged the Quapaws that only three hundred warriors remained. The residents of Kappa and Tongigua had combined to establish a single village on the west bank of the river below where Marquette and La Salle had first encountered the tribe. Yet even here they had found no immunity from the disease. In this new settlement, wrote Father St. Cosme, "There was nothing to be seen . . . but graves," because "all the children and a great number of the women were dead." Within the year still another population shift occurred, with the people of Tourima joining those of "New Kappa." By late 1700, therefore, the Quapaw enthusiasm for the white man had reaped little more than wholesale destruction. Instead of thousands, there were now only hundreds; instead of four villages, only two remained.[12]

Despite the grim reward, the Downstream People had appealed to the black-robed missionaries to stay among them. The priests, though, were skeptical, for Tonti's men, a corrupting force in the wilderness, were nearby. More significant, the tribe was not assembled in a single village, a situation that would impede the work of any missionary. The Quapaws were not anxious to rid themselves of the traders, but they were willing to concentrate their settlements and even to build a house for a priest. Indeed, the combination of New Kappa and Tourima occurred the following spring. Given such a demonstration, Catholic officials could hardly refuse to send a missionary, and in 1701 Father Nicholas Foucault was dispatched to begin work among the Quapaws.[13]

The coming of the French priest had more than just spiritual implications. By the end of the seventeenth century, France's claim to the lower Mississippi, upheld by no more than two isolated missions, was being challenged by other European powers. Settling Charles Town, Carolina, in 1670, British citizens inaugurated a vigorous trade with the southeastern Indians that within three decades had extended to the Chickasaws on the east bank of the Mississippi River. Not satisfied with this accomplishment, Carolina Governor Joseph Blake late in 1699 delegated a group of traders to carry presents of ammunition and merchandise to other Mississippi tribes who might welcome a commercial and political relationship with

Britain. Descending the Tennessee River and guided by Jean Couture, a deserter now from Tonti's post, the party reached the Quapaw villages in February, 1700. The Downstream People were so favorably impressed by the Carolinians and so enticed by their presents that they immediately set forth to obtain what the British demanded as the basis of any trade—slaves. Warriors, crossing the Mississippi to the upper Yazoo River, raided settlements and took captive a number of Chakchiumas, a Muskogean-speaking people later incorporated among the Chickasaws. Such human merchandise the Carolina traders later sold along the Atlantic coast.[14]

The presence of the English in the very heart of Louisiana and the specter of Spanish expansion north and west from Pensacola stirred the French to action. Convinced now that La Salle's and Tonti's vision was not as grandiose as once presumed, the crown commissioned Pierre Le Moyne d'Iberville to establish a permanent outpost at Biloxi on the Gulf coast, a mission he completed in 1699. Three years later the French also settled Mobile Bay. Despite such signal accomplishments, Iberville knew that the success of his sovereign's colonial ambitions required more than nominal control of the coast line. Specifically, France also had to dominate the Mississippi Valley, a task that would require the full cooperation of the Quapaws and other river tribes.

The governor preferred to win the interior of Louisiana by establishing military posts where the Missouri, Ohio, and Arkansas rivers entered the Mississippi. He successfully implemented his plan at the more northern locations, but in the domain of the Downstream People lack of funds and personnel forced him to adopt another strategy—the use of missionaries, diplomacy, and commerce. Father Foucault's work on the Arkansas stemmed from this context, combining in the same effort the objectives of both church and state.[15] But in 1702 the Koras, a tribe situated near Natchez, killed the pious priest. When the Quapaws retaliated with a punishing attack upon the smaller tribe, Iberville sought to perpetuate French influence by sending them "a little present," hardly a major diplomatic initiative but the only one that circumstances permitted.[16] Thereafter the governor had to rely on nameless *coureurs de bois* and *voyageurs* as France's representatives to the Arkansas people. Fiercely independent, these men had fallen heir to Tonti's commercial empire, bringing to the Quapaw villages guns, utensils, metal tools, creature comforts, and alcoholic beverages. In exchange, they took bear and deer skins, buffalo hides, some beaver pelts, bear's grease, and buffalo suet. Many of these traders intermarried with the tribe.[17]

As a group, though, they were poor diplomats, for personal rather than national aggrandizement was their objective. As a consequence, they failed to persuade the Downstream People that their best interests could be served by a French alliance. In the spring of 1708, for example, Thomas Welch, a Carolina trader, convened on the Yazoo River a council of the Quapaws and other Indian peoples. By convincing them that the Louisiana French were only deserters, he won from the tribes a commitment of peace and friendship. This defection, along with the more spectacular success of English diplomacy among the Chickasaws, came in the midst of Queen Anne's War, a larger colonial conflict between France and England. Had it not been for the leadership of Jean Baptiste le Moyne d'Bienville, the brother and successor of Iberville, Louisiana might very well have slipped from French control. Gracious, suave, and fluent in aboriginal languages, he was able to regain the confidence of the Indians and to negotiate a peace with the English-allied Chickasaws. Thus when Queen Anne's War terminated in 1713, France's preeminence in the Mississippi Valley was unquestioned.[18]

Although the Downstream People had played a minor role, the war represented a turning point in Quapaw-French relations. Since the Chickasaws were wholly within the British orbit, the ultimate realization of France's colonial objectives demanded that the Arkansas natives be used as a bulwark against that tribe's expansive forays.[19] The good will of the Quapaws was necessary as well because their villages were on the Arkansas River, a water route that provided easy access to the rich mines of northern New Spain and presumably flowed by mineral deposits as rich as those in Mexico and Peru. Finally, located midway between New Orleans, the new administrative center of Louisiana, and Kaskaskia, headquarters of the Illinois country, the tribal domain was desirable as a place where river convoys could pause and regroup. After 1717, therefore, when John Law's Compagnie des Indies took charge of Louisiana's economic affairs from the bankrupt Antoine Crozat, the Arkansas country became a center of activity.

The renewed interest in the Downstream People and their domain had various manifestations. To confirm the French alliance and to establish a way station in the summer of 1721, Second Lieutenant de la Boulaye and a company of thirteen soldiers took up residence among the Quapaws who had recently situated all of their villages on the Arkansas River, apparently for protection from the Chickasaws. The Lieutenant and his men promptly erected the first alien military facility ever constructed on tribal soil. Later that year at least eighty German colonists sent by John Law to develop a personal concession of 24,000 acres arrived to establish a settlement on the Grand Prairie adjacent to the tribal settlements. The Downstream People watched curiously as the immigrants applied "superior" Old World agricultural techniques in an attempt to make the prairie bloom. When those efforts failed, they graciously permitted the Germans to cultivate some of their old fields. This timely assistance staved off certain starvation and temporarily perpetuated the colony.[20]

The disturbing presence of the white settlers may have accounted for the cool reception that the tribe gave to Bernard de la Harpe in February, 1722. Already an explorer of some renown, La Harpe had been ordered by the company to search out the gold rumored to exist up the Arkansas and also to determine the navigability of the river as a route toward the more distant plains tribes. The Quapaws tried to discourage the Frenchman by informing him that some deserters from Law's concession had gone upriver the previous year to trade with the more distant Osages and had been killed for their efforts. When La Harpe refused to be intimidated, they reluctantly provided his expedition with some provisions. But when they found that one of their canoes had been expropriated they pursued the French party, bent upon retrieving the vessel. Rather than chance "a rupture" with the Downstream People, the explorer returned the canoe and halted his journey until another one could be constructed. After ascending the Arkansas some 250 miles, although no more than 130 miles by land, and reconnoitering the mountains southwest of the river, La Harpe was back in the Quapaw villages in early May. "Barely escaping a surprise by a Chickasaw war party," he departed for New Orleans convinced that the Arkansas River was navigable to the Spanish settlements in New Mexico and drained lands "of the finest description."[21]

Despite this assessment, company-sponsored activity in the domain of the Downstream People was short-lived. Because of isolation, expense, and reality, officials in France ordered that the soldiers be withdrawn from Arkansas Post and that the agricultural experiment be all but abandoned. Commandant-general Bienville delayed execution of the order, but only for a time. Accordingly, when Father Paul du Poisson re-established a mission among the Quapaws in 1727, he found no soldiers at the fort, only a few colonists, and no evidence of gold or precious stones.[22]

It fell to Father du Poisson, then, to remind the Downstream People of their French alliance. Finding the tribe collected in three villages and numbering no more than 1,200 souls, he had been received with enthusiasm. He turned down the "honor" of participating in a calumet dance but did permit the performance of the discovery dance, which he presumed would require fewer gifts in return. Shortly after his arrival, du Poisson began to study the Quapaw language and to observe tribal customs. He won few converts, but long-range prospects were apparently good, for he formulated plans to congregate the entire tribe in a single village on the Mississippi. In November, 1729, he set out for New Orleans to get official approval for his project and paused briefly at Fort Rosalie. As fate would have it, the day after his arrival the Natchez and their allied tribes attacked the settlement, killing du Poisson and 250 others.[23] When news of the disaster reached the Quapaws, they went into mourning and sought an opportunity to avenge the priest's death. The following spring some of their warriors attacked a party of Yazoos and Koras, taking four scalps and making several women prisoners. On their return they declared to French hunters that as long as one Quapaw was alive the Natchez and the Yazoo would not be without an enemy. They also displayed a bell and some books that had belonged to du Poisson which they expected to present to the next "black chief" who would reside among them. Ten years elapsed, however, before another priest, Father Avond, resumed the mission.[24]

The French attributed the crippling Natchez raid to English intrigue among the Indians. Obviously, if that threat were to be curtailed, prompt action was required. In 1731, therefore, the king of France took direct responsibility for Louisiana and two years later recalled Bienville to serve as governor. Simultaneously with the assertion of royal authority, Arkansas Post was again garrisoned with twelve men, commanded by First Ensign de Coulange. The presence of the French troopers so inspired the Quapaws that three hundred of their warriors busied themselves with repeated attacks upon the expansive Chickasaws and once even refused to make peace with their enemy. This concerted warfare endeared the

Downstream People to New Orleans officials, especially since the latter "had nothing to give them except promises." Since the tribe was at the same time being subjected to attacks from the west by the Osages, its struggle against the Chickasaws was even more valorous.[25]

Unfortunately, the frequent Quapaw sallies against the British-allied Indians were never major defeats for the enemy. They may very well have been counterproductive, for the Chickasaws increased their raids upon French river convoys. Concluding that France's policy had not been sufficiently punitive, Bienville in late 1735 laid plans to attack the Chickasaws from both the south and west. The southern army he placed under his personal command, but he assigned the leadership of the western army to Major Pierre D'Artaquette, the commandant of Fort Charters in Illinois. D'Artaquette assembled some 140 regular and militia troops and an equal number of Indian auxiliaries before descending the Mississippi to present Memphis. Arriving there on March 4, 1736, he was joined by some twenty-eight Quapaws who had been instructed by the commandant of Arkansas Post to notify him once the position of the Chickasaws had been determined. At that point and prior to any battle, the commandant would move forward with the entire warrior population of the Downstream People. Yet D'Artaquette was eager to attack, and when Bienville's army failed to appear, he was persuaded to assault the Chickasaw town of Chocolissa. He would have been better advised to wait for reinforcements, even if they were only a small number of Quapaws. Five to six hundred of the enemy, including twenty Englishmen, cut his army to ribbons. Had it not been for the few Quapaw and Iroquois warriors with him, none would have escaped alive. As it was, one hundred Frenchmen were killed. Of the twenty prisoners taken by the enemy, D'Artaquette and thirteen others were burned alive. Yet this disaster hardly compared to that suffered by Bienville before the Chickasaw town of Akia in late May. His even larger army was decisively defeated and forced to take refuge in the Choctaw nation.[26]

Although the battle had been lost, the Louisiana governor was determined not to lose the war. The glory of France and the success of her colonial ambitions required that the Chickasaws be brought to terms. Bienville immediately set to work planning a second invasion. In 1737 he sent Bernard de Vergès and a party of Quapaws to locate the most accessible route to the enemy towns via the Mississippi. At the direction of his scouts, de Vergès beached his canoes on the east bank just opposite and north of the St. Francis River and pushed eastward some fifteen miles. Upon reaching the highlands, the Arkansas natives asserted that the Chickasaw villages were not more than thirty miles distant. On the basis of this survey the governor opted for a western invasion rather than one from the south, although for a time he did entertain the idea of sending a contingent of Quapaw warriors by way of the Yazoo River to attack the Chickasaws. In September, 1738, the French constructed a base camp just north of the St. Francis, from which teams of soldiers were sent out with Quapaw guides to mark a road to the enemy villages. Throughout the next year provisions, armaments, and troops were gathered at the St. Francis encampment. Some two dozen Arkansas Indians were employed to provide meat for the army, which by the fall numbered 3,600 men—the largest military force ever assembled in the Mississippi Valley. In early November, Governor Bienville came upriver to join the expedition and paused briefly at the villages of the Downstream People to invite all of the warriors to join in the expedition. After surveying the scene, he ordered that the temporary camp be removed across the river to the base of a bluff near present-day Memphis. He named the new post Fort Assumption.[27]

The governor, though, was never able to capitalize upon his elaborate preparations. The Chickasaws were a good deal farther away than first expected; the location of a suitable road proved extremely difficult; and rains made the terrain almost impassable. As weeks slipped into months without any combat, the Indian allies of the French lost interest. This loss of enthusiasm, along with an ancient animosity for the Iroquois, induced many of the Quapaws to abandon the camp and return to their own villages. With his position deteriorating, in order to save the honor of the expedition Bienville eventually invited the Chickasaws to treat with him. In February, 1739, an enemy delegation began negotiations that resulted in a decision to end hostilities and to exchange prisoners. An anticlimax to his efforts was the governor's order for the destruction of Forts Assumption and St. Francis, removal of his army, and return downriver to New Orleans.[28]

Although Bienville had been aggravated by the untimely desertion by the Quapaws, the French were in no position to retaliate. They needed their Arkansas friends to contain the British-allied Chickasaws whom they themselves could not destroy. This was especially true after 1740, when the two European powers resumed another formal colonial conflict known as King George's War. As a consequence, Louisiana officials strengthened the garrison at Arkansas Post and a new governor, Marquis de Vaudreuil, frequently entertained the Quapaw chiefs in New Orleans. During the course of the war, moreover, the local commandant removed the fort down the Arkansas to better facilitate the resupply of convoys on the Mississippi and the Quapaw attacks upon the Chickasaws. To all of this the Downstream People responded by continuing their raids, two of the most effective occurring in 1744 and 1747.[29] Unfortunately, these forays brought frequent counterattacks from English-allied Indians, especially the Chickasaws but also the Missouri. Of these raids, the most celebrated took place in May, 1748, when Payah Matahah, a Chickasaw chief, and a party of 150 warriors struck and burned the French settlement at Arkansas Post. Payah Matahah was gravely wounded during the battle, but not before his people had killed several enemies and captured thirteen white women and children. Coming in the wake of an epidemic disease that had reduced their warrior strength to no more than 250, the raid so frightened the Quapaws that they removed their villages further up the Arkansas and requested that the fort be relocated nearby.[30] King George's War ended the same year, and somewhat later the Downstream People avenged the intrusion, but on the whole the tribe paid dearly for its involvement in the conflict.[31]

In addition to curtailing British expansion, the Downstream People served France's colonial ambitions in other ways. Their villages commanded the approach to the Arkansas River, which had its headwaters in northern New Spain. To use this highway to tap the rich resources of the Spanish province had been a goal of Louisiana officials from the beginning. Such a motive had spawned the La Harpe expedition in 1722, but it was not until 1739 that Pierre and Paul Mallet reached Santa Fe via a route along the Platte River to the Rocky Mountains and then south. After receiving a favorable reception from New Mexican officials, the brothers returned to Louisiana by way of the Canadian and Arkansas rivers. Arriving at the Quapaw villages in July, 1740, they were convinced that profitable trade with the distant province via their shorter return route was possible. This was good news to the governor, Bienville, and the following year he sent Andry Fabry de la Bruyère, a subaltern, on an official expedition to verify the information. Although Fabry was interrupted by wary Osages and forced to turn back, other adventurers, perhaps as many as a hundred, soon gathered among the Downstream People in anticipation of upstream journeys that would bring them fame and fortune. With a treaty between the Comanches and the Jumanos in 1746 or 1747 making travel less dangerous, three deserters from Arkansas Post departed from the Quapaw villages and reached Santa Fe in early 1749. Thereafter, other Frenchmen followed, but with different results: their goods were confiscated and they were imprisoned.[32]

Despite the wholesale opposition of Spain to commerce via the Arkansas, France for a time favored the contraband trade. Governor Louis Kerlerec even proposed that trade relations be established with the interior provinces of Mexico. But given the attitude of Spain and the fact that another war with England required her support, in 1754 the French court ordered Kerlerec to curtail the trade with New Mexico. Unable to spare regular troops for such duty, the governor summoned Guedetonguay, the Quapaw medal chief, to New Orleans and persuaded him to interdict the Arkansas River commerce. As international police, the Downstream People proved most effective. Thereafter little or no trade via their nation reached Santa Fe.[33]

The accommodation with Spain, of course, occurred on the eve of the conflict that would determine France's destiny in North America—the French and Indian War. In anticipation of this climactic event, Louisiana officials as early as 1750 began to strengthen their military posture in the Mississippi Valley. A visit in 1751 to Arkansas Post by Jean-Bernard Bossu, a captain of French Marines, confirmed that the facility had fallen into decay. Only an ensign and seven men garrisoned the fort and held the Quapaws to their traditional alliance. Moreover, disease had again ravaged the Downstream People, reducing their warrior complement by one-third, from 225 to 150 men. Accordingly, the next year Governor Vaudreuil assigned a full company to Arkansas Post, directed Captain de la Houssaye to rebuild the fortifications, sent François Sarrazin to serve as interpreter, and encouraged Father Carette to occupy the long-abandoned mission. During the summer of 1753 Vaudreuil also brought Guedetonguay and seventeen minor chiefs to the capitol, entertained them royally, and cautioned them against any intrigue with the British.[34]

The governor, from the point of view of the French, did not act any too soon. For the first time the Quapaws were showing signs of possible desertion. They had been subjected to Osage attacks, raids that Louisiana officials seemed unable to curtail despite an alliance with the larger tribe. Supposing that they were on their own, the Downstream People had received war belts from British-dominated Illinois Indians. Vaudreuil's speech to Guedetonguay in 1753 and the activity at Arkansas Post undoubtedly counteracted a part of this slippage, but not much. In 1754 some Quapaw warriors joined with their ancient enemy, the Chickasaws, and raided a party of French-allied Indians in Illinois.[35] Indeed, so alienated had the Quapaws become that when Governor Kerlerec called the chiefs to New Orleans in 1756 to enlist their aid in stopping the Arkansas river traffic to Santa Fe, the medal chief boldly threatened to join the British in the conflict that was then two years old. In light of the strategic importance of the Downstream People, the governor took the chief at his word. The next spring he sent another detachment to Arkansas Post, rebuilt the facility, and struggled to regain the confidence of the Quapaws.[36]

Kerlerec, however, could do little to correct that which antagonized the Indians most—the trade system. Although some independent operators trafficked with the Quapaws, the commandant of the post generally had a monopoly of the trade, the profits of which were used to maintain the post or supplement his income. Frequently, therefore, the tribe had to accept poor quality trade goods at high prices. Twenty deerskins bought one and a half yards of stroud, sixty buffalo hides purchased a single gun, and one buffalo hide paid for only ten bullets.[37] The British had better goods at cheaper prices, a condition that would have affected the Downstream People had their allegiance been determined by economics alone. But other interests motivated them. They were genuinely attached to the French and took pride in never having "soaked their hands in French blood." As a consequence, they lived with the trade system, albeit fitfully. "[O]ne can make them see the impossibility of furnishing them certain merchandise in time of war or in times of scarcity," wrote Governor Kerlerec. "It is in general a brave nation, which merits friendship and bounties from the French."[38]

The Quapaws, then, kept the faith with the brethren of La Salle. In the decisive contest that began at the forks of the Ohio and ended on the Plains of Abraham, the tribe never wavered in its support. Yet such steadfastness had little impact upon the results of the French and Indian War. The larger British population on the Atlantic coast and the superiority of King George's navy spelled the eventual defeat of French arms, a defeat that was admitted in the Peace of Paris of 1763. By terms of the settlement, France ceded her possessions in North America east of the Mississippi River to England and, as compensation for losses suffered elsewhere, gave to her ally, Spain, that area claimed west of the river. The Downstream People did not learn of the significance of France's defeat until the summer of 1763. When they did, their chiefs went down to New Orleans to plead with the governor not to deliver them up to the Spanish. That official could only commiserate with them, for an era had come to an end.[39]

The century of French domination had brought perceptible and profound changes to the Quapaws. Of all, the most remarkable was demographic. Estimated as 6,000 to 15,000 strong in 1682, by 1763 they numbered less than 700, of whom 160 were warriors. Their use as raiders and auxiliary troops by the French accounted for some of the decrease, but their reduction was mostly a consequence of European introduced disease that reached epidemic proportions in 1698, 1747, and 1751. The epidemic of 1698 had the most disastrous consequence, reducing the population of the tribe by at least two-thirds. Sadly, in terms of population the Quapaws had reached the zenith of their power before 1700. The dramatic reduction also directly affected the tribe's settlement pattern. Initially, the Quapaws resided in four large villages, but by the end of the French period only three small villages remained. And where the focus of population was at first on the Mississippi, in 1763 it had transferred to the Arkansas. The governmental organization of the Downstream People had reflected the four-part division, hence it too was altered. Rather than four chiefs who acted in concert only when national interests required it, a great chief emerged to claim special hereditary prerogatives. No doubt their social structure was equally altered in other ways by the decimation of population.

Less apparent but equally important were economic changes wrought by commerce with the white man. Once predominantly agriculturalists, the Quapaws became so infatuated with the white-supplied creature comforts that they came to spend more time on the hunt than in the field. Moreover, in search of buffalo and deer hides, hunters ranged even further west, simultaneously sapping the strength of the tribe at home and eliciting the enmity of the Indians upon whose territory they encroached. The European commerce also meant that many white men took Quapaw women as mates, a fact that further altered the cultural integrity of the tribe. Finally, the alcohol supplied by the traders debauched many proud warriors and left them senseless when clear heads and sharp wits were demanded.

Only in their spirit life, apparently, did the Downstream People resist dramatic culture change. The mission efforts of Fathers Foucault, du Poisson, Avond, and Carette resulted in friends rather than converts. For that matter, toward the end of the French period the black robes seemed more interested in the resident white population than in the Quapaws. The inability to sustain a mission obviously reflected the continued allegiance of the tribe to traditional gods. Given the decimation of their population and the radical changes in their lifeways, only the faith of their fathers assured their perpetuation as a people.

CHAPTER III
A VALUABLE ALLY
1763-1819

The Treaty of Paris of 1763 had little immediate impact on the Quapaws. Spain occupied Louisiana only slowly, and even then made few changes in the policy that had governed France's relations with the Indians living west of the Mississippi River. As previously, therefore, the friendship of the Downstream People was prized because of their bravery in battle and their strategic location on the Arkansas River. Apparently, it made little difference that their warrior population was ever decreasing. The status of the Quapaws as valuable and meritorious allies did not change, even after the United States purchased Louisiana in 1803, although the role assigned to them did. Both France and Spain had looked to the tribe to restrict access to the region west of the Mississippi, but American officials charged the Quapaws with facilitating the limited exploitation and settlement of the province. As inconceivable as it seems to later observers, the Downstream People willingly accepted the role assigned to them. As a consequence, they interpreted the Treaty of 1818, in which they ceded most of their territorial claims to the United States, not as an act of dispossession but as a contribution made by an independent and equal people to the national purposes of their esteemed ally. Given this rather unique perspective, it was no wonder that the American government considered the Quapaws to be particularly valuable partners in war and peace.

Although Louisiana technically belonged to Spain after 1763, not until March, 1766, did Antonio de Ulloa and a force of ninety men arrive in New Orleans to institute Spanish authority. In the interim, Louisiana had been administered by a lame-duck French government which was not fully convinced that a transfer of the province had actually occurred. Two major problems confronted these New

Orleans officials. One concerned the transition of power from France to Spain, while the other related to England's peaceful occupation of the region east of the Mississippi, including Florida. The latter problem had particular significance for the Quapaws.[1]

In August, 1763, the British occupied Pensacola and two months later, Mobile. Early the next year they planned to take possession of the Illinois country by sending a convoy of troops and supplies up the Mississippi. In anticipation of that event, French authorities in New Orleans instructed the commandant of Arkansas Post to provide whatever assistance was necessary and to inform the Quapaws that the English were now their friends and should be permitted to pass without molestation.[2] That the Downstream People might impede the English convoys was a distinct possibility. For more than half a century they had warred constantly with the British-allied Chickasaws, and they found it difficult to extend the hand of friendship just because diplomats had signed a document far across the sea. Moreover, they were in communication with the Ottawa chief, Pontiac, who continued to stir up resistance to England's occupation of the Ohio Valley even though his conspiracy had been quelled in 1763.[3] According to General Thomas Gage, the Quapaws were "so exasperated by the influence" of Pontiac that they even searched friendly French convoys for Englishmen. Gage was absolutely certain, as a consequence, that the tribe would harass and perhaps block any British movement on the Mississippi.[4] Because he was convinced that the Quapaws were a threat, attacks upon convoys were attributed to the Downstream People whether they were guilty or not.[5]

Both French and English officials acted to thwart this presumed threat. In early 1765 Charles Philippe Aubry, the French governor in New Orleans, sent an officer with presents to the Quapaws to seek their acquiescence to British occupation.[6] In the meantime John Stuart, England's Indian agent in the South, dispatched two representatives to negotiate a general peace with the Quapaws and other Mississippi River tribes. He also sent two experienced frontiersmen directly to the villages of the Downstream People in an effort to secure free passage of English troops.[7] Moreover, at a congress in Mobile in April, 1765, Stuart persuaded the Choctaws and Chickasaws to send embassies to the Quapaws and other Indians for essentially the same purpose. These two tribes also agreed to station a large party of warriors near Natchez to patrol the banks of the river once a British convoy reached the domain of the Downstream People.[8]

All of this—the presents, negotiations, and Indian embassies—had the desired effect. In September, when Major Robert Farmar and his command reached the Arkansas River on their way north to occupy the Illinois country, the Quapaws let them pass. The only discordant note was struck by the French commandant of Arkansas Post. He refused to let Farmar employ an interpreter through whom he could communicate with the Quapaws and to distribute presents to the tribe in their village. The English major, therefore, had to assemble the Downstream People on the east bank of the Mississippi where he passed out gifts and learned that the commandant had told his charges that they would be better served "to strike upon English, than to take presents from them."[9] Nevertheless, Farmar was impressed by the reception the Indians gave him and concluded that the Quapaws appeared to be a "faithfull [sic] Nation and great Friends to the English."[10] This latter assessment undoubtedly accounted for John Stuart's proposal of the following year to settle the tribe on the English side of the river and to incorporate them in a defensive network that would protect the exposed southwestern flank of the British colonies. That the plan was never implemented was not due as much to its misjudgment of the Quapaws as its non-approval by authorities in London.[11]

The English convoy was safely up the river when Governor de Ulloa arrived in New Orleans the next year. The few Spanish troops that accompanied him, however, were of insufficient number to occupy the province militarily. Ulloa, therefore, was required to muster into Spain's service men of French extraction, one of whom, Alexander de Clouet, was sent to Arkansas Post as commandant. The governor also adopted the French system of winning the allegiance of the Indians through the use of annual presents, permanent forts, medals, and commerce. The importance of the tribe generally dictated the number of presents, the size of the fort, the amount of medals, and the quality of the trade. Judging from what the Quapaws received, they were considered most important by Spain. Gifts distributed to them in 1769 amounted in value to one peso per person, or the price of two barrels of rum. In all they received about 16 per cent of the cost of all the goods distributed in Spanish Louisiana, proportionately more than any other forest tribe. Moreover, Arkansas Post was rebuilt on the Mississippi and rechristened

Fort Carlos III. Some fifty soldiers were stationed there in 1769, one of the largest contingents in the Spanish province.[12]

Aside from presents and forts, Spain also relied upon medals and trade to win the Indians. During the French era the Quapaw chiefs had generally gone down to New Orleans to pledge their fidelity and to receive from the hands of the governor the prized medals. But during Ulloa's administration such a journey proved impossible, and the chiefs had to content themselves with gifts instead of medals. As a consequence, when the governor was forced to abandon the capital by virtue of a local rebellion, the Quapaws' friendship for Spain cooled visibly. Only by detaining the grand chief at Fort Carlos until another cargo of presents arrived in July, 1769, was the commandant able to prevent a serious revolt. Thus when Alexandro O'Reilly restored Spain's authority in Louisiana the following month, the commandant did not discourage the Quapaw leaders from going to New Orleans to receive presents directly from the new governor.[13] Medals, though, apparently were not distributed. Two more years passed before the Spanish got around to that important detail, and only then with precious little finesse. In a ceremony designed to confirm tribal allegiance with Louisiana's new rulers, the grand chief was asked to exchange his large French medallion for a smaller Spanish one. When the flags were raised on the morning of June 6, 1771, a cannon was fired, and three more boomed when the medal was placed on the chief. Thereafter speeches and the consumption of fifty-seven bottles of aguardiente by the Quapaw leader assuaged his disappointment over the different sizes of the medals. By such rituals did Spain hope to win the Downstream People![14]

Trade, of course, was another important element of Spanish Indian policy. Although Governor O'Reilly ordered that commerce be opened to all, in reality it was controlled by the local commandant. In the single store at Fort Carlos, for example, the commandant set the prices of all articles sold, and he received 5 per cent of the profits. With his own prosperity in the balance, he was thus deaf to complaints that prices were too high, a fact that made trade on the Arkansas River counterproductive to Spanish colonial goals. For their part, the Quapaws were so incensed that they actively sought to engage in commerce with the British. Ironically, in addition to costly goods and belated presents, Louisiana officials had paved the way for this subversive trade by encouraging the Downstream People to receive the English as friends.[15]

As early as 1768 British traders had established a post on the west side of the Mississippi where the White River emptied into the Arkansas. Known as Ozark, this establishment was supervised by a woman of questionable reputation—a "Magdelon," said the Spanish commandant—who distributed liquor in the Quapaw villages.[16] Another trader active at Ozark was John Blommart, a prosperous Natchez merchant who later established on the east bank of the Mississippi the community of Concordia, which was also designed to tap the Indian commerce of Louisiana. For a time in the late 1760's and early 1770's the trade of the Downstream People was channeled almost entirely to these two facilities. Indeed, the Quapaws were so pleased with the better goods and lower prices that they sought a permanent alliance with the British. At Mobile in 1771, for example, one tribal chief requested just such an arrangement. The following year, other Arkansas warriors visited that city again, apparently for the same purpose. Moreover, in 1774 thirty-five Quapaws visited Natchez and proposed to the governor of West Florida that the Downstream People and Britain negotiate a treaty of peace and friendship. Because any formal accord would have been a diplomatic affront to Spain, these petitions were rejected by the English, although no effort was made to curtail the commerce that existed with the Quapaws.[17]

Spanish officials could do little to counteract this erosion of influence. In 1773 the commandant at Fort Carlos did arrest his Quapaw interpreter, Nicolas Labauxiere, for serving as a British agent among the tribe. But even that was accomplished with difficulty. The Downstream People surrounded the post and demanded Labauxiere's release, a request they relinquished only after the commandant distributed gifts and exhorted the tribe to "settle down and make a crop." Yet such advice was hardly sufficient to pacify the Quapaw leaders. By 1777 Great Chief Angaska had made a secret alliance with the British traders and had accepted Britain's medal and flag. Caiguaioataniga, the chief of the Kappa village, followed the example of his leader and, despite orders from Fort Carlos, allowed 5,000 deerskins to pass through the tribal domain to an English market in return for a barrel of whiskey. Only with these affronts did Spain take decisive action. At the suggestion of the commandant, Kaskaskia Indians in the spring of 1777 raided Ozark and dispossessed the merchants of their goods, forcing the British to withdraw east of the Mississippi and the Quapaws to look to the store at Fort Carlos for trade items. Economic necessity, therefore, brought the tribe back to the fold, although their enthusiasm for Spain was always measured.[18]

The commercial success of England among the Downstream People weakened more than just the defensive posture of Spain in Louisiana. It also threatened her domination of tribes farther west, particularly the Osages. Situated in what is now southwestern Missouri and northeastern Oklahoma, these near kinsmen of the Quapaws were skillful hunters and brave warriors, ranging an area that extended as far south as Red River. If the proud Osages were to be integrated into the colonial system and their trade channeled to New Orleans, Spain required the cooperation of the Downstream People. They alone, it seemed, were willing to challenge the warlike spirit of their kinsmen. As a consequence, when a tripartite agreement (concluded in March, 1764, between the Osages, the Quapaws, and the French) failed to produce a lasting peace, Spanish officials looked to the Downstream People to organize war parties that would avenge the pillaging by the more western tribe.[19] To encourage such activity they even agreed to compensate the Quapaws for any Osage scalps delivered to Fort Carlos.[20] By March, 1777, apparently, the Osages had had enough, for one of their chiefs, two headmen, two warriors, and a woman appeared in the Quapaw settlements to petition for peace. Chief Angaska reproached the delegates for their bad conduct, argued that his people had taken up arms to avenge their Spanish brethren, and indicated a reluctance to terminate the war. The commandant of Fort Carlos, Balthazar de Villiers, hastened to assure Angaska that Louisiana officials desired that all Indian nations live in tranquility. As a result, the Quapaw chief reluctantly agreed to a cessation of hostilities. The following month an Osage delegation of three chiefs and forty warriors came down the Arkansas River to confirm the peace.[21]

That the Osages continued to terrorize the southwestern plains and that little commerce resulted from the agreement distressed Commandant de Villiers. But because Spain involved herself in the American Revolutionary War, his attention was directed elsewhere. Of more immediate importance was the British menace emanating from the east bank of the Mississippi. Indeed, Spain supported the American cause primarily as a means of limiting England's expansion in North America and decreasing her influence among such tribes as the Quapaws. For these reasons the rebellious colonials were permitted to purchase supplies in New Orleans and to use Fort Carlos as a way station and resupply depot. Lieutenant William Linn, for example, wintered on the Arkansas River in 1776 and 1777 before moving on to the Illinois country with New Orleans powder and shot obtained for General George Rogers Clark. The following year Captain James Willing paused at the fort before continuing his expedition that resulted in the destruction of the British settlements of Concordia and Natchez. With the conflict reaching such proportions, Spanish officials ordered that Fort Carlos be rebuilt at a site some thirty miles farther up the Arkansas and nearer the Quapaw villages. The new post, constructed because of the obvious importance of the Downstream People to Louisiana's strategy for defense, had been completed by 1779 when Madrid formally recognized America's independence and declared war upon England.[22]

The Quapaws were more witnesses to than participants in the ensuing conflict. Indeed, they demonstrated such little interest in the activity of the post that Commandant de Villiers requested that a drummer be assigned to his garrison, thinking that the military noise might amuse and impress them. Yet the tribe remained apathetic, hardly taking notice when on November 22, 1780, de Villiers crossed the Mississippi and, at the site of Concordia, "took possession" of the east bank for Spain.[23] At the same time the Downstream People made no attempt to aid and abet the English enemy. Angaska had fully repented of his earlier alliance with them and upon request of the commandant even sent out parties to scout British defenses among the Chickasaws. Such minimal effort won high praise from de Villiers. "I shall never cease, Sir," he wrote to Governor Bernardo de Galvez in July, 1781, "recommending to you this brave and faithful nation, and above all that you should send a commission of great chief and a standard with a coat of arms to this Chief Angaslkha [sic] who is most useful to me."[24] The Quapaw leader apparently got the recognition he deserved, for the following spring he and his colleagues journeyed to New Orleans to visit acting Governor Esteban Miró. But even on that occasion the Quapaws manifested their lofty indifference to the Spanish war effort. They were more concerned about their official interpreter's embezzlement of a portion of the government presents forwarded the previous year.[25]

In spite of all the activity at Fort Carlos, actual warfare did not come to the Arkansas country until 1783. Following an unsuccessful revolt at Natchez in 1781, the leader of the English insurgents, John Blommart, was arrested and sent to New Orleans, although others successfully escaped to the Chickasaw country where they were protected by James Colbert. An intermarried English trader who had become a Chickasaw leader, Colbert was determined to win the release of Blommart. In May of the following year, he sought to exchange for Blommart the wife and family of the lieutenant governor of Spanish Illinois, whom he had captured in a famous raid on the Mississippi River. When that did not work, the Chickasaw chief let it be known that his next target was Fort Carlos. Feverish activity followed at the Arkansas post. Its walls were reinforced and its four cannons mounted on new carriages. Quapaw scouts were sent out to discover just when the attack would come. But nearly a year elapsed before Colbert was ready.[26]

Accompanied by a hundred white men and fourteen Indians, the Chickasaw leader arrived at the mouth of the Arkansas River on the evening of April 16, 1783. At the Quapaw village of Osotouy he found that most of the men were out hunting and that Chief Angaska was intoxicated. Colbert calmed the befuddled mind of the great chief by telling him that he and twelve Americans had come to shake the hand of Captain Jacob Dubreuil, the new commandant of Fort Carlos. Paddling swiftly up the still waters of the Arkansas, Colbert arrived at the post at 2:30 on the morning of the seventeenth. He first overran the white settlement and captured not only Lieutenant de Villiers and his family but also the household of six habitants. Hearing the shots, Captain Dubreuil sent his interpreter to raise the nearby Kappa village, but Chief Caiguaioataniga refused to take part in the white man's war. At daylight Colbert fired upon the fort itself; the commandant answered by discharging his cannons. Rather than surrender the post as Colbert demanded, Dubreuil sent Sergeant Pastor, a handful of Spanish soldiers, and four Quapaw warriors who happened to be in the fort to mount a counterattack. This, along with the disconcerting war whoops of the Quapaws, forced the British sympathizers to retreat to their boats and in the confusion to release all of their captives except Lieutenant and Madame de Villiers, their three Negro servants, and two white women. By 9 o'clock Arkansas's Revolutionary War battle was over.[27]

At noon Chief Angaska belatedly appeared at Fort Carlos, somewhat hung over but full of contrition. With a hundred warriors and twenty Spanish troops, he set out to rescue the captives. Seven miles above the mouth of White River he overtook Colbert's fleet. Confronted by a superior force, the Chickasaw leader was compelled to surrender most of his captives, retaining the Negroes as security for a $2,000 promissory note exacted as ransom from de Villiers. Four Spanish soldiers and a habitant boy at that time volunteered to join his party to serve as hostages for the release of John Blommart. If Blommart was Colbert's principal concern, he had acted hastily. The Natchez loyalist had already been released by Spanish officials. If, on the other hand, his motive had been to aid the British in their war with the American revolutionaries, his effort was as belated as it was futile. Four months before, England had terminated the conflict and recognized the independence of the United States. By the terms of the Treaty of Paris of 1783, Britain ceded the east bank of the Mississippi to the new republic and returned both East and West Florida to Spain.[28]

No doubt Spain believed that the withdrawal of England would ensure her domination of the Mississippi Valley. But as a matter of fact, the contest for the control of that region had just begun. The United States, Spain's erstwhile ally, was expansion minded, a compulsion that had no respect for lines on a map or rivers on a continent. To combat this new, unexpected competitor for empire, Louisiana officials needed the full, undistracted support of their Indian allies. Among other things, there followed a concerted Spanish effort to negotiate a permanent peace between the Quapaws and the Chickasaws, the fruits of which would terminate a contest that had consumed the energies of the Downstream People for more than a century. In June, 1784, at Mobile, this diplomatic campaign won from a Chickasaw delegation a pledge to end hostilities, a commitment confirmed later that year by the entire tribe. Following this intertribal pact, the Downstream People and their neighbors lived in peace.[29]

With the specter of Chickasaw hostility removed, the Quapaws were free to enjoy the presents lavished upon them and to engage in the commerce now confined to Fort Carlos. One of the annual gifts and an important item of the trade was liquor. By 1786 the Quapaws were consuming so much of the fiery liquid that drunkenness was more the rule than the exception. Because of the widespread dissipation, in August of that year the Quapaw chiefs visited New Orleans and begged Governor Miró to prohibit the further introduction of

Don Joseph Vallier, Spanish commander of Arkansas Post, 1787–1791, at the time of the Colbert incident in the wake of the American Revolution.

strong drink into the Arkansas district. But Miró, more concerned with the profits of the traders than the sobriety of the Downstream People, ignored the request. Disaster resulted. By June, 1787, five Quapaws had died in drunken brawls. One of the dead was Joseph Cignide, a minor chief of Osotouy, who upon visiting the Kappa village was murdered and his mutilated body thrown into the river. Assured that "Rum [was] the cause of it all," Miró reversed himself and in October ordered the cessation of liquor traffic at Fort Carlos. Although the trade diminished, it was never completely abandoned.[30]

Had it not been for the Osages, the decade following the American Revolution would have been the most tranquil period the Quapaws experienced while dominated by Spain. But the peace concluded between the Downstream People and their kinsmen in 1777 was soon ignored by the more western tribe, endangering Spain's first line of defense against American expansion. When the Quapaw chiefs were in New Orleans in 1786, Governor Miró took the opportunity to encourage them to make war upon the Osages and later provided guns and ammunition.[31] Yet, for some reason, the tribe was more inclined to shelter their kinsmen than to fight them, a proclivity which Miró described as tantamount to "protecting a viper which [would] gnaw their entrails."[32] After 1790 Louisiana officials did persuade the Downstream People—"the only tribe that the Osage fear[ed],"[33]—to make honest warfare. Even then their attacks were limited to isolated, retaliatory raids that generally redounded to their disadvantage. By 1793 no Quapaw hunter could venture safely into the Osage country in search of game.[34]

For the new governor of Louisiana, Francisco Luis Hector, Baron de Carondelet, Spain's inability to curtail Osage depredations was intolerable. Without much thought as to consequences, in May, 1793, he declared war upon the tribe, directing the Quapaws to participate in a general attack upon their villages.[35] Before the blow was struck, however, Osage warriors fell upon the Missouri frontier with such ferocity that Carondelet was compelled to change his plans. He promptly abandoned the war and sought to win the cooperation of his adversary through presents and trade.[36] Taken as a whole, the conflict with the Osages had been an exercise in futility, sapping the strength of the Quapaws and making it impossible for them to live in peace with their kinsmen.

In addition to the response of the Osages, Governor Carondelet dropped his war plans because a more serious threat to Louisiana's security had emerged. In 1793 Edmond Genêt arrived in the United States to represent the republican government of France. He had ambitions of involving the Americans in the war then raging in Europe between France and Spain; failing that, he determined at least to enlist local aid in attacking the Spanish provinces of Florida and Louisiana. Genêt, therefore, commissioned George Rogers Clark to recruit an army that would march south, perhaps to New Orleans itself. Although this particular threat soon passed, it did induce considerable consternation among officials both in the lower Mississippi Valley and in Spain. Fort Carlos was put on alert and the Supreme Council of State in Madrid learned just how vulnerable Louisiana was to invasion from the east.[37]

Unfortunately for Spain, the lesson was of little benefit. In 1795 she signed the Treaty of San Lorenzo with the United States, whereby American citizens were granted the right of free navigation on the Mississippi River. Louisiana officials had hoped that the accord would pacify individuals like James Wilkinson, who threatened to march against the Spanish province unless a commercial outlet to the sea was arranged.[38] They badly miscalculated, however. The treaty only increased the danger to Louisiana, because the number of Americans on the Mississippi River multiplied. These brash frontiersmen began to covet the fertile lands of the west bank, the profitable Indian trade, and even the commerce with distant Santa Fe. To protect their dominion and to awe the natives, New Orleans officials strengthened Fort Carlos, exhorted the "valiant" Quapaw warriors "to harass the enemy greatly," intrigued with the Indians south of Kentucky, and during the 1790's patrolled the river below St. Louis with a fleet of war vessels.[39] Such defensive measures, though, were more expensive than effective. By 1801 Spain had had enough and to cut her losses agreed to cede Louisiana back to France. The French government, under Napoleon's leadership, was determined to restore its North American empire. How the Downstream People reacted to this retrocession was never recorded, but given their earlier support of the French, they must have received the news with a degree of enthusiasm.

Yet the French never returned to Louisiana. Serious reverses to his colonial schemes made the Emperor amenable to President Thomas Jefferson's frantic efforts to purchase at least part of the province. Rather than release just a segment, Napoleon offered to sell the whole of Louisiana. Jefferson's constitutional scruples were severely strained, but in 1803 the transaction was consummated, with the United States paying a mere fifteen million dollars for the entire domain. To soothe his legal conscience and to provide a rationale for the purchase, Jefferson envisioned Louisiana as a resettlement area for Indian tribes east of the Mississippi River who refused to accommodate the frontiersman's lust for inexpensive and already partially developed land. It was a plan fraught with serious implications for the Quapaw Indians.[40]

The United States did not formally take control of New Orleans until December, 1803, nor of upper Louisiana until March, 1804. With St. Louis as its administrative center, the latter region encompassed the present state of Arkansas and, of course, the domain of the Downstream People. Of the various officials at the district and later territorial capital, the superintendent of Indian affairs, or William Clark after 1806, wielded the most conspicuous authority. Clark's decisions had particular significance for the Quapaws and for the traders residing at Arkansas Post, then a sleepy settlement of no more than 160 whites of French and Spanish extraction and twelve Negroes.[41] For their part, the Quapaws were situated in three villages on the south bank of the Arkansas and numbered less than 575 men, women, and children. Located nearer the mouth of the Arkansas, a fourth village was made up of Choctaws who had crossed the Mississippi in search of more abundant game and, having intermarried with the Quapaws, called the host tribe "bridal people." A single chief continued to preside over each Quapaw village council, although one—Wahpahtesah—acted as principal chief of the entire tribe. Although their lifeways had been radically altered during the previous century, the Downstream People continued to engage in skillful agriculture, supplying the corn required for their own needs and those of the white settlement. Moreover, they provided the trading community with many horses bred from animals originally obtained in commerce with tribes farther west.[42]

Given the fact that domination of the Quapaws had seemed crucial to both France and Spain, American officials formulated policy on the basis of the same assumption. As early as May, 1804, presents of two hogsheads of tobacco and four barrels of whiskey were delivered to the tribal villages.[43] Somewhat later the Department of War stationed a captain and sixteen troops at Arkansas Post, rechristened Fort Madison.[44] Of more significance, in 1805 the United States established a factory or Indian trading post adjacent to the Quapaw settlements. A nonprofit operation designed to secure the friendship of the Indians by a commerce in cheaper and higher quality merchandise,[45] this facility was managed by John B. Treat and stocked with $10,000 worth of trade goods. Unfortunately it never prospered. Competition from resident traders and from the firm of Morgan and Bright, a Philadelphia-based company, was stiff.[46] Treat also was unable to grant credit to the Indians and did not always have in stock the merchandise most desired by his customers, namely silverware, rifles, and scarlet cloth. Nor could he alter the traditional trading patterns of the Downstream People, who preferred to deal with entrepreneurs of French extraction.[47] As a consequence, between 1806 and 1808 Quapaw hunters exchanged only ten packs of skins at the government post, and it was closed in 1810.[48]

Despite the military contingent at Fort Madison and the factory at Arkansas Post, the Downstream People believed that they were largely ignored by the United States. Both France and Spain had lavished presents upon them and summoned them to New Orleans to receive messages directly from the governor. Yet, except for Treat, whose duties were commercial, no American had visited them in an official capacity. The chiefs frequently complained that, unlike other tribes, they had not received "either talks or presents from their present Father," which was obviously a slight, for the Quapaws were willing "to place less dependence upon the Chase for a Livelihood" and to renew their war with the Osages.[49] Treat dutifully passed these complaints on to the secretary of war with the recommendation that the Quapaws be given special consideration. Yet not until the spring of 1808 did his superior authorize him to distribute presents with a value of up to $1,000 a year and to hire an interpreter to act as liaison with the tribe. Since Treat soon left his post, the Downstream People never received the presents, although Baptiste Saussie did serve for a time as official interpreter.[50]

Officials were willing in part to mollify the Quapaws because the United States needed to win the good will of the tribe in order to build up a profitable public and private commerce. This was especially the case since President Jefferson's plan to induce Indians east of the Mississippi River to exchange some or all of their tribal domains for homes in Louisiana had encountered an unexpected obstacle. Emigrating Cherokees, for example, found themselves harassed by the warlike Osages, who considered the newcomers to be intruders at best and deadly enemies at worst. For a time the Quapaws threatened to join the emigrants in this red war for the West, but when the United States ignored their requests for presents and "talks," they moved to establish an alliance with their kinsmen.[51] Which tribe the Downstream People supported, however, was not very important to them. By joining the contest, they hoped to exacerbate the turmoil and endanger American efforts to curtail the fighting. With bloodshed looming at the end of the trail, the Cherokees could hardly be expected to exchange their homeland for a new one in Louisiana. In other words, the Quapaws threatened to undermine the government's policy of Indian removal.

Still another menace to the removal scheme resulted from the establishment of white settlements in the Arkansas country during and after the War of 1812. The war with Britain had by-passed the region and was apparent to the Quapaws and others only in the abandonment of Fort Madison. With hostilities elsewhere, the southern district of Missouri Territory was an attractive haven to hundreds of white settlers, who took up homesteads along the Arkansas and especially in the Ouachita River Valley somewhat farther south. Organizing Arkansas County, these frontiersmen by October, 1815, complained that the Quapaws and Choctaws were "daily in the habit of killing their cattle, hogs, and stealing horses, and committing personal abuse on the Inhabitants...."[52] That white settlements should flourish among the Downstream People, though, was contrary to stated government policy. Secretary of War William H. Crawford declared that, considering the amount of land available for development by American agriculturalists, "the public interest" did "not require any additional cessions from the Indians." Indeed, Crawford insisted that "the propensity of our frontier settlers to spread over the surface" of the lands of distant tribes should "be restrained by the timely vigilance of the Government" in order to prevent disputes with the native Americans.[53] It followed that the whites in the Arkansas country threatened to disturb the peace necessary to induce large numbers of eastern Indians to exchange their aboriginal domains for ones in the West. Moreover, such an exchange would be impossible if white men already occupied the land.

With the government's cherished removal policy in jeopardy, Missouri's territorial governor, William Clark, took decisive action.

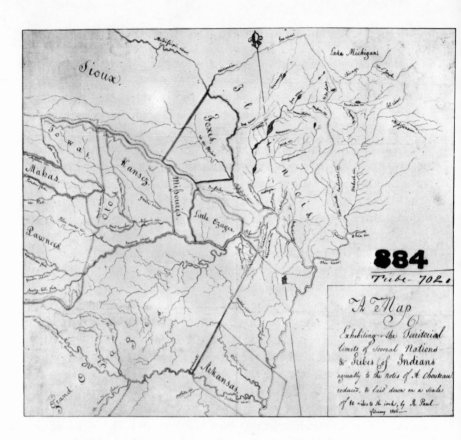

Map exhibiting the territorial limits of several nations and tribes of Indians, February, 1816. Note that the Quapaws (Arkansas) are assigned boundaries north of the Arkansas River and east of the Mississippi River. Courtesy National Archives.

In May, 1816, he sent David Musick and William Parker to the Arkansas country to deliver an order instructing the several hundred white families to remove from the lands claimed by the Downstream People. The two also carried an invitation to the Quapaw chiefs requesting them to meet in St. Louis with representatives of the Cherokees and Osages early that fall.[54] Such measures, undoubtedly, were based on certain fundamental assumptions. First, Clark believed that the Quapaws were an influential people numbering at least 1,000 and that they had a well-established claim to the territory between the Arkansas and Canadian Rivers on the north and the Red River on the south.[55] Second, he assumed that the tribe had dominion over a tract of land on which some emigrant

Cherokees had already settled, the title to which would have to be extinguished if the recent arrivals—some 2,600 strong—were to be assured of a homeland unfettered by prior tribal claim.[56] Finally, Clark believed that the white settlers not only were illegal intruders but also were pre-empting lands that could later be assigned to eastern Indians other than Cherokees.[57] These assumptions prompted the governor's actions and accounted for the Quapaw chiefs' visit to St. Louis in early November, 1816. A Cherokee delegation accompanied them, although the Osage tribe declined to send one.

The negotiations that followed represented the first official discussions that the Downstream People had with the United States. From the beginning, their delegates made it clear that they wished to be accommodating. Although they complained bitterly about the white intrusion and the failure of the government to distribute gifts, they seemed interested in adopting the habits and improvements of the emigrant Cherokees. To obtain stock, farming implements, and also an annuity, the chiefs agreed to cede over half of their land, which could then be used by the Cherokees or even the white settlers. Ironically, Governor Clark and his associate commissioners found themselves unable to take advantage of this opportunity. Their instructions from Secretary of War Crawford enjoined them to accept no cession of land motivated only by the desire of the Indians to win an annuity from the government. Moreover, since the secretary had stated that public interest and protection of the frontier required a compact settlement pattern, a Quapaw cession for no reason other than to protect the interests of the whites in the Arkansas country was undesirable. Finally, Crawford had insisted that no effort be made to provide lands for the Cherokee emigrants until the parent body in the southern Appalachians agreed to exchange an equal amount of their eastern domain. Despite the willingness of the Downstream People to part with much of their own territory, then, Clark's hands were tied. He could do no more than assure the Quapaw and western Cherokee delegates "that their situation should be correctly represented to the President," entertain them, and then, in late November, send them back to Arkansas pending a more propitious opportunity for discussions. The Quapaws were most disappointed but, according to Clark, did not despair "of eventually obtaining from our Government that Justice to which they [thought] themselves entitled."[58]

The conditions which doomed the negotiations to failure altered within the next few months, making "justice" for the Downstream People more imminent than the governor might have thought. The white settlers in Arkansas County had registered a vigorous complaint against Clark's order that they remove from tribal lands, even before the St. Louis conclave.[59] Immediately after, the territorial assembly came to their support in a resolution objecting to only "160" Indians holding title to such a vast extent of land, especially since "they never pretended to claim more than about fifty miles square until within about two years."[60] In early 1817 the long-smoldering conflict between the Cherokees and the Osages flared into open warfare, and by joining the emigrants, the Quapaws threatened to add to the turmoil.[61] Moreover, in July the eastern Cherokees finally agreed to accommodate their Arkansas brethren and exchange a portion of their lands for a western domain, the title to which the United States promised to perfect.[62] And finally, John C. Calhoun became the new secretary of war and brought to the office a decided commitment to some form of removal of the eastern tribes. He had no scruples against accepting Indian land cessions that might result in an irregular frontier settlement pattern. Indeed, the conviction was growing that instead of expelling the whites in the Arkansas country, they should be encouraged to stay. The defense of the republic seemed to require an unbroken chain of settlements on the west bank of the Mississippi from St. Louis to New Orleans.[63] Given the pressure from settlers, the Cherokee-Osage war, the need to provide a clear title to emigrants, defense considerations, and a new administration, the necessity to renew negotiations with the Quapaws was clear.

Secretary Calhoun, therefore, in February, 1818, instructed Governor Clark and Auguste Chouteau, a noted St. Louis trader, to solicit from the Downstream People a land cession that could be exchanged for the homelands of eastern Indians who chose to emigrate to the West. Three thousand dollars was set aside to cover the expense of the negotiations. Upon the basis of these instructions, in early July, Governor Clark dispatched his nephew, Benjamin O'Fallon, to the Quapaw villages to invite tribal leaders to meet in St. Louis. The following month a delegation led by Chief Heckaton arrived in the territorial capitol. The delegates were undoubtedly anxious that this time they should not fail to secure the annuity that had escaped them two years earlier. Working with this attitude, lavish entertainment, and the distribution of gifts that included a military uniform for Heckaton, a treaty was quickly negotiated and signed August 24, 1818. By its terms the Downstream People ceded to the United States all claims to the east bank of the Mississippi River and to the north bank of the Arkansas River. Of more significance, they relinquished title to a tract encompassed by a line that began at the mouth of the Arkansas, followed it to the South Canadian, continued along the latter to its source, turned south to Red River, extended down that stream to the great raft (a log jam well known as a landmark) and east to the Mississippi, from whence it went back to the Arkansas. Within this immense tract "which at all times heretofore has been considered their property," the Quapaws retained for themselves a reservation that was bounded on the north by the Arkansas River, on the southeast by a line extending from the Post of Arkansas to the Ouachita River, on the southwest by the Ouachita and Saline rivers, and on the northwest by a line that followed a "due northeast" course from Little Rock on the Arkansas to the Saline. Altogether, the tribe ceded an estimated thirty million acres and reserved for themselves a tract of about two million acres. In return the United States guaranteed the accommodating Quapaws the perpetual right to hunt in the relinquished territory, made them an immediate gift of manufactured items valued at $4,000, and promised them an annuity of $1,000 to be paid in goods and merchandise.[64]

The significance of the Treaty of 1818 cannot be overestimated. For the United States it spelled the success of the increasingly popular removal policy, securing an area which was unfettered with prior tribal claims and which could be exchanged for Indian lands east of the Mississippi. For the Quapaws the treaty tacitly recognized that their cooperation was necessary if the American government was to successfully incorporate Louisiana into its national purposes. That this contribution differed dramatically from that made to France and Spain was apparently lost upon Heckaton and his colleagues. Judging from the way the chief later ostentatiously produced his copy of the treaty for Thomas Nuttall, the renowned American traveler and naturalist, the Downstream People believed that the terms of the document confirmed their status as valuable allies of the United States.[65] The American government had, after all, pledged to the Quapaws a perpetual annuity of greater value than the gifts bestowed annually by the two European powers. Moreover, the tribe had ceded nothing more than hunting territory, which was hardly a

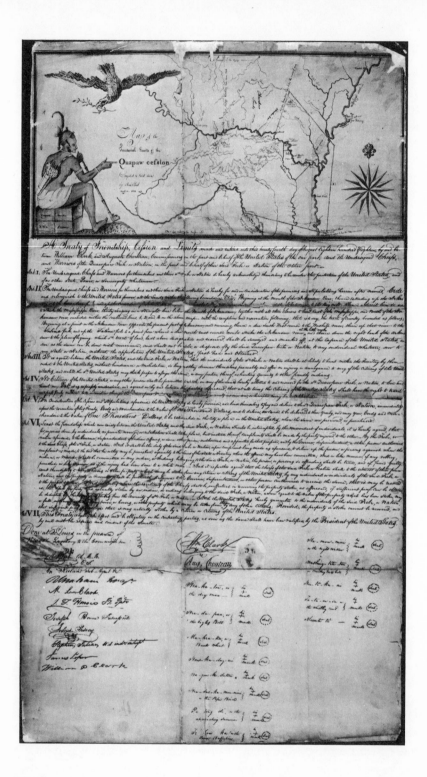

Photograph of the Quapaw–United States Treaty, August 24, 1818, facing page. Detail enlarged, this page. Courtesy National Archives.

significant loss, for the right to hunt in it had been continued under the treaty. The Quapaws deduced that the United States believed them to be a people of worth, meriting consideration and perpetuation. Had they been able to foresee the future, they might have reached a different conclusion.

CHAPTER IV
INTO THE WILDERNESS
1819-39

United States policy affecting Quapaw-American relations prior to 1818 was conceived within the context of national interests. On the basis of information compiled at St. Louis, the Downstream People were seen as prospective commercial partners who held one of the keys to successful removal of eastern Indians. Such views enabled the tribe to remain undisturbed in its ancestral domain and to maintain the fundamental character of its society. To be sure, the preservation of the Arkansas natives was not a primary consideration of the United States; yet it was a logical derivative of policy conceived and administered by bureaucrats situated far from the Quapaw villages. With the formation of Arkansas Territory in 1819, however, local, instead of national, considerations became paramount in determining the tribe's relationship with the American government. The result was a dramatic reversal of traditional policy, a change of status for the Quapaws, and eventual dispossession.

The reaction of white settlers in the Arkansas country to the size of the reservation retained by the Downstream People in the Treaty of 1818 marked the beginning of the new era. "[W]hile we highly approve the Benevolence and liberality of the government in Making Provision for that Peaceable and inoffensive tribe of Indians," wrote one group of petitioners, "We Deprocate [sic] the measure and Protest against . . . unnecessarily lavishing large Portions of Public and Private Property on Savages while total indifference or neglect is manifested towards their fellow citizens. . . ."[1] The Quapaw reserve, which Governor Clark had once labeled as good but swampy land, was to them the "gardin [sic] of Louisiana" and some "of the best soil" west of the Mississippi River.[2] Indeed, deprived of such an Eden, the nation's newest Territory could hardly expect to prosper

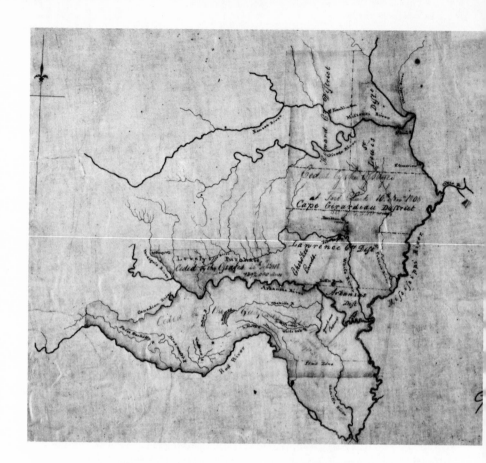

Map showing cession of the Quapaw Indians as made in the Treaty of August 24, 1818, and as plotted by the General Land Office of the United States, 1821. Courtesy National Archives.

and take its rightful place in the sisterhood of states. The *Arkansas Gazette,* therefore, in one of its earliest issues opined the absolute necessity of acquiring the remaining Quapaw lands. The first territorial legislature was of the same mind and petitioned the president of the United States to reduce the Indian reserve to no more than twelve square miles. And the first territorial delegate, J. Woodson Bates, introduced legislation in the national Congress to implement the request.[3]

For a time, however, federal officials ignored the pleas of the Arkansas settlers. Indeed, they demonstrated little interest in all matters relating to the Quapaws. James Miller, the first territorial governor, had been supplied with gifts to be distributed among the

Downstream People and other Indians in his jurisdiction, but by early 1820 the $1,000 annuity guaranteed the tribe in the recent treaty remained unpaid. The promised merchandise, diverted for a time to St. Louis, eventually arrived at Arkansas Post, but hardly in time to alleviate the suffering caused by the lack of supplies.[4] This unfortunate delay, as well as succeeding ones, did cause the government to change its procedures and pay the $1,000 directly to the territorial governor, who then converted the annuity into goods, a practice that was also a boon to local merchants.[5] Yet the new system was not foolproof. The annual payment was seldom forwarded with regularity. In 1824, when territorial officials pointed this out, Secretary of War Calhoun insisted that requisitions upon the treasury were regularly made and if any remained unpaid it was "from causes unknown to, or not within the control of this Department."[6]

This official unconcern manifested itself in other matters important to the Quapaws. Although sub-agents were assigned to the tribe between 1820 and 1822, Calhoun determined in the latter year that the Downstream People did not merit a resident government agent. His quest for economy also led him to deny the tribe access to a blacksmith who could repair guns, hoes, and axes.[7] Nor did the government protect the Arkansas natives from Osage depredations or support their efforts to gain redress from their warlike kinsmen. In April, 1821, for example, when the Osages murdered three Quapaw hunters just west of Fort Smith, Robert Crittenden, the acting territorial governor, directed the chiefs "to stay at home and tend their crops."[8] On other occasions when the Downstream People offered to join the Cherokees in a combined attack upon the Osages, they were similarly admonished. Quapaw retaliation, of course, would have contributed substantially to the turmoil in the Territory and jeopardized the removal policy cherished by Washington officials.[9]

That the tribe no longer claimed the attention of the federal government and had lost its status as a valuable ally became especially apparent when the boundaries of its diminished reserve were marked. The manuscript copy of the Treaty of 1818, that ratified by the United States Senate, had described the tract retained by the Quapaws as bounded by the following line: "Beginning at a point on the Arkansaw river opposite the present post of Arkansaw, and running thence a due South West course to the Washita river, thence up that river to the Saline fork, and up the Saline fork to a point from whence a due *North East* [italics mine] course would strike the Arkansaw river at the Little Rock, and thence down the right bank of the Arkansaw to the place of beginning. . . ."[10] As the map drawn at the top of the original treaty showed a north-south line from Little Rock rather than one "due North East" from the Saline and as William Clark had certified the former as the intended line, instructions to the surveyor directed that it be marked as the western boundary of the diminished reserve.[11] Despite the actual language of the treaty, therefore, the line surveyed in early 1819 effectively deprived the Quapaws of some 800 square miles of territory. Fearful of criticism but given the map and Clark's interpretation, Washington officials acted to make the official description conform to the surveyed line. Accordingly, when the published edition of the treaty appeared, "due North East course" became "due *north* [italics mine] course."[12] Governor Miller pointed out the discrepancy and the Downstream People protested it, but all to no avail. The north-south line as surveyed remained the western border of the tribal reserve, the original language of the treaty notwithstanding.

Although the government could ignore issues considered important by the Quapaws themselves, it could not for long dismiss the demands of settlers and territorial officials that relations with the Indians be reviewed. That the tribe might have a legal claim to lands beyond the borders recently surveyed was reason enough to insist upon a reassessment. Just as important was the government's removal policy, which had resulted in the resettlement of large numbers of eastern Indians along the Territory's western limits. Resentful because they had been forced to leave their native domain, these "fierce and savage" people, wrote the editor of the *Arkansas Gazette*, were bent "on glutting [their] vengence on a weak and defenseless" white population. "Over-run by marauding savages," with Arkansas a veritable "Botany Bay," and with more Indians than could "well be kept in subjection," territorial residents believed that the least the government could do was to acquire the remainder of the lands possessed by the Quapaws.[13] Moreover, since the Downstream People were threatening to side with the Cherokees in their war against the Osages, white Arkansans saw the Quapaws as endangering their own peace and security as well as impeding their statehood ambitions. As they saw it, the federal government was obligated to help the Territory combat the Quapaw "menace."[14]

But to persuade Washington officials to act was another matter, requiring a campaign of deceitfulness and half-truths. As early as October, 1821, the territorial legislature informed the United States Congress that the tribe was willing to cede its diminished reserve and combine with other Indian peoples.[15] In December, "One of the People" declared in the *Gazette* that the Quapaws should "*be allowed* [italics mine] to join the Caddoes, south of Red River."[16] Jedediah Morse, the father of American geography, in his 1822 report to the secretary of war on Indian affairs gave such sentiments national publicity by including a letter from a Little Rock correspondent that asked rhetorically if it would not be good policy for the government to acquire the domain of the Quapaws and pay for it in agricultural implements.[17] Moreover, in June, 1822, Henry W. Conway, a candidate for territorial delegate, advised the War Department that the tribe was anxious to amalgamate with the Caddoes and could be persuaded to sell their reserve for no more than $50,000. The tract could then be resold for a profit of not less than $500,000![18] Anxious that there be tangible evidence of the accuracy of this report, in mid-1823 Acting Governor Robert Crittenden informed Secretary Calhoun that he had the Downstream People—"a poor, indolent, miserable, remnant of a nation, insignificant and inconsiderable"—in "training for a Treaty." He also estimated that only $25,000 would "rid the Government of them" forever.[19] Finally, to demonstrate the earnestness of the Territory, Delegate Conway in December introduced legislation calling upon the president to appoint commissioners to treat with the Quapaws and providing $5,000 to defray the expenses of the negotiations.[20]

Even if the administration of President James Monroe had wished to do so, it could not have protected the Downstream People from the determined demands that they cede their diminished reserve. By January, 1824, Calhoun was ready to accede to the wishes of territorial residents, especially given the "willingness" of the Quapaws to remove elsewhere. Accordingly, he endorsed the frantic efforts of Conway on Capitol Hill and adopted measures designed to secure an appropriation adequate for the purchase of the tribal domain.[21] On May 26, 1824, Congress authorized $7,500 to carry out the negotiations; one month later Calhoun commissioned Robert Crittenden to secure the desired cession and amalgamation. And as a testimony to Conway's role in pushing the measure through Congress, the secretary entrusted a $7,000 warrant to him that would cover the expenses of the transaction.[22]

*Henry W. Conway, territorial delegate of Arkansas,
won the appropriation from the United States Congress
that resulted in the first removal treaty of 1824.*

Despite the expectations and communications of territorial officials, however, the Downstream People proved less than eager to
cede the remainder of their ancestral homeland. Indeed, in May,
1824, when seventy-nine Quapaws visited Little Rock—the new
capital of the Territory—for one of Crittenden's "training" exer-
cises, they demonstrated that they were in no "humor for parting
with their lands."[23] Nor, for that matter, did they appear to relish
the opportunity to join the Caddoes, among whom they had hunted
but with whom they had little else in common. But the acting governor was undaunted and at a long delayed annuity payment the
following month sought to gain the tribe's assent to removal. Apparently considering the talks formal negotiations, Chief Heckaton
and his people adamantly refused to abandon their diminished reserve, although they did agree to a diminution of its current borders.
At the very least, they insisted, the Quapaws would retain a ten mile
wide tract that extended from the Arkansas River south to the
Ouachita. Considering this a rather modest requirement, Crittenden
agreed to the partial cession, whereupon the Indians returned to
their villages convinced that they had preserved their right to remain in their homeland.[24]

Unfortunately, these negotiations were completed prior to Crittenden's receipt of his official instructions. Those orders, written in
light of the demonstrably false information received from the Territory, envisioned the total acquisition of the tribe's domain and the
incorporation of the native Arkansans with the Indians on Red
River. Confronted now with instructions that contradicted his con-
cessions to the Quapaws, the acting governor could only reassemble
the Downstream People and resume negotiations. Although Crittenden was somewhat embarrassed by the turn of events, the editor
of the *Gazette* decidedly was not. "This interesting news will be
highly gratifying to our citizens," he wrote. "We could scarcely wish
for more pleasing prospects for this section of the country."[25]

In response to the acting governor's request for further discussion,
in November, 1824, Chief Heckaton and his people gathered at Har-
rington's, a white settlement near their villages. If the vast quantities of provisions and presents shipped in from Kentucky suggested
to them that more than just friendly talks were anticipated, it was
not recorded. They apparently expected nothing more than to for-
malize the partial cession agreed upon the previous July. When Crittenden informed them that the earlier agreement was inoperative

and that the tribe was now expected to remove to Red River, the Quapaws were stunned. Heckaton declared himself deceived and insisted that he could not possibly go:

The land we now live on, belonged to our forefathers. If we leave it, where shall we go to? All of my nation, friends and relatives, are there buried. Myself am old, and in the same place I wish to deposit my bones. Since you have expressed a desire for us to remove, the tears have flowed copiously from my aged eyes. To leave my natal soil, and go among red men who are aliens to our race, is throwing us like outcasts upon the world.... Have mercy—send us not there.[26]

Forced to beg, the chief pleaded with the acting governor to honor his earlier commitment and permit the Quapaws to remain. "The land you wish to send us to now," he said, "is inhabited by many tribes; and to go there this winter, is terrifying to us."[27]

Unmoved and apparently undisturbed that he had reneged on a personal pledge, Crittenden seized upon Heckaton's reluctance to migrate *that winter*. He informed the chief that he did not anticipate the tribe's immediate removal; for that matter it might remain in its villages an additional year. Moreover, when the time for emigration arrived, the Quapaws would be abundantly supplied with powder, lead, and provisions sufficient to procure for them a "manly and independent livelihood," in sharp contrast to their "intoxicated ... , useless and effeminate" life in Arkansas. And finally, the president of the United States would speak to the Caddoes and "intercede with them to receive and treat [the Quapaws] as brethern."[28]

Despite their profound opposition, the Downstream People had no other alternative than to accept Crittenden's treaty. On the next day, November 15, 1824, fifteen chiefs and headmen signed a document whereby they ceded the reserve as described in the original manuscript of the Treaty of 1818—a tacit admission that the official version in the United States Statutes was in error—and agreed to join the Caddoes on Red River. As compensation for the cession, the government promised to pay $500 to each of four chiefs, to distribute immediately $4,000 in merchandise, to provide six months of subsistence on Red River, to pay annually for eleven years $1,000 in specie, and to assign some 2,320 acres to twelve persons of Indian descent named in the document.[29] But that was all. Contrary to existing federal policy whereby eastern emigrant tribes were allotted well-defined reserves further west, the treaty contained no provision for assigning a reservation to the Quapaws in exchange for their two million acres.[30] The tribe was simply to merge itself with the Caddoes and lose not only its ancestral home but its identity as well. No wonder Secretary Calhoun reputedly termed the treaty "the best ever made with an Indian tribe."[31]

Permitted to remain in Arkansas throughout the winter of 1824–25, the following June, Chief Heckaton appealed to a new territorial governor, George Izard, to allow his people to postpone removal. Izard refused the request, but as a counter proposal he encouraged the chief to send a party to investigate the site of the tribe's new home on the Red River. The governor also agreed that Antoine Barraque, a recent French emigrant who traded with the Quapaws and who had once served in Napoleon's army, should accompany the exploratory expedition.[32] In August, 1825, therefore, the tribal chiefs and headmen journeyed southwest to reconnoiter the Caddo lands. Upon reaching Red River, they learned that, contrary to promises made by Crittenden, neither the Caddoes nor their agent, George Gray, had received any official instructions with regard to the impending removal. Despite this confusion, which Governor Izard attributed to the "characteristic improvidence of the Indian," the Caddo chief was persuaded to accept the planned Quapaw settlement among his people, although he did not agree to the amalgamation of the two tribes.[33]

Meanwhile, Governor Izard made final preparations for the removal of the Downstream People. A congressional appropriation enabled him to budget $500 for a sub-agent to organize the emigration, $1,000 for transportation, and $10,000 for six months of rations. In early November the governor contracted with John Clark to provide fresh beef at three cents a pound, salt at five cents a pound, and corn meal at three cents a pound to be delivered at strategic locations along the removal route and on Red River. He also prepared a tribal role that enumerated 455 individuals (158 men, 123 women, and 174 children). Appointing Barraque to lead the tribe to the Caddo domain, Izard directed, finally, that emigration would commence on December 12, 1825.[34]

When the appointed date arrived, the Quapaws proved reluctant to go. Preemptory measures were required in order to effect actual departure, and one inducement apparently was payment of the 1825 annuity just before the trek began. Here again the white Arkansans were nonchalant when it came to conforming with treaty stipulations. Although the accord of 1818 had provided that a $1,000 annuity be paid in merchandise, the accord of 1824 had stipulated that another $1,000 be paid in specie, or coin. Yet in December the entire $2,000 was converted to trade goods before it was distributed.[35] Ultimately, in early January, 1826, the Quapaws, in groups of fifty individuals or more, slowly moved southwest from their ancestral domain. Inclement weather hampered their progress, but by the thirteenth of February advance parties were on the north bank of Red River in northwestern Louisiana. There they learned from Choctaw Indians that the Caddo chief had had second thoughts about permitting the Quapaws to settle among his people. Not until March 1 did Barraque finally induce the emigrants to cross the river, and then only after he had converted the rations due for the next four months into cash and distributed the balance per capita.[36]

Once over the river the Quapaws became embroiled in a dispute among themselves, the Caddoes, Barraque, and Agent George Gray. Concerned that the host tribe had indeed determined not to admit the emigrants, Barraque summoned the Caddo chief to the Quapaw camp in order to clarify the situation. He did this, unfortunately, without consulting Gray. Considering such action a threat to his own authority, the agent confronted Barraque, reminded him that he had no jurisdiction in the Caddo nation, and demanded that the Frenchman account for the rations supplied the Quapaws. Although neither man would accommodate the other, both had legitimate concerns. Barraque wanted the Quapaws to have a home which would not depend on the whim of the Caddoes, and he wanted the removal to be accomplished with as much economy as possible. On the other hand, Gray desired to maintain peace among the Indians, a peace which was threatened when the Downstream People insisted that they were more than the mere guests of the Caddoes. Additionally, the agent was convinced that the Quapaws would squander the money received for their rations and in their destitution would commit unsettling depredations in the white community.[37]

By mid-April the turmoil associated with the Quapaws' arrival on Red River had all but subsided. The accusations and counter-accusations made by Barraque and Gray were largely ignored by

Washington officials. It was of more concern to them that the removal had been completed with dispatch and thrift. Of the $10,000 allotted for six months of provisions, only $6,950.29, or eight and one-half cents per person per day, had been spent, considerably less than anticipated.[38] The Downstream People established themselves near the agency compound on Caddo Prairie some thirty miles northwest of present Shreveport, Louisiana. They built there three villages which corresponded to the tribal units in the Arkansas Valley. With seed furnished by the agent, they planted small fields of corn and watched with anticipation as green shoots pushed through the fertile soil. But in May, Red River flooded and inundated their crops. Undaunted, the Quapaws replanted their fields, only to have the fruit of their labor washed away again in June. Whether they might have profitably planted for a third time was beside the point. They no longer had the will. Starvation reigned. Sixty of their number, most of whom were women and children, died.[39]

The Quapaws also encountered other difficulties. The Caddoes proved less than hospitable hosts, and the assertion by Mexico of her sovereignty south and west of Red River seemingly placed the tribe beyond the protection of the United States. Moreover, when a portion of the 1826 annuity was allocated for the purchase of corn, the per capita payment to each Quapaw was markedly reduced.[40] Ravaged by nature, unwelcomed by the Caddoes, claimed by the Mexicans, and deprived of a large part of their personal funds, the tribe repented the decision to leave the Arkansas Valley. After only six months in Louisiana, approximately one-fourth of the tribe followed Sarasin, a half-blood chief elevated to authority by Governor Miller, back to their ancestral home.[41]

Tales of the recent distress of the returned Quapaws touched the hearts of the residents of Arkansas Territory. The *Gazette* editorialized that "humanity requires that some further provision should be made . . . for their relief."[42] Governor Izard promptly furnished Sarasin's band 500 bushels of corn, and in December, 1826, Henry Conway pushed through the United States House of Representatives a resolution requesting information as to "the present condition of the Quapaw Nation of Indians, and the measures, if any, that have been taken to alleviate their distresses." Conway's action prompted the Department of War to allocate $2,000 from contingent funds for the relief of that part of the tribe still on Red River.[43]

However timely the assistance, one tragic fact could not be obscured. The ancient unity of the Quapaw tribe was broken. Indeed, in January, 1827, Sarasin and his people petitioned the secretary of war to be permitted to remain in Arkansas, to be made American citizens, and to be granted land on equal terms with the white settlers. Although the government ignored the substantive requests, it did permit the Arkansas band to stay temporarily in the Territory and agreed to allocate one-fourth of the $2,000 tribal annuity to it. At the same time Washington officials also recommended that the returned Quapaws consider incorporating with the Cherokees.[44]

With the tribe and its annuity tragically divided, those of the Downstream People still on Red River confronted their destiny with resignation. Failing in an attempt to force Sarasin's band to rejoin the main body, they continued to plant their fields and struggled to maintain the tempo of their traditional life. But in June, 1828, just after their corn had sprouted, Red River rose again and inundated their fields. As they had two years before, the Quapaws once more found themselves totally destitute. The critical condition of the tribe prompted the agent to recommend their removal south of the so-called raft, or log jam, in the river to a location just southwest of modern Shreveport. Although the agency was later moved to that spot, whether the Quapaws under Heckaton ever made the southward trek was never recorded.[45]

Despite the return to Arkansas, Sarasin's small party fared little better. In their haste to demonstrate their worthiness to be American citizens, they cut themselves off from the immediate benefit of the annuity assigned them. At Sarasin's request, Governor Izard held most of the funds in order to accumulate monies sufficient to purchase land for the use of the band. With the remainder he acquired hoes, axes, and plows, and arranged to send some tribal youngsters to school.[46] Deprived of their annual stipends and declining to join either the Cherokees or the Osages—the latter suggested by the governor—,the returned Quapaws built homes in isolated areas, cultivated small fields, and hired themselves out as hunters and cotton pickers.[47] They were so inconspicuous and unobtrusive that the Arkansas Gazette, ordinarily alert to any "Indian problem," failed to report upon them. For that matter, the federal government ignored them too, taking cognizance only to recommend the band's amalgamation with still another tribe. From Washing-

Robert Crittenden, secretary and acting governor
of Arkansas Territory, who negotiated the
Quapaw Removal Treaty of 1824.
Courtesy Arkansas History Commission.

ton's point of view the Downstream People were in Arkansas by courtesy of the Territory only and not by any official sanction.[48]

That Sarasin's band was permitted to remain on ancestral lands did not go unnoticed by the remainder of the tribe on Red River. What they knew of the Quapaws in Arkansas seemed to contrast sharply with their own situation: their crops were regularly flooded, they were encouraged to make still another removal, their annuity seldom arrived promptly, they were demoralized by contraband whiskey, and their agent had died recently. No wonder, then, that throughout 1829 and 1830 small parties left Louisiana and rejoined their brethren on the Arkansas River. So complete was the migration that in September, 1830, no more than forty Quapaws remained in the Caddo country. By the end of the following month, "almost to a man" they were gone. It is notable, though, that one of the last to leave was the principal chief, Heckaton.[49]

Though a joyous event for the tribe, its reunification brought unanticipated hardships. Administrative red tape and the economic conditions of the frontier made it impossible to have that part of the annuity recently distributed on Red River paid instead in Arkansas. Thus, the Quapaws were left without funds.[50] Combined with the general physical distress, this economic problem reduced the tribe to begging the federal government for relief. Indeed, Chief Heckaton determined personally to explain the plight of his people to President Andrew Jackson, and in December, 1830, accompanied Arkansas's territorial delegate, Ambrose H. Sevier, to Washington. The chief probably never saw Jackson, but once on the Potomac he did enter into correspondence with Secretary of War John Eaton. Heckaton appealed to him to assign the tribe lands in the vicinity of Arkansas Post and to permit the Quapaws to live as American citizens. To underscore the good intentions of the tribe he also asked that a portion of its annuity be set aside to finance the education of young men he had just enrolled in the famous Choctaw Academy at Blue Springs, Kentucky. He requested as well that a sub-agent and an interpreter be appointed to assist the tribe in its development and in communications with the federal government.[51]

The secretary of war proved partially amenable to Heckaton's requests. He directed that $900, or almost half, of the tribe's annuity be applied each year toward educational purposes and that a sub-agent be appointed. Yet Eaton refused to assign the returned Quapaws a permanent residence in Arkansas, although he did agree that they could remain until the land upon which they were squatting was sold or until a more suitable home could be selected for them elsewhere.[52]

If Secretary Eaton believed that he had complied with the basic wishes of the tribe, the Quapaws certainly did not. Their satisfaction with the assignment of a sub-agent was dimmed when Wharton Rector, a prominent territorial politician, received the appointment instead of their choice, Antoine Barraque. Chief Heckaton, they believed, had agreed to the naming of Rector only with "the assistance of spirits." They also complained that despite the chief's visit to Washington the government did not have an accurate picture of their grievances, that the $900 set aside for educational purposes would emasculate their annuity, and that funds solemnly promised by treaty were not regularly paid.[53]

But their objections were ignored, and the Downstream People could only make the best of an increasingly difficult situation. Most burdensome was their inability to receive annuity payments. To be sure, in 1830 two $1,000 warrants were issued; but because the sub-agent had not yet been bonded, he could not receive them. Unaware of the administrative problem, the Quapaws accused Rector of intentional fraud.[54] When advised that the tribe had not received its money, the government again cavalierly declared that the annuities had been regularly issued and if they were not paid it was no fault of Washington officials. To compound the problem, in January, 1832, a new commissioner of Indian affairs, Elbert Herring, ordered that future annuity payments be suspended, insisting that the tribe had forfeited rights to them by returning to Arkansas.[55]

Such an order placed the Quapaws in an untenable position. They needed the money if they were to survive, but at the same time they had no desire to return to Louisiana. Fortunately the crisis was eased by the timely intervention of a new territorial governor, John Pope of Kentucky. Considering the Quapaws harmless, inoffensive, and much defrauded, Pope sought permission to purchase public lands in Arkansas for the benefit of the Indians. So untypically Jacksonian was this request that the government took pause and determined to reassess its policy with regard to the tribe. Officials reasoned that if the governor saw the Quapaws as meriting special consideration, perhaps policy changes were in order. Accordingly, to decide the course of future relations with the tribe the Indian office submitted the case to the so-called Stokes Commission, a three-member delegation authorized in July, 1832, to adjust all Indian problems west of the Mississippi. Also, rather than make the payment of annuities to the tribe contingent upon its return to Red River, government officials determined only to suspend payment until the Stokes Commission acted.[56]

As the Quapaws awaited their fate, their situation in Arkansas continued to deteriorate. The payment in the spring of 1832 of the annuity so long denied them, the distribution of a $1,500 annuity the following year, and a supplemental donation of $1,000 neither paid their debts nor supplied their wants. Land-hungry whites also rudely evicted the Quapaws from their isolated cabins and forced them off of their fields.[57] Previously ignored by the *Arkansas Gazette,* the Downstream People were now labeled as troublesome and described as "drunken vagabond savages."[58] Dispossessed and demeaned, the Quapaws could only retreat into the swamps, hoping to find in those recesses the refuge that had heretofore eluded them.

Touched by their plight, Richard Hannum, whose recent appointment as sub-agent was a tacit admission by the government that it had some responsibility toward the Indians, took it upon himself to press for an immediate disposition of the Quapaw case. In early May, 1833, he made a special trip up the Arkansas River to Fort Gibson where the Stokes Commission was then assembling and persuaded the members to make the status of his charges one of their first items of business. The Reverend Mr. J. F. Schermerhorn and the commission's secretary, S. C. Stambaugh, then accompanied Hannum back downriver to New Gascony, near present Pine Bluff, Arkansas, where the Quapaws had previously assembled, having anticipated the success of the agent's mission.[59]

Discussions with the tribe began on Saturday, May 11, 1833. In his opening statement, Commissioner Schermerhorn informed the Quapaws that the president of the United States was aware of their difficulties and wanted to remove them to more western lands, set apart by Congress as permanent homes for different Indian peoples. In their new domain the government would take care of them, protect them from all harm, and provide them with the necessary implements to engage successfully in agriculture. Characteristically, Chief Heckaton responded that his people had haunting doubts about removing farther west, having heard, among other things, that the winters were so cold that livestock would die. Instead, he proposed that the Quapaws be permitted to remain in the land of their nativity, where the bones of their ancestors were buried. They would even be willing to take up homes in the swamps, far removed from the fertile fields desired by white men. Without giving a reason Schermerhorn responded that such a request could not be granted. It was best, he said, that the tribe should live by itself beyond the influences of evil whites. The old chief, however, had heard such language before and was not persuaded.[60]

Because the next day was Sunday, the commissioner's day of worship, negotiations were recessed until Monday, May 13. When they resumed, Heckaton had relented in his opposition to removal to the point where he could declare: "I know I have to die[.] [I]t matters not where it is[,] here[,] on Red River or at the new home promised us."[61] Seeing his opportunity, Schermerhorn immediately presented a draft of a proposed treaty. The agreement called for the assignment to the Quapaws of 150 sections of land west of the state line of Missouri and between the reservations recently assigned to the Senecas and Shawnees. It called for the United States to bear the expenses of removal and for the government to provide subsistence for one year upon completion of emigration. In addition to livestock of various kinds, agricultural implements, and firearms, the treaty also authorized the employment of a farmer and a blacksmith for the benefit of the tribe and stipulated that $1,000 a year be allocated for educational purposes. The perpetual and limited annuities provided in previous treaties were commuted to pay the tribe's debts, amounting to $4,180, while a new $2,000 annuity was authorized for twenty years.[62] Altogether the treaty terms were liberal, especially in light of those accepted in 1824. The Quapaws had to leave their ancestral domain, but at least this time they would have an assigned homeland and retain their identity as a separate people. Accordingly, they turned their faces toward the west.

The implementation of the treaty, of course, depended upon its ratification by the United States Senate. This was not accomplished until April 12, 1834, some eleven months after the initial negotiations. The delay was most unfortunate, for in the spring of 1833 the Arkansas River flooded and drove the Quapaws from their homes yet another time.[63] Even worse, the tribe again found itself divided. A part of an annuity to have been paid in 1830 on Red River had remained undistributed by virtue of the tribe's return to Arkansas. Following an official inquiry as to the disposition of the money, the Caddo agent, Jehiel Brooks, in the spring of 1833 informed those few of the Downstream People remaining in his jurisdiction that if the tribe presented itself at his agency, a distribution would be made. These Quapaws took the information to the majority of the tribe in Arkansas.[64] Dispossessed by the cruelties of nature, uncertain of their future because of the inaction of the Senate, and informed that the Osages would kill them in Indian Territory, some three hundred Indians in June followed Sarasin back to Red River. Upon their arrival, the Quapaws even petitioned the government to be permitted to remain among the Caddoes, a request that was rejected. Brooks nonetheless paid out the funds previously entrusted to him and later distributed another $1,000—actions not calculated to force a return of Sarasin to Arkansas.[65]

Despite the unfortunate division of the tribe, the government proceeded·with its plan to remove to Indian Territory those Quapaws remaining in Arkansas. Wharton Rector was appointed as the agent responsible for the emigration. In September, 1834, near Pine Bluff, he collected and enrolled the 176 Quapaws, including Heckaton, whom he would conduct west. Rector also arranged for rations at a cost of eight cents each and settled upon a route. On September 16, he departed the rendezvous point and after a thirty-day journey arrived in Indian Territory with 161 Indians. He settled the Quapaws in what is now the northeast corner of Oklahoma on lands he took to be those assigned the tribe in the recent treaty. After Rector returned to Little Rock, George Fletcher, the Commissary General of Subsistence, appointed an agent to issue to Heckaton and his people the subsistence provisions promised in the treaty as well as the livestock and agricultural implements. The wool cards, looms, and spinning wheels that were also to have been delivered to the Quapaws were, unfortunately, lost when the *Neosho* sank in the Arkansas River.[66]

According to the Treaty of 1833 the new Quapaw reserve was to have been situated between that of the Senecas and Shawnees. Given this description and his general knowledge of the region, Rector properly located his charges near the Neosho River just west of the Missouri border. The Downstream People, having no reason to question his decision, established their villages, and the following spring they planted their common field to corn and pumpkins.[67] Unknown to them and, for that matter, to Rector, the government had determined once again to ignore boundaries specifically stated in a treaty. As the Senecas and Shawnees had "become contiguous to each other," wrote the commissioner of Indian affairs, "[t]he reservation of the Quapaws ... will be located west of the Missouri State line, and north of the Senecas and Shawnees."[68] On the basis of this decision, the "approved" reserve of the Downstream People was surveyed in the spring of 1836 when, to the surprise of no one, it was ascertained that the Quapaws had been improperly located.[69] In the fall of 1839, therefore, the government directed yet another removal of the tribe.[70] And this time, at least for Heckaton's band, it was the last.

During the course of the emigration to Indian Territory, the 300 Quapaws still in the Caddo country steadfastly refused to join their brothers. This decision was made despite the closing of the Red River agency in July, 1834, the admonitions of the government, and the pleas of a deputation sent by Chief Heckaton. In late 1835 more than fifty Quapaws did join those on the assigned reserve, but the remainder—who had apparently comprised one entire village—either crossed into Texas to join Chief Bowles's Cherokees or took up temporary residences among the Choctaws in what is now southern Oklahoma.[71] Among those declining to reside in Indian Territory was Sarasin. Sometime after 1834 he returned to Arkansas to live out the remainder of his days and to become something of a folkhero. Fifty years later a memorial window in his honor was placed in St. Joseph's church in Pine Bluff, and his body was removed to the church's cemetery. Since Sarasin was a mixed-blood whose motives were usually economic rather than patriotic, such honors may have been more than he deserved.[72]

The removal of the Downstream People from their ancestral domain was accomplished within twenty years after the creation of Arkansas Territory. As filled with pathos as it was, the story of the tribe's dispossession had additional significance beyond its immediate impact upon the Quapaws. It illustrated, for example, how objectives of federal Indian policy frequently changed at the Mississippi River. Secretary of War John C. Calhoun insisted that when eastern Indians ceded part of their homeland they should receive as compensation tracts of land—sometimes of immense proportions—beyond the Mississippi. Yet western Indians received no such consideration. In 1824 the Quapaws relinquished their entire reservation but were granted nothing in exchange. Rather than be preserved as a separate people, like the eastern tribes, they were expected to become extinct as a tribe.

The removal of the Quapaws also indicated how a detached and moderate Indian policy formulated in a national context could on the local level become corrupted and perverted. Before 1824, dealing with officials resident in St. Louis and Washington, the Downstream People were neither maltreated nor maligned. But with territorial status for Arkansas and with the governor becoming superintendent of Indian affairs, the nature of Indian policy changed. Local white residents insisted that the tribe was a nuisance in that it occupied valuable lands and jeopardized statehood ambitions. As a consequence, territorial officials not only ignored treaty provisions and engaged in deceit but pressured the federal government to expel the Quapaws. A temperate policy thus became wholly intemperate, particularly in 1824 but also in 1833.

Dispossession of the Indian was a national theme in the 1830s. Andrew Jackson had been elected in 1828 on a platform that had as its principal plank just such a goal. Yet the Quapaw story during those troubled years made it clear that there was a humane side to some of the officials responsible for making Indian policy. Governor John Pope and sub-agent Richard Hannum, both Jackson appointees, were most sensitive to the needs of the tribe and championed a course of action that sought to alleviate its unfortunate condition. The Reverend Mr. Schermerhorn, another appointee, included language in the Treaty of 1833 that restored a measure of dignity to the Downstream People and guaranteed their preservation as a separate entity.

Finally, the removal of the Quapaws illustrated the inconsistency and ineptness of federal Indian policy. Having settled upon removal of the tribe to Red River in 1824, the government effectively negated that objective two years later when it permitted Sarasin to remain in Arkansas. When the balance of the tribe joined Sarasin's band, the Indian bureau reversed itself and demanded that all of the Quapaws go back to Louisiana. But when Governor Pope interceded for the tribe, the government negotiated a new treaty that directed the resettlement of the Indians west of Missouri. Sarasin promptly subverted the intent of that agreement by returning to Red River, where federal officials not only disbursed the unclaimed annuity but other funds as well. The result of such vacillation was to reduce the Quapaws from an independent to a pathetically dependent and di-

*George Izard, territorial governor of Arkansas
at the time the Quapaws were forced to
remove to Red River in December, 1825.
Courtesy Arkansas History Commission.*

vided people. That they survived at all was miraculous, a testimony
to the efforts of a few humane, untypical Jacksonian appointees and
to the timeless traditions of the Downstream People themselves.

CHAPTER V
THE DISPOSSESSED
1839-65

Given the provisions of the Treaty of 1833, the Downstream People assumed that removal to a new homeland would herald a marked improvement in the quality of their life. With rich, dark soils, deep flowing streams, abundant timber, and luxuriant prairie grasses, the assigned reserve was most promising. Moreover, the Quapaws would have the advantages of an agent, a farmer, a blacksmith, and an annuity. These benefits certainly did prevent the dramatic suffering characteristic of the decade prior to removal, but they failed to insulate the Arkansas natives from a comparable end—wholesale dispossession. The difference was only in the nature of the process that accomplished the reduction. Before 1835 it had been swift and spectacular; after, it was slow and almost imperceptible.

Whether intentional or not, government policy generally contributed to the dispossession. The official desire to resettle eastern Indians west of the Mississippi had accounted for the tribe's relinquishment of most of its ancestral domain, and its eventual removal resulted from government efforts to accommodate the economic and political aspirations of territorial Arkansas. Once the Quapaws were assembled on their assigned reservation, Washington officials of Jacksonian vintage attempted to isolate them from the corrupt influences of the white man by adhering to the provisions of the 1834 Indian Trade and Intercourse law. Ironically, they simultaneously sought to recast the Downstream People in the image of the predominant white population by turning them into agriculturalists imbued with the precepts of Christianity, individual toil, and private property. To produce a "civilized" Indian was dispossession of another variety; yet, given the government's policy objectives, such dispossession was more insidious and perhaps just as effective as a traumatic removal. The deprivations and displacement suffered by the Quapaws during the Civil War further weakened their cultural integrity and economic independence. By 1865, therefore, the extinction of the tribe as a proud and unique people was nearly complete.

The official will of the government, though, was not always clear, and it filtered down to the Quapaws through a sometimes mystifying bureaucratic structure. Along with the Osages, the Senecas, and the mixed Senecas and Shawnees, the Downstream People comprised first a sub-agency and after 1851 an agency. Known initially as the Neosho Agency but later as the Quapaw Agency, it was attached to a superintendency (which was at first the Western and then, after 1867, the Central), one of several regional offices that reported directly to the Bureau of Indian Affairs in Washington. Originally a part of the War Department, the Indian office in 1849 was transferred to the Department of the Interior. Presumably the bureaucracy implemented policy legislated by the United States Congress, but its administration of the congressional will frequently resulted in action that had a different, perhaps contrary, emphasis. Often inconsistent, policy became even more confused when applied by a succession of different agents. With contrasting backgrounds, personalities, and concepts of office, these functionaries made their own interpretations of official directives, applied them unevenly, and made radically varying conclusions as to their effectiveness. For the Downstream People the bureaucratic structure and the uncertainties of policy produced a confusion of torturous proportions that left them all but impotent in their struggle for self-preservation.

In the thirty years following the removal of the Quapaws to Indian Territory, at no time was the government more heavy-handed than at the beginning. After Heckaton and his people had established their customary villages and laid out a common field near the Neosho River in the fall of 1834, subsistence provisions were regularly provided, the first $2,000 annuity was delivered, and they were joined by more than a hundred of their kinsmen who had abandoned the Red River settlement. Yet all of this happened before their 150-section reservation was officially marked according to the instructions of the commissioner of Indian affairs rather than the language of the treaty.[1] Although the official survey in the spring of 1836 confirmed the necessity of another removal, the government did not carry through with the relocation until late 1838. Instead, the Downstream People were permitted to languish in uncertainty at the site of their initial settlements. And when the belated removal actually occurred, members of the tribe were not permitted to re-establish their traditional villages. Instead the Quapaws were located on widely dispersed individual homesteads. An action calculated to disrupt their social patterns and to encourage an alien agricultural system, this resettlement of the Quapaws was wholly unexpected and had devastating consequences. Many of the tribe abandoned the reservation, causing a political division that remained somewhat permanent throughout the nineteenth century.[2]

Those one hundred or so of the Downstream People who now found life on the reserve untenable sought refuge among their brethren then living in northeastern Texas. Representing one of the three traditional villages and the remnants of Sarasin's band, the latter group had recently crossed into Texas and joined Chief Bowles's Cherokees and associated bands who had been in the vicinity of present Nacogdoches for more than a decade. The southern Quapaws—at least one hundred strong as well—had also been party to the so-called Consultation of November 13, 1835, by which Texas leaders assigned to the Indians lands now comprising Cherokee and Smith counties. On February 23 of the following year this agreement had been formalized in a treaty with the Texas Provisional Government.[3] The Quapaw dissidents from the reservation in Indian Territory, then, joined their southern brethren at a time when harmony between the various associated tribes under Chief Bowles and the Texans prevailed.

Peace and good will did not last for long, however. Following independence from Mexico and the creation of the Republic of Texas, the Indians found themselves accused of pre-empting valuable agricultural land and of joining in a military effort designed to return the province to Mexico. Sam Houston was able to shield the tribes from eviction during his presidency, but his successor, Mirabeau B. Lamar, considered the Indians a menace and lent his influence to a movement intended to dispossess them. When Bowles and his people refused to remove peacefully from Texas, Lamar applied force. The Republic's army, commanded by Joseph E. Johnston, attacked the Indians on July 15 and 16, 1839, defeated them decisively, and pursued them until most of them had crossed the Red River into the Choctaw nation. Thus did the southern

Quapaws learn that dispossession was also the policy of a government other than that of the United States.[4]

Despite their unhappy sojourn on Texas soil, the fleeing Downstream People elected not to return to the reservation. Whether from lingering intratribal animosities or disillusionment with life on the reserve, they elected instead to establish homes in the western part of the Choctaw domain on streams tributary to Red River. The host tribe, unfortunately, considered the refugees to be unwelcome intruders and prevailed upon United States troops to evict them.[5] Wanderers once again, they moved northward across the Canadian River, where the Creek Indians granted them permission to establish a village. By 1842, 250 Quapaws were located eight miles west of where Little River empties into the Canadian, just south of present Holdenville, Oklahoma.[6] From this site they ventured west to the Plains, hunted buffalo, and even engaged in commerce with the Comanches and other tribes. They proved to be valuable allies for the Creeks, defending their western frontier from depredations by raiding Indians such as the Pawnees.[7] In the late 1840's some of the southern Quapaws also established a village on the False Washita west of modern Chickasha. When the Chickasaws complained, in 1852 they relocated on Chouteau's Creek where Lexington, Oklahoma, would later be established.[8] By the following year at least some of these Quapaws had returned to the Little River encampment, where members of Lieutenant A. W. Whipple's expedition observed them and counted twenty-five warriors, suggesting a total population of somewhat less than one hundred.[9]

As their fellow tribesmen established themselves along the Canadian River and adopted a somewhat different lifestyle, the Downstream People on the reservation struggled with the myriad adjustments demanded by government officials. One of these changes was diplomatic in nature. The Quapaws and various other recent Indian emigrants were deemed intruders by many of the Plains tribes who ranged over much of what is now western Oklahoma. Consequently, when the newcomers ventured west of the so-called Cross Timbers, it was at the risk of life and property. As early as August, 1835, the United States sought to mediate this dispute by negotiating a tripartite agreement between the government, the emigrants, and the Plains tribes at Camp Holmes in present McClain County. Chief Heckaton and twenty-two other delegates represented the Quapaws at the conclave, which was also attended by members of the Cherokee, Creek, Choctaw, Osage, Seneca, Comanche, and Wichita tribes. Proclamations of good will and exhortations of peace marked the occasion. Heckaton declared, for example, that "There must not be any blood . . . unless it be the blood of the Buffalo."[10] With such sentiments predominating, the Treaty of Camp Holmes was concluded on August 4, with the Plains tribes pledging to live at peace with their new neighbors.

The 1835 meeting was only one of many negotiations designed to adjust problems unique to an Indian territory. Between 1837 and 1845, six other meetings were also hosted by the Cherokees or the Creeks, all of which were attended by Quapaw delegates. Invariably the objectives of these meetings were to further peace and friendship, to perpetuate tribal customs, and to discourage participation in Mexican intrigues. Although not always successful, they more often than not eased intertribal tensions and represented a remarkable attempt to solve problems that emanated from the government's forced resettlement of eastern Indians adjacent to tribes who considered all intruders enemies. Had reconciliation of differences with the Plains tribes been the only adjustment necessary in the wake of removal or, put differently, if removal had been the culmination rather than the genesis of government policy, the Quapaws and other emigrants might have fared well. As it was, intertribal diplomacy was only tangential to the alterations of traditional patterns anticipated by American officials.[11]

While the long-range goal of the Bureau of Indian Affairs was to remake the Downstream People in the image of the white man, the immediate objective was to turn them into self-sufficient agriculturalists. To facilitate the conversion, the Treaty of 1833 had provided for a farmer, a blacksmith, and thirty cabins to be located on individual homesteads. After the cabins were constructed in 1839,[12] some of the Quapaws felt secure enough to break fields for planting and to place at least one hundred acres of corn under cultivation. But over the next six years the area in production increased only twenty acres, hardly an impressive showing for a people who before the advent of the white man had been farmers of note.[13] Various agents attributed this disinterest in agriculture to the lazy and indolent habits of the Quapaws, to their insistence that the agency farmer do their work rather than show them how to do it, and to their belief that it was a disgrace to labor.[14] "They say," reported one, "that they are brave warriors and good hunters, and never will acknowledge their inability to make a living by hunting, by working with their hands like a *squaw*."[15] It was such sentiment, no doubt, that prompted the tribal chiefs in 1848 to request that the position of farmer be discontinued and that the government make presents of blankets instead.[16] While it was true that some Quapaws on the reservation continued to make annual trips to the plains to kill buffalo and that most of them hunted the adjacent woodlands for bear, deer, beaver, and raccoon, the lack of interest in agriculture also stemmed from the cultural disorientation that followed a traumatic removal. Still, by 1850 some 228 acres—just less than one acre per person—were being cultivated, producing a harvest of 3,840 bushels of corn, lesser amounts of wheat, potatoes, and beans, and 5,000 melons. Moreover, some 1,000 fruit trees dotted the reservation landscape, a clear indication that the Quapaws had not forgotten their horticultural talents.[17] The harvest from the field and the orchard and the natural abundance of the plains and the woodland provided the Downstream People with ample foodstuffs. Only when periodic floods and severe droughts visited the reservation was the tribe in want and were official charges of indolence relevant.

Even when agriculture was insufficient, the tribe during its first twenty years in Indian Territory could always rely for economic assistance upon the $2,000 annuity provided in the 1833 treaty. At first these funds were apparently distributed in merchandise, but after 1840 they were paid per capita in specie. In 1844, for example, 224 Quapaws received payments of $7.50 each. Also, from these funds the agent paid $50 apiece to four chiefs, and to cover outstanding tribal debts he disbursed $120 to licensed traders.[18] Although in this instance only 6 per cent went directly to traders, more than likely the largest portions of the individual payments went to them as well. Obviously, then, commerce with white entrepreneurs provided the tribe with an economic cushion as well as an adequate measure of creature comforts.

In addition to its economic significance, the payment of the annuity had important social implications. As the occasion of its distribution was announced well in advance, all of the Downstream People, including those living on the Canadian River, made an effort to be present. At least 224 gathered in 1844, 264 in 1846, 221 in 1848, 271 in 1850, and as many as 314 in 1852.[19] Virtually a tribal reunion, the distribution of funds was always a festive occasion. Whiskey sellers from the Cherokee neutral lands in what is now southeastern Kansas contributed to the merrymaking by supplying a barrel or two of their best stock. The Quapaw agents struggled— usually in vain—to prevent such traffic, spilling the liquid when found and forcibly expelling the vendor. A confrontation in 1842 between Agent John B. Luce and S. P. Gillespie, a whiskey peddler, resulted in the death of the latter. Luce was eventually acquitted of a murder charge, but the incident so tarnished his record that he was forced out of the Indian service.[20] Yet from the reports of other agents, the intemperance common to Luce's administration was more the exception than the rule. His observation, for example, that the tribe passed "days and even weeks together in a state of intoxication," contrasted sharply with B. B. R. Barker's view that the Quapaws "drank less whiskey this year [1843] than formerly" and with James S. Raines's view that "These people do not hunt after nor drink whiskey [in 1845] as they used to do."[21] The Downstream People never became abstemious, but the "bacchanalian row[s]" associated with early annuity payments and drinking bouts that ended in bloodshed were common only during the early reservation years.[22]

When government officials admonished the Quapaws to become "civilized," of course, it was not expected that they should prefer the form that came in bottles. But once intemperance was curbed, at least two agents believed that the tribe aspired to the more acceptable attributes of civilization. The Downstream People were, said one, "kindhearted and agreeable, fully meriting the assistance and protection of the United States."[23] They were "An uncommonly docile people," another wrote, "inclined to listen to advice, easily managed, and if properly encouraged and assisted, will no doubt continue to improve."[24] And according to Agent Barker, they did. He pridefully noted in 1844 that the tribe had condemned and banned one of their members who had killed another and that they were imitating the whites in their dress, "wearing pantaloon, shoes, &c., in place of their former rude apparel." To Barker all of this meant that the Downstream People were "rapidly approaching to civilization and contentment."[25]

Yet the changes in tribal lifeways were hardly that profound. Barker's successor, James Raines, declared that previous accounts of the advancement of the Quapaws were "most exaggerated." From the perspective of policy objectives, Raines was probably more accurate, because the Arkansas natives had retained many of their social, cultural, and political institutions. Although village life had been made impossible, the tribe preserved the three basic social units once reflected in its settlement pattern. A chief presided over each group, and one of these chiefs was the hereditary leader of the entire tribe.[26] Heckaton held the latter post, known as the First Chief, until 1842, when upon his death he was succeeded by War-te-she, perhaps the older man's son. At least through 1854 a fourth chief also existed, an anachronistic position stipulated in the Treaty of 1833 because of Sarasin's prominence. As previously, the chiefs meeting in council deliberated upon matters of importance to the tribe, collectively making decisions on different issues.

In addition to their political structure, the Quapaws also retained many of their social and cultural customs. Most remarkable of these was the annual corn dance. On or about August 20 the whole nation assembled, with each family bringing produce raised during the year. For two or three days they ate and danced, all "for the purpose of returning thanks to the 'Great Spirit' for a plentiful harvest."[27] In addition to this ancient festival, polygamy apparently survived the trauma of removal, as did the tribe's spiritual system.[28] The clan structure, no doubt, also remained unaffected, although in view of the division of the Downstream People it must have been under severe strain.

That the Quapaws failed to shed their cultural baggage did not surprise thoughtful officials. To make them into "civilized" Indians would require time and, particularly, education. Thus the government was at pains to encourage the tribe to take advantage of all instructional opportunities. The $1,000 authorized annually by the Treaty of 1833 for educational purposes was, therefore, applied toward the support of the four male youths enrolled in 1830 at the Choctaw Academy at the request of Chief Heckaton. But even here, government authorities met with some resistance. In 1841 two of the boys left the Kentucky school, one rejoining the tribe, the other making his home among the Omahas. The former, despite his ten years in school, could speak neither English nor Quapaw, while the latter was so confused that he could not find his own people.[29] "If he had been taught to read like the whites," Heckaton complained about the boy living with the Omahas, "he would have known better than to go up the Missouri to look for his people. They teach our boys nothing. That is the reason why they do not know how to come home."[30] Convinced that the educational experience of the youngsters was both deficient and harmful, the old chief refused to send any more students to the boarding school. Instead he urged that the children of his tribe be educated at an institution located on the reservation. "If we cannot have a teacher here," he declared, "our Grand father can keep the thousand dollars if he wants it."[31]

When Washington officials continued to believe that administrative efficiency demanded a pooling of educational resources,[32] Heckaton took matters into his own hands. In 1840 he requested Samuel G. Patterson, a Methodist minister of Sarcoxie, Missouri, to open a school near the Quapaw settlements. After the Annual Conference of Missouri Methodists approved the project, the missionary-teacher began his labors in December, 1842. Heckaton had died the previous fall, but Chief War-te-she and a tribal council gave Patterson a "hearty welcome." Although Agent Luce was sympathetic to the tribe's desire for a local school, he viewed the action of the leadership as unauthorized and in an ugly scene declared the teacher to be in violation of the trade and intercourse laws. The Methodist hierarchy promptly appealed the decision to the secretary of war, who forthwith reversed the agent's decision, enabling Patterson to establish his Quapaw Mission on March 27, 1843.[33]

Situated on the east bank of Spring River and financed by church and individual contributions, the school enrolled twenty-three students during its first term.[34] The scholars began their academic career with the alphabet, since most of the students had never before seen a book. In time they could spell in one, two, and three syllables and understand a measure of common conversation. Patterson also clothed and boarded his students, expecting in return that they share in the daily chores necessary to the maintenance of the institution. The results of the effort so impressed Agent Barker that he was virtually enraptured. "This school will be of lasting benefit to the Quapaw nation," he wrote, and he believed it would prove that the Indian could be civilized and enlightened. For Barker, failure would result only if facilities lacked.[35] Because of his enthusiasm, the Bureau of Indian Affairs allocated money from its Civilization Fund for a small school building adjacent to the mission. In ceremonies on October 1, 1844, War-te-she and others received the completed structure and christened it "Crawford Seminary" in honor of Commissioner of Indian Affairs Thomas H. Crawford.[36] If sentiment accounted for the name, so, too, did politics. Barker and the Quapaws hoped to persuade the commissioner to apply the $1,000 educational stipend toward the support of the school and to secure Patterson's employment as teacher at the sum of $500 per annum. The strategy worked perfectly. In December, 1844, Crawford authorized the desired financial arrangements and expressed his appreciation for "[t]he compliment which the chiefs have thought proper to confer on me" by naming the institution in his honor.[37]

As Commissioner Crawford and Agent Barker left office in March, 1845, the money and Patterson's appointment were not immediately forthcoming. Indeed, the Bureau of Indian Affairs under Commissioner William Medill withheld all educational funds of the Quapaws until the spring of 1847, at which time it made arrangements with the Methodist Episcopal Church South to receive the annual appropriation and operate Crawford Seminary.[38] This action was taken without consulting either the Downstream People or Patterson, the latter in the meantime having kept the school in operation with his own resources. When the Methodist teacher finally made a claim for his services as per the 1844 authorization, Commissioner Medill professed total surprise and directed that Agent James S. Raines investigate.[39] Raines confirmed the merit of the claim, whereupon the commissioner ordered that Patterson receive $1,217 in back pay and that all accrued funds as well as future educational appropriations be allocated for the support of Quapaw students at Crawford Seminary.[40] The tribal agent unfortunately marred this modest victory by demanding from the educator a $217 payment, a sum he said he had paid to get the claim approved. This and charges of malfeasance in office resulted in the dismissal of Raines, later a Know Nothing candidate for governor of Missouri and a Confederate general.[41]

The release of accumulated funds and the assurance of future appropriations enabled Patterson to expand his educational program. In late 1847 he erected new buildings at a site near the east bank of Spring River and on the military road leading from Fort Leavenworth to Fort Smith, some five miles west of Newton County, Missouri. Capable of accommodating forty students, the new seminary opened its doors on April 1, 1848. By September, twenty-eight youngsters had enrolled and were receiving instruction in the 3-R's, spelling, geography, and the elements of vocal music. Each child was permitted to visit his home on Saturday but was required to attend Bible school and public worship every Sunday. The school term ended with a public examination, usually conducted by the agent and witnessed by interested Quapaws.[42]

Despite the hopes of its founder, Crawford Seminary and the adjacent Methodist Mission never really prospered. Parents were reluctant to force their children to maintain constant attendance, and Patterson was frequently absent in order to perform his missionary duties elsewhere in Indian Territory. These facts and perhaps a measles epidemic in early 1852 that left forty of the Downstream People dead spelled the end of the school. In February, 1852, it closed its doors for the last time. Noble in purpose and conducted at great sacrifice, the institution had touched the lives of only a few Quapaws, and those very slightly. "All who have been educated at this school, except the present United States interpreter," wrote Agent W. J. J. Morrow in 1852, "have resumed all their original habits, and are now as wild and untamed as though they had never been within the classic walls of Crawford Seminary."[43]

Morrow's assessment notwithstanding, the ten-year experience of the Quapaws with formal education had not been wholly sterile. Their own school had no more than closed when they were at pains to find a replacement, namely the Osage Manual Labor School conducted by the Jesuit Fathers at what is now St. Paul, Kansas. Founded in 1847, this institution had been the focal point of an energetic mission effort that extended to the Quapaws as well as other Indian Territory tribes. In late December, 1847, for example, Father John Baptist Bax baptized at least five of the Downstream People who became the nucleus of a mission established on the reservation the following year. A virtual revival followed, resulting in the baptism of forty-three members of the tribe in 1850. At the same time or shortly thereafter, Chief War-te-she also submitted to the rite. If this reemergence of Catholic sentiment did not account directly for the demise of Crawford Seminary, it was certainly responsible for the selection of its successor. In February, 1853, the Quapaw chiefs prevailed upon Father John Schoenmakers to admit twenty-four of their youngsters to the Kansas school. The following May, they petitioned Commissioner of Indian Affairs George W. Manypenny to pay their educational annuity to Schoenmakers, who had consented to maintain at least thirty students at a cost of $55 each per year. Unlike some of his predecessors, Manypenny responded quickly and also positively. By August, he had agreed to apply the tribal funds as requested.[44]

For the next seventeen years Father Schoenmakers, his brother priests, and the Sisters of Loretto nurtured the educational interest manifested by the Downstream People. No more than twenty-two male and female children were ever enrolled in the school at any one time, but these and their Osage counterparts had the benefit of dedicated instruction in academics, Christian doctrine, manual arts, and housewifery.[45] The religious influence of the faculty extended even to the tribe, and between 1853 and 1855 an additional 130 adults and children were baptized.[46] Thus, although their educational impact was undoubtedly limited, the Jesuit Fathers did rekindle the Catholic sentiment latent within the tribe, cultivating it to the extent that many Quapaws abandoned their traditional spirit life. For government officials interested in restructuring the tribe, it was a development that should have been applauded but, since most officials were Protestants, it was rarely even mentioned. For the Downstream People it represented the first successful attack upon their cultural integrity and, although the converts would not have admitted it, stripped them of one important link with the past that had enabled the tribe to survive the traumatic adjustments demanded by United States Indian policy.

The Quapaws had need of all the strength that viable traditions could afford. This was especially true after 1854, when the $2,000 annuity authorized by the removal treaty for twenty years only was no longer paid. On the one hand, the cessation of the payment left the Downstream People without the economic cushion that had supplied many of their wants and needs. On the other, it intensified the factionalism within the tribe that had plagued it since 1825. No longer, for example, were the effects of the geographical separation of the Quapaws neutralized by the festivities of an annual reunion. Worse yet, many from the reservation, previously held to the assigned domain by a cash payment, actually joined the settlements on the Canadian River, a migration that left only half of the estimated 400 members of the tribe near the agency.[47] Without funds and abandoned by many of their brethren, the Quapaws who remained confronted a crisis of major proportions.

How to replace the funds supplied by the expired annuity was the most pressing concern of the reservation-based Quapaws. If that could be done, then presumably economic security would be achieved, and some of the dissidents would be given reason to return to the parent body. With so much at stake the Downstream People were prepared to make unusual sacrifices—even the ultimate one of

Quapaw Stomp Dance. Courtesy Oklahoma Historical Society.

selling their land. The tribe revealed this inclination at a council called in November, 1853, by Agent Andrew Dorn. The agent had been instructed by Commissioner of Indian Affairs Manypenny to determine whether or not the Downstream People would relinquish their reserve, remove farther west to the plains, and endorse a territorial government for the Indian country. In the course of the discussions, Chief War-te-she indicated the willingness of his people to entertain such proposals and, more specifically, to negotiate a new treaty. Moreover, there would be no question about selling if his "big brothers"—the Choctaws, Creeks, and others—also sold, although he did fear that the wild tribes of the plains might kill the Quapaws if they moved among them.[48]

Not until August, 1854, did the United States take advantage of the economic and political crisis confronting the Downstream

People. On the twelfth, Dorn submitted to them a draft of a treaty prepared in Washington that would commit the tribe to cede its whole domain, reserving only an eighty-acre homestead for "each soul" and a tract of twelve sections to be held as common property and apportioned to absentees who might later claim an individual allotment. Once surveyed, the remainder of the 150-section reserve would be declared as public lands and sold to white farmers, the net proceeds of the sale accruing to the credit of the tribe. Furthermore, for a $3,000 payment the Quapaws would release the United States from claims of noncompliance with former treaties or from claims resulting from injuries by its citizens. And finally, the measure stipulated that if the treaty proved imperfect in its application, the president or the Congress could unilaterally make adjustments. Whatever the insidious implications of the provisions of the draft, particularly the last two, War-te-she and seven other Quapaw headmen ignored them and "cheerfully entered into the treaty." They did not act out of desperation or because there was no realistic alternative. Given their objectives of economic security and political unity, their action was a creative response to the current crisis.[49] Unfortunately, the effort was in vain. Although approved by the secretary of the interior, the treaty was never submitted to the Senate for ratification by President Franklin Pierce.[50]

However unlikely it may appear to later observers, the Downstream People were disappointed that the proposed sale of part of their reserve did not materialize. The leadership, therefore, soon renewed their offer to dispose of a portion of the tribe's landed estate when the crisis confronting them was compounded by periodic crop failures. Following confirmation by a United States Army survey that a half-mile-wide strip along their northern border lay in Kansas Territory, they proposed in 1857 to sell it as well as the eastern part of their domain.[51] But this proposition was also rejected by the government, perhaps for the same unexplained reason that the treaty signed in 1854 was never perfected.[52] In this and other instances federal officials apparently missed the point that the tribe's basic objective was to create a capital fund that would replace the expired annuity. As a consequence, in early 1860 the commissioner of Indian affairs directed Agent Dorn to propose to the Quapaws that their reserve be surveyed and apportioned to members of the tribe in severalty. War-te-she rejected this option as wholly unrealistic.[53] Because the tribe had "not been drawing anything for a long time," he said, they wished to sell their lands, not allot them.[54] With money the major goal, early the next year the chief and other headmen agreed to transfer to the Shawnees of Kansas one township (36 sections) of land for $20,000. Although completed under the auspices of Agent Dorn, this accord, too, was not approved by the Bureau of Indian Affairs, primarily because the Shawnees had no monies from which they could make the payment.[55] The rejection was a keen rebuff for the Quapaw leadership, but their efforts to deal realistically with a serious economic and political crisis had not been entirely fruitless. By 1859 the population on the reservation had increased to 350.[56] To be sure the regathering of the tribe was in anticipation of a cash payment, but it was also a testimony to the soundness of tribal policy.

The failure of the government to purchase or to approve a transfer of the Quapaw reserve was the result of more than mere insensitiveness. Given the turmoil in Kansas following its organization as a Territory in 1854, federal officials justifiably balked at opening up new lands for settlement into which the controversy over slavery might spread. After the election of Abraham Lincoln in November, 1860, the situation in Kansas and throughout the nation was even more unsettled. When the southern states made good their threat to secede from the union, it was obvious that the financial needs of the Downstream People would have to wait. And of even more importance, it became apparent that the Quapaws and other tribes in Indian Territory would be drawn into the general devastation of the American Civil War.

Although bound by various treaties to protect Indian Territory from foreign incursions, the Union government withdrew its military forces from the region south of Kansas in May, 1861. The Confederate States, on the other hand, considered the occupation and control of the Territory as essential to its over-all military strategy.[57] Indeed, as early as March, three commissioners from Texas had visited the different Indian peoples—including the Quapaws residing on the Canadian—in an attempt to secure their support of the secession movement.[58] An even more important Confederate embassy occurred during the summer and fall of 1861. Instructed by President Jefferson Davis to negotiate treaties of alliance with the different tribes, Albert Pike, an erudite Arkansas editor and attorney, began an extended tour of the Territory in June with a stop at Tahlequah, the Cherokee capitol. Finding Chief John Ross determined to follow a neutral course, Pike turned south and by mid-August had signed treaties with the Creeks, Choctaws, Chickasaws, Seminoles, Comanches, and Wichitas. In the meantime, a Confederate victory at Wilson's Creek in Missouri and the formation of a Cherokee Confederate battalion under Stand Watie had caused Chief Ross to have second thoughts about neutrality. In mid-September he sent word to Pike that the Cherokees were ready to negotiate a treaty with the southern states.[59]

In preparation for the Confederate commissioner's return to Tahlequah, Chief Ross dispatched messengers to the Quapaws, Osages, and Senecas and Shawnees. If these tribes and the Cherokees all signed treaties with Pike, the chief reasoned, then the Indian conversion to the Confederacy would be unanimous, a hedge of some importance should the decision ever be challenged. Andrew Dorn, having only recently submitted his resignation as United States agent, carried the invitation to the Downstream People.[60] A trusted friend, he persuaded a four-member delegation headed by Chiefs War-te-she and Ki-he-cah-te-da to accompany him back to the Cherokee capitol. When Pike arrived in early October, therefore, the ground was well prepared for a Quapaw-Confederate alliance. On October 4, 1861, War-te-she and his colleagues accepted a formal treaty prepared by the commissioner whereby they acknowledged the authority of the southern government, recognized slavery, and agreed to become parties to the existing war. In return for this commitment, Pike pledged the southern states to continue the $1,000 annually paid the tribe for educational purposes by the United States, to construct a grist mill and, most significant, to provide $2,000 in goods annually for twenty years.[61] The Quapaws had been forced to switch alliances to accomplish it, but the treasured annuity was once again assured them.

If the Downstream People embraced the Confederacy for reasons other than practical considerations, they did not demonstrate it in the succeeding months. That part of the tribe residing on the Canadian River joined 7,000 neutral Indians led by the Creek fullblood, Opothleyahola, who refused to recognize the treaties negotiated by Pike. Throughout November and December, 1861, these Quapaws and their Creek and Seminole counterparts heroically defended themselves against attacks by Confederate Indian troops commanded by Colonel Douglas H. Cooper. The battles of Round Mountain and Chusto Talasah resulted in victories for the neutrals, but the battle at Chustenalah on December 26 ended in defeat. With snow and the bitter winds of winter compounding their misery, Opothleyahola's people were forced to seek refuge over the northern border into Kansas.[62] Moreover, as southern arms surged even closer to the assigned reservation of the Downstream People, Chief War-te-she and those still on the reserve in February, 1862, abandoned their homes and fled northward to endure with their kinsmen the deprivations of refugee life near LeRoy, Kansas, in present Coffey County.[63] Ironically, the white man's war had reunited the Quapaws for the first time in twenty-seven years.

Surely a joyful event, reunification of the tribe could hardly ease the realities of the tragic situation. Without personal possessions, only scantily clad, and lacking any means of support, the Downstream People were wholly dependent for survival upon the "hospitality" of the federal government. Subsistence rations and other essentials were distributed first by the United States Army and then by officers of the Indian bureau. But such assistance was seldom adequate or timely, because the bureaucracy was not structured to meet the unique needs of wartime. Moreover, Agent P. P. Elder at Fort Scott and Superintendent W. G. Coffin at Lawrence were both some fifty miles distant from the refugee camps. For the Quapaws the situation meant unimagined hardships, exposure, sickness, and even death. Given these conditions, the cost of provisions, and the administrative confusion, government officials saw only one course of action as a means of relief—the Downstream People and other refugees had to be promptly returned to Indian Territory.[64]

To implement such a plan required vigorous military operations south of Kansas. In the spring of 1862 the United States Army organized the so-called Indian Expedition under the command of Colonel William Wear of Kansas, ordered it to penetrate south of the border, and directed that it demonstrate the ability of federal forces to protect the various tribes who remained loyal to the United States. At least sixty Quapaw warriors and a thousand other refugees combined with two white regiments to form the command, which in June pushed successfully to Tahlequah.[65] And as previously planned, the Quapaw noncombatants followed in the wake of the column and reestablished themselves on their reservation.[66] Unfortunately, their homecoming proved to be premature. Charging Wear with intemperance and even insanity, Colonel Fredrick Solomon assumed control of the expedition and despite its success withdrew his white units to Fort Scott, pausing only to plunder the returned Quapaws of their stock, corn, and other possessions. War-te-she and his people, mystified by the turn of events, had no recourse but to follow the troops back into Kansas, this time establishing encampments on the Ottawa reservation near Ohio City.[67]

Especially concerned about the expense of refugee life, Agent Elder sought to persuade the Quapaws to go back to Indian Territory despite the failure of the expedition.[68] But given their recent experience, they preferred to remain in their temporary camps until the success of Union arms was certain. At the same time, the tribe was willing to cooperate in the attainment of that goal. In late 1862 some eighty of their young warriors joined the 2nd Indian Regiment of Colonel William A. Phillips' Indian Home Guard.[69] The contribution of this group to the Union war effort was similar to that made by their ancestors to Bienville's second Chickasaw campaign. When Phillips moved south in the spring of 1863, most of the Quapaws were absent, or, as one white officer kindly put it, they had gone "buffalo hunting."[70]

That the Downstream People slowly lost interest in the Civil War simply reflected the depth of their own suffering. Not only were they physically and economically distressed, but their political and cultural institutions had been weakened by geographical dislocation and the absence of able-bodied males assigned to distant military units. Furthermore, the Ottawa Indian agent had protested their presence in his jurisdiction and prevailed upon the commissioner of Indian affairs in June, 1863, to order their removal.[71] Fortunately, the Ottawas themselves did not share the views of their agent and agreed that the Quapaws should remain among them until at least the spring of 1864. When Agent Elder also declared that "no greater injustice to those harrassed and unfortunate Indians could befall them, than a removal at this time,"[72] the commissioner rescinded his edict and permitted the Quapaws to remain on the Ottawa reserve for one more year. He was not so amenable, however, to requests made by the tribe that the government comply fully with commitments made in previous treaties.

Always sensitive to how well the United States met its obligations, the Downstream People were convinced that a substantial amount of money guaranteed by the removal treaty of 1833 was yet due them, which if paid could alleviate some of their distress. For

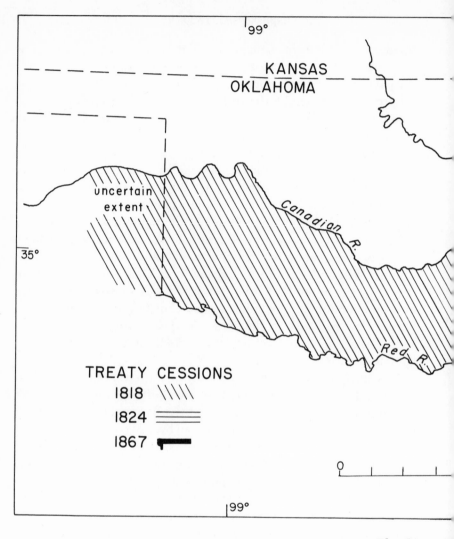

The Quapaw

this reason in April, 1863, War-te-she and other chiefs authorized
Perry Fuller, then Sac and Fox agent but later an influential government contractor, to seek a congressional appropriation of all unpaid
funds.[73] After at least two trips to Washington, Fuller established
that financial commitments made to the tribe totalled $15,578, of
which $9,726 was yet unappropriated.[74] In the spring of 1864 he
secured congressional consideration of the Quapaw claim and, despite an adverse report by the Senate Committee on Indian Affairs,
later that year obtained an appropriation for the unpaid balance.[75]
Unfortunately, Congress stipulated that the money should be used

aty cessions.

"for payment of expenses incident to the removal of the Quapaw Indians from Kansas," obviously a contravention of the intent of the 1833 accord.[76] Even so, if all the money had been applied according to the new stipulations, the tribe would have received some benefit. As it turned out, one-third of the appropriation was claimed by and paid to Fuller for his timely assistance.[77]

To return the Downstream People to Indian Territory had been the objective of the United States since the beginning of the war. When the commissioner of Indian affairs in 1863 permitted the tribe to remain among the Ottawas for an additional year, he assumed

that the military situation south of Kansas would improve enough
to permit a safe removal. In the interval, Union troops under General James G. Blunt did push as far south as the Canadian River and
take Fort Smith, but Confederate forces led by Stand Watie continued to raid behind Union lines. Given the still unsettled conditions, it was apparent that any return of the Quapaws in 1864 would
subject them to unreasonable dangers. When Agent Elder reported
that the Ottawas were willing to allow the tribe to remain beyond
the date originally stipulated, that the Downstream People had
planted some crops, and that the burden of removal would fall upon
old men, women, and children, the commissioner agreed to postpone a southward migration for yet another year.[78]

When spring came to the Kansas plains in 1865, federal officials
saw no reason to delay further the long-anticipated removal. As in
Virginia, Confederate arms in Indian Territory were all but defeated.
Furthermore, white men claimed the lands upon which the
Quapaws had made their encampments,[79] and the cost of subsisting
the Indians was straining the resources of the Washington government. Accordingly, a new agent, George C. Snow, was delegated the
task of implementing removal. In April, he assigned George Mitchell as special agent to gather the Quapaws, who since the death of
War-te-she in January were led by aged Ki-he-cah-te-da, and transport them south. Pending a reconnoiter of the reserve, Mitchell
halted the column after only eighty miles and encouraged his
charges to plant small gardens. Then in early June, Agent Snow led
an advance party of fifty Indians and a contingent of the 25th Kansas
Volunteer Cavalry on ahead to survey what would confront the tribe
upon its final return. Devastation greeted him. Houses had been
looted, fences destroyed, stock carried off, and the agency buildings
burned. Despite these conditions, Snow believed that once the
Quapaws had harvested their small crop, nothing should prevent
them from resuming a "happy and prosperous" life on their assigned
reservation. But as insurance he recommended that they be provided
with a mowing machine and that a company of soldiers be stationed
nearby.[80]

The regathering of the Downstream People in Indian Territory,
though, did not immediately follow. Instead, the tribe became involved in negotiations that had important implications for them
once they did manage to reassemble on the reserve. In July, 1865,
and with the approval of Agent Snow, Chief Ki-he-cah-te-da and

other Quapaw headmen leased a portion of their yet unoccupied lands to the Kansas Shawnees. Intended to provide those beleaguered people with new homes, the lease nonetheless elicited a good deal of opposition among the Downstream People, in part, apparently, because some white speculators also had designs upon the territory. A letter bearing the very marks of the chiefs who had originally approved the lease was sent to the commissioner of Indian affairs asking that the agreement not be approved and condemning Snow for his part in the affair. A later communication absolved the agent of any blame, yet at the same time it did not reflect any support for the lease. Whether the first letter had been forged, as Snow believed, or the Quapaws had simply changed their minds, was never made clear. In any event, the commissioner elected not to approve the lease and learned that elements within the tribe, despite commitments by the leadership, would not easily be separated from their lands.[81]

An even more important negotiation respecting the future welfare of the Downstream People occurred in September at Fort Smith, Arkansas. With the collapse of the Richmond government, Confederate military units in Indian Territory admitted the inevitable and surrendered to federal forces. Yet, for the rebel tribes to simply cease hostilities against the United States was wholly insufficient insofar as the secretary of the interior was concerned. The cabinet officer responsible for Indian affairs, he insisted that those tribes recently allied with the Confederacy must declare their peaceful intentions and enter into new treaties with the federal government. Accordingly, he sent Commissioner of Indian Affairs D. N. Cooley to Fort Smith to convene a conference of the rebel Indians and to negotiate appropriate accords. Among the delegates present at the Arkansas fort when the commissioner arrived were three Quapaw headmen— George Lane (Wa-te-sha), Ka-she-ka, and John Hunker (Wa-she-honca)—and the tribal interpreter, Samuel G. Vallier. Along with their colleagues from other tribes, they listened with incredulity when Cooley opened the conference on September 8 by declaring that because the Indians had joined the Confederacy, they had "rightfully forfeited" all of their annuities and lands. Still, he asserted, the president was disposed "to hear his erring children in the extenuation of their great crime" and make new treaties that would, among other things, provide for a permanent peace, adoption of the freedmen, and some form of territorial government.[82]

In so far as Cooley's demands related to the Downstream People, he obviously had been misinformed. To be sure the tribe had signed Pike's treaty, but it had done so only after repeated attempts to obtain funds from the United States had failed and federal troops had abandoned Indian Territory. Moreover, some Quapaws had actively fought the Confederacy, while others had fled to refugee camps to endure unspeakable deprivations. None, of course, had owned slaves. When the tribal delegates and other spokesmen persuasively stated the actual facts, Commissioner Cooley moderated his expectations and insisted only that the Indians sign a brief protocal calling for an immediate peace. All other issues were to be left to subsequent adjudication. To this request the representatives of the Downstream People could agree, and they set their marks to the document on September 14, 1865.[83]

When adopted by other tribes, the Fort Smith accord marked the end of the Civil War in Indian Territory. Thus, there was no reason why the Quapaws who settled in temporary camps in southern Kansas could not cross the border to their own reservation. In November, nearly four years after they had been forced to flee northward, Chief Ki-he-cah-te-da led his people—numbering no more than 265—back to their treaty lands.[84] It was undoubtedly a melancholy homecoming, for the improvements of thirty years lay in utter ruin. As they had been when they had emigrated from Arkansas, the Downstream People were without possessions save for the land itself. With past labors having been in vain and without the reservoir of strength once derived from ancient traditions and cultural unity, it was no wonder that they began the task of reconstruction with little enthusiasm.

CHAPTER VI
PEACE AND ACCOMMODATION
1866-88

I f the first thirty years in Indian Territory perceptibly changed the lifeways of the Downstream People, the next twenty-two brought even more significant transformations. In the postwar era the Quapaws were exempted from the punitive measures levied upon rebel Indians by the government, but following the negotiation of a new treaty, they were directly affected by the so-called Quaker peace policy. Formulated during the administration of President U. S. Grant, this approach aimed to persuade the Indians by love and the tireless ministrations of God-fearing agents to assume the economic and cultural patterns of western civilization. Grant and other reformers realized that such an objective would not be accomplished immediately. However, isolating the tribes on reservations where they could be properly instructed in Christianity, in the necessity of individual effort, and in the value of private property, seemed to be the way to assure ultimate success. Once the goal of a "civilized" Indian was attained, the reservation could be abolished, and the government could retire from the Indian business. For the Quapaws, the Quaker policy and the reservation system further dispossessed them of their traditional institutions and paved the way for cultural accommodation. Predictably, although this fact was not fully appreciated by white observers, by 1888 many of the Downstream People had adopted, at least externally, patterns of conduct generally ascribed to civilized society.

To implement official policy among the Quapaws, the Bureau of Indian Affairs continued to rely on its field officers. After 1864, Special Agent George Mitchell had immediate responsibility for the tribe, although it and others in northeastern Indian Territory were technically attached to the Neosho agency. In 1871, when the latter office was given exclusive authority over Osage affairs, Mitchell's jurisdictions were reorganized into the Quapaw agency.[1] Hiram W. Jones, a Quaker, replaced Mitchell and was given the rank of agent. At the regional level, the Central superintendency, with headquarters at Lawrence, Kansas, exercised supervision over the new agency. In accordance with current policy, this office was under the control of the Quakers, since Superintendent Enoch Hoag had been nominated for his post by the Associated Executive Committee of Friends on Indian Affairs. That the Quapaw agent was also a Quaker was no accident, for the Friends were permitted to select most agency officials included within the superintendency. Government policy affecting the Downstream People, as a consequence, was generally implemented and on occasion conceived by field personnel sharing a common faith and similar social objectives. Because recognition and vindication of their religious precepts depended in part on their achievements as administrators, the Quakers seemed determined to succeed—with or without the cooperation of the Indians.

The peace policy notwithstanding, in 1866 the Quapaws were hardly prepared to assume the image of the white man. Chief Ki-he-cah-te-da and his people had only recently returned to the tribal reserve and with difficulty erected crude shelters along Spring River and its tributaries. They suffered severely for want of clothing and food, and had it not been for the timely assistance of George Mitchell and the monthly rations issued until June, starvation would have resulted. Crops were planted, but floods annulled the effort, forcing the tribe to subsist wholly upon roots and berries. After all rations were discontinued, the chiefs and headmen sought relief by proposing that the money usually allocated for the farmer be used to purchase provisions. When this request was ignored, they were left with only one recourse: to sell a part of their reservation. Although the tribe's similar proposals in the midst of the recent national crisis had not been accepted, on this occasion the government would not fail to take advantage of the Quapaws' distress.[2]

At least two considerations made the Bureau of Indian Affairs amenable to negotiations. On the one hand, no definitive treaty marking the restoration of peace yet existed; and on the other, the government desired to relocate, on reservations in Indian Territory, tribes then obstructing the white settlement of Kansas. As a consequence, Neosho Agent George Snow was instructed in December, 1866, to dispatch a Quapaw delegation to Washington. The following month the tribe selected Chiefs John Hunker and Ka-she-ka and interpreter Samuel Vallier to undertake the negotiations, authorizing them to sell a portion of their reserve to the United States. Hunker died en route, but the remaining two delegates, along with representatives from other agency tribes and those slated to remove from Kansas, reached the capital in February, 1867.[3] Before substantive discussions began, however, the Quapaw, Seneca, and Seneca and Shawnee delegates—probably upon the recommendation of Agent Snow—engaged General James G. Blunt to advise them. Commander of Union troops in Kansas during the late war and an attorney, Blunt was widely recognized as a man of influence who frequently represented Indian tribes with claims against the government.[4] His employment was not at all sinister, but conformed to procedures then current in the federal city.

Negotiations opened on February 9, 1867, with statements by members of the different tribal delegations. Speaking in turn, Ka-she-ka made clear the willingness of the Quapaws to sell that part of their reservation lying north of the Kansas border and just east of the Neosho River. On the basis of this information and that provided by other spokesmen, the government representatives prepared a draft of an agreement that embodied the objectives of the Indians. The language of the so-called Omnibus Treaty was made final some days later, and then, on February 23, signed by the different tribal delegations.[5] By its terms the Quapaws agreed to sell the 7,600 acres of their reserve situated in Kansas to the United States for $1.25 per acre, and a tract of 18,522 acres, the western one-fourth of the reservation, to the Peoria Indians for $1.15 per acre. Of the proceeds from the sales, $5,000 would be paid to the tribe upon ratification of the treaty to relieve immediate distress. The balance would be invested at 5 per cent, the interest therefrom distributed per capita semiannually. Moreover, the treaty directed that the tribe's $1,000 educational annuity be applied toward the tuition of students at the Osage Manual Labor School until a suitable facility could be constructed on the diminished reserve. It also stipulated that unpaid funds due the farmer could be used to purchase provisions, implements, and seed; future appropriations for that office would be applied toward the general improvement of agriculture. Finally, the accord authorized a commission to adjudicate the claims of the Quapaws, Senecas, and mixed Senecas and Shawnees for property losses suffered during the war, a stipulation made on the theory that the government had been "under obligations to protect them, but for the time [was] unable to do so.... "Probably because of Blunt's influence, this provision directed the payment of up to $90,000 in satisfaction of various claims.[6] Given the terms of the treaty, the Quapaw delegates left Washington convinced that the immediate needs of their people had been met and that future economic crises would be eased with revenue realized from invested funds.

The expectations of the Downstream People never fully materialized. Impeachment proceedings against President Andrew Johnson distracted the United States Senate from early ratification of the treaty. Moreover, the Senate Committee on Indian Affairs demonstrated reluctance to accept those provisions whereby the government acknowledged responsibility for the wartime property losses and pledged $90,000 as compensation. The timely intervention of General Blunt counteracted some of this sentiment, but the committee nevertheless did strike the clause by which the United States admitted culpability, and the committee refused to authorize a specific payment. Instead, an amendment was inserted which only directed the secretary of the interior to report the findings of the investigating commission directly to Congress.[7] The full Senate adopted this and other suggested amendments on June 18, 1868, whereupon the commissioner of Indian affairs dispatched a messenger to Indian Territory to secure the consent of the tribes affected. Those delegates who had signed the treaty vigorously objected to the amendment respecting claims but, fearful of losing other advantages that had been approved, accepted the language as altered.[8] President Johnson proclaimed the treaty on October 14, some twenty months after it had been originally negotiated.

The great lapse of time between signing the treaty and proclaiming it worked an unexpected hardship upon the Downstream People. They had anticipated that the funds provided in the treaty would enable them to successfully overcome their economic crisis and physical distress. When the money was not forthcoming, they were reduced in the winter of 1867–68 to a "suffering condition from want of sufficient clothing ... and from want of food," even though they had "struggled manfully."[9] Government rations of beef, bacon, flour, and corn meal eased their plight, but a drought the next summer resulted in another crop failure and the starvation of most of the tribe's stock.[10] In March, 1869, the Quapaws were reported as being "in a desperate starving condition, ... living on corn meal, roots and

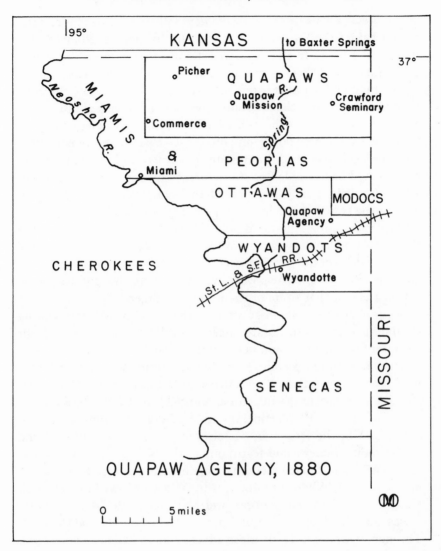

Quapaw Agency in 1880.

nuts."[11] Had the Senate acted with dispatch, of course, much of this trauma could have been avoided. Unfortunately, these conditions were not immediately alleviated even after the treaty was ratified, at which time the Downstream People were to have received $5,000. Congress did not make the appropriation until the spring of 1869, and bureaucratic red tape, despite the vehement protest of Agent

Snow, prevented payment until the next fall.[12] Still three more years passed before the Quapaws received any further benefit from the sale of their lands. In 1872 Congress finally appropriated $25,801.24 to pay for the ceded acres, monies that were to have been invested in a trust fund at 5 per cent interest.[13] Curiously, and despite the clear intent of the treaty, the appropriation was not invested but apparently paid directly to the tribe.[14] Chief Ki-he-cah-te-da and other Quapaw headmen no doubt supported such a payment, for per capita portions exceeded $100. Interest from a trust fund, by way of contrast, would have yielded no more than $2.69 per person semiannually. Although it may have eased the symptoms of poverty, enhanced the status of the leadership, and quieted dissident elements within the tribe, hundred-dollar payments to each of the Downstream People were hardly sufficient compensation for the loss of a fourth of the tribal reserve. When the money was spent (as it quickly was), the Quapaws were even poorer, for the land was gone. It was a lesson that some of them did not forget.

In contrast to its administration of the treaty provisions relating to land sales, the United States acted more decisively in carrying out the intent of the agreement pertaining to wartime losses. Even here, though, it required prodding by General Blunt, who continued to represent the interests of the Quapaws and other tribes.[15] Eventually, the secretary of the interior appointed J. W. Caldwell of Illinois and Landon Carter of Tennessee to the investigative commission authorized in the treaty. In March and April, 1869, Caldwell and Carter took affidavits and testimony at the Neosho agency relating to seventy-eight Quapaw claims, documenting property losses valued at $48,601. When combined with damages allowed the Senecas, Shawnees, and mixed Senecas and Shawnees, the total wartime losses sustained by the four different tribes totalled $110,809.[16] Throughout the course of these investigations, George Snow, the former Neosho agent, was present as General Blunt's representative. He worked actively not only to substantiate each claim but also to secure from the individual Indian a contract assigning to Blunt one-third of whatever award Congress might appropriate to satisfy the different losses. Thus, after the report of the two commissioners was submitted to Congress in early 1870, Blunt was able to work for an appropriation with the full confidence that he would be amply rewarded. A skillful and capable lobbyist, in July he won a congressional allocation of $90,000, a sum that would be distributed pro rata to the claimants.[17]

James A. Williamson, an employee of the Bureau of Indian Affairs in Washington, was assigned the task of delivering the money. Setting out for the Neosho agency in October, he was joined at Leavenworth by General Blunt, who had determined to be present at the payment in order to collect his fee. Upon their arrival they found that J. L. Long, a member of the Board of Indian Commissioners, Enoch Hoag, and William Nicholson, later Hoag's successor as Central superintendent, had preceded them to the agency. Blunt promptly assembled the Indians and reminded them of his efforts on their behalf and of their contracts with him. Objecting particularly to the size of the fee, Long and Hoag apparently remonstrated with the general. Insisting that his expense had been huge, Blunt could not be dissuaded from his intended course. Accordingly, when each Indian was paid his share, he immediately handed the money back to Special Agent George Mitchell, who then deducted one-third for Blunt and whatever amount was due the agency trader before returning it. One claimant, for example, was scheduled to receive $338.21, but payments of $112.73 to Blunt and $40 to the trader reduced that amount to $175.48. Through such divisions the general received some $30,000 for his efforts.[18] Once the transaction became public, men of good will protested, particularly the chairman of the Board of Indian Commissioners, Felix Brunot, and the head of the Indian Rights Association, Herbert Welsh.[19] Their outcry resulted in a congressional investigation, the published report of which labeled Blunt's fee as "extortion"; but it did not prevent the general from keeping his money.[20] Ironically, the Quapaws and other Indians never protested. Without Blunt's services there doubtlessly would have been no appropriation, and whether it was good or bad, they had struck a bargain which good faith demanded that they keep.

In addition to negotiating definitive peace treaties and adjudicating claims, another important postwar objective of the United States in Indian Territory was organization of the resident tribes into some type of cooperative government. At first reluctant to support any program that might impair their autonomy, the Indians realized by 1870 that they must take action before an alien and perhaps repugnant scheme was imposed on them. Meeting in September at Okmulgee in the Creek Nation, George Lane, as representative of the

Downstream People, and other delegates selected a committee to draw up a suitable document that would provide the basis for intertribal cooperation and action. Adjourning until the committee could complete its work, they reassembled in December to adopt the famous Okmulgee constitution, with Robert Lombard instead of Lane signing for the Quapaws. Chief Ki-he-cah-te-da and other headmen ratified the compact the following year and tribal delegates attended annual meetings of the council until it disbanded in 1875.[21] The contribution of the Quapaws was only minor, but that they were involved at all was remarkable. Poverty-stricken people seldom exhibit interest in matters not related directly to the stomach.

Although some type of territorial government was an important policy objective, even more basic was an educational program. Transformation of the Downstream People into pseudo white men depended upon proper instruction in the ways of "civilization." In pursuit of this objective, the Treaty of 1867 had provided that the $1,000 educational stipend paid the tribe since 1833 should be continued. Father Schoenmakers' Osage Manual Labor School remained as the beneficiary of the annuity, but the growing influence of the Quakers within the Central superintendency resulted in the discontinuation of any further payment to the Kansas institution in March, 1870.[22] The Friends were convinced that Catholicism was inimical to their objectives, which required supervision not only of the Indian's person but of his mind as well. Accordingly, after three years of planning, Hiram Jones used government funds in 1872 to erect buildings for a Quapaw boarding school that would accommodate a hundred students. As principal teacher, he appointed Emaline Tuttle, a Quaker of Dover, New Hampshire, recently assigned to the Ottawa mission school and the sister-in-law of Enoch Hoag. Joined later by her husband, A. C., who served intermittently as superintendent, Mrs. Tuttle opened the school in September, only to be keenly disappointed and apparently embarrassed by the initial indifference of the Downstream People.[23] After two years the institution managed an average enrollment of only fifty students, half the number that could be accommodated, and the majority of whom were not Quapaws.[24] The modest size of the student body became critical after 1874 when the Tuttles, at first agency employees, were forced to operate the school on a contract basis whereby they received $2.00 per week per student.[25] For the institution to have sufficient financial support required a full complement of scholars. Perhaps this accounted for Mrs. Tuttle's praise of Agent Jones, who had, she wrote, "encouraged and admonished and in some instances almost compelled the children to be kept in school," and for her belief that "compulsory education would have a salutary effect among the Indians."[26] Yet despite the agent's exertions, in 1877 only forty-six students were enrolled, of whom just seventeen were Quapaws.[27]

Mr. and Mrs. Tuttle remained at the Quapaw mission school until 1879, when they retired from the work.[28] Thereafter the institution was reorganized with different financial arrangements. Identified as the Quapaw Industrial Boarding School, it was financed by the educational stipend of the Downstream People, allocations from funds of other tribes whose children attended the school, and government appropriations.[29] In the 1890's thirteen different buildings and a farm of 160 acres represented the principal physical features of the institution, which in 1892 had an average daily attendance of 112—an all-time high.[30] The number of Quapaws enrolled at any one time, though, seldom exceeded twenty. With a strong academic curriculum through nine grades and instruction in agriculture and housewifery, the school inspired in the tribe an increasing appreciation of a structured education.[31] Some students even continued their training at Carlisle Indian School in Pennsylvania and Haskell Institute in Lawrence, Kansas.[32] Many others—such as Victor Griffin, Harry Whitebird, Frank Buck, and John and Frank Buffalo, all of whom played an important role in twentieth-century tribal affairs—learned to read and write at the boarding school.[33] When, in the interest of economy, the government closed the institution in 1900, the tribe was at pains to find a worthy successor.

Whatever the long-range implications of educational efforts among the Downstream People, during Mr. and Mrs. Tuttle's tenure they were nearly imperceptible. Mrs. Tuttle was especially discouraged because few Quapaw students enrolled in the Quaker mission school. Hoping to make better use of the facilities and to salvage her pride, she sought another source of prospective students. If other more populous tribes could be settled on the Quapaw reservation, she reasoned, her empty school could be filled to capacity.[34] Happily, Mrs. Tuttle found widespread acceptance for her idea. Indeed, Agent Jones reported in 1873 that the Downstream People had a much larger reserve than they needed. "I think much greater benefit would accrue to them," he wrote, "if at least half of their lands could be disposed of to some other tribe. . . . "³⁵ And Enoch Hoag, Mrs. Tuttle's kinsman who, as Central superintendent, was in a position to implement her scheme, did not disagree with the agent. In late 1873 when the Bureau of Indian Affairs sought a new homeland for the remnants of Captain Jack's Modoc band, he recommended the Quapaw reservation as a relocation site. The presumed indolent habits of the Downstream People and the proximity of whiskey peddlers in Kansas and Missouri thwarted this plan, however, and the Modocs were located farther south and nearer the agency. Yet, not all was lost. At least thirty Modoc children enrolled in Mrs. Tuttle's school, more than doubling the enrollment but leaving it still only half filled.³⁶

Although the Quapaws apparently were never consulted, a high-level campaign developed that had as its objective not only the assignment of much of their reserve to other Indians but their own relocation as well. In his annual report for 1874, for example, Enoch Hoag informed his superiors that the tribe had "too much land" and recommended that a part of it be purchased and assigned to displaced Indians. Simultaneously, Agent Jones accused the Quapaws of having "lazy [and] indolent habits," a charge he made repeatedly in succeeding years.³⁷ Such demeaning assessments were also made known to the Quapaws, who in time came to doubt their own self-image and the propriety of continuing to occupy their reservation. Indeed, in 1874 a few began to drift west into the Osage country, among them the hereditary chief, Louis Angel (Tallchief), who had succeeded to authority upon the death of Ki-he-cah-te-da in the fall of that year.³⁸

This trickle of emigration only confirmed for Superintendent Hoag and Agent Jones the wisdom of the resettlement plan. After the southern plains wars against the Cheyennes, Comanches, and Kiowas, therefore, Hoag recommended that some 3,000 members of these "Captive Nations" be relocated upon Quapaw lands. John P. C. Shank, recently a member of Congress from Indiana, was dispatched to Fort Sill in what is now southern Oklahoma to secure the consent of the three plains tribes, and C. F. Larrabee, an Indian office employee, was sent to the Quapaw agency, where he was to make preparations for the actual resettlement.³⁹ In early April, 1875, Larrabee assembled a poorly attended council of the Downstream People, informed it of the plans, and requested that the tribe relin-

Tallchief, with sacred eagle-feather fan.
Courtesy Oklahoma Historical Society.

quish a part of its reserve to the government for the civilizing experiment. The Quapaws refused to agree to a formal sale, but the special agent did secure the assent of eight headmen to a cession of 40,000 acres with "the compensation to be fixed by the government at a just and equitable rate at an early day hereafter."[40] Larrabee was delighted with his accomplishment and promptly contracted to have 350 acres of prairie sod broken for cultivation and to have a stone structure erected as a storehouse.[41] Such advance preparations would meet the physical needs of the emigrants, and with the mission school available to supply their spiritual and intellectual requirements, the special agent looked forward to a successful career as head of the Agency for Captive Indians.

Yet Larrabee's expectations never materialized. After a thorough investigation at Fort Sill, John Shanks recommended that the Cheyennes, Comanches, and Kiowas be permitted to remain on a reservation in what is now southwestern Oklahoma. They had been sufficiently chastised for their recent rebellion, were now peacefully engaged in agriculture, and had recently received an annuity. "A separation of these people and their removal now," he reported, "is only a matter of force without cause...."[42] Moreover, the United States Army opposed the resettlement scheme, which, according to General Philip Sheridan, would result in dissatisfaction and mortality from homesickness.[43] With Shanks and the Army both opposed to removal, the Bureau of Indian Affairs abandoned the plan. Special Agent Larrabee was keenly disappointed, but no more than Mrs. Tuttle.[44]

In one way, at least from the point of view of the Quaker-dominated Central superintendency, the resettlement scheme had not been a failure. Discouraged, demeaned, without annuity funds, and with agricultural efforts generally unsuccessful, most of the Downstream People abandoned their homeland. The trickle of immigration to the Osage reserve which had begun in 1874 became a flood following the captive nations experiment. By 1876 at least half of the tribe, or about 115 Quapaws, had settled among their kinsmen.[45] After twelve more months, the number had increased to about two-thirds, of whom almost all were members of two of the three tribal divisions first observed by the French and once organized into village units.[46] If there had been any doubt among government officials about previous recommendations as to the disposition of the reservation, this new development entirely erased them. Convinced that the absentee Quapaws desired to sell the reserve which they had abandoned, Agent Jones in 1876 revived his suggestion that the tribal domain be assigned to other Indians and that all of the Downstream People be transferred "either to the Osages or to some small tract suitable for them."[47] Those few Quapaws still on the reservation, ironically, endorsed the proposal in a belated protest to the captive nations experiment. According to one, John Hotel, the home band was not willing to permit resettlement of other tribes until payment for the land relinquished in the Larrabee agreement had been made.[48] Although Hotel did not envision the total displacement of his people, his seeming readiness to welcome others upon certain conditions was not lost upon the Bureau of Indian Affairs.[49] Perhaps Mrs. Tuttle's school would yet be filled.

A sure opportunity to bring to fruition the Quaker hopes for the Quapaw agency presented itself unexpectedly in early 1877. Troubles with the Sioux forced the Ponca Indians led by Chief Standing Bear to consent to removal to Indian Territory. In February, a Ponca delegation counseled with the Osages about settling among them, but the negotiations were so disappointing that eight of the delegates abandoned the group and returned home. Two others, however, went with Inspector Kemble to Mrs. Tuttle's Quapaw mission, where "they were *made to believe* that the Quapaw Reserve was as *good as vacated*" and thus a suitable relocation site.[50] So informed, Kemble persuaded the delegates to accept the reservation of the Downstream People as their new homeland. Although no effort was made to secure the consent of the Quapaws—the government assuming apparently that the 1875 agreement with Larrabee was still operative—in June, Kemble returned with 170 emigrants. Only then did he convene a council of the Quapaw home band; but his objective was not to win their consent. Instead he informed them somewhat peremptorily that the great father had given their lands to the Poncas and that they must go and live with the Osages.[51] In light of his earlier indoctrination at the Quapaw mission, Kemble must have been surprised by the reaction. The Quapaw home band was not about to remove nor even relinquish a part of the tribal domain without sufficient compensation fixed well in advance.[52]

In their resistance to Ponca occupation of the reserve, the Downstream People had the help of Lewis F. Hadley. A member of the Friend fellowship and a skilled linguist, in 1876 he had been appointed as a teacher at the Quapaw mission and thus had been privy to the ambitions of Mrs. Tuttle.[53] Either out of compassion or pique, Hadley agreed to write up the grievances of the Quapaws and to conduct their correspondence even though he remained on the staff of the school. In letters signed by John Hotel, he reminded both the president and the commissioner of Indian affairs that the Downstream People had been granted their reservation forever, that at least 103 persons still occupied the land, and that the destitution of the tribe was due in part to the purposeful design of Quaker policy. The Quapaws, Hadley wrote, had no objection to selling up to two-thirds of their reserve, but they would not sell all of it, nor would the home band join the absentees in the Osage country. Such a removal reminded them of an earlier one to Caddo lands, he declared. Besides, the Quapaws were "Civilized Indians" and did not propose to join "half wild tribes."[54] Hadley's lengthy and reasoned letters undoubtedly articulated the objections of the home band and did not necessarily represent "unscrupulous intermeddling," the oblique charge of Agent Jones.[55] This was certainly the view of John Hotel and his people who, following Hadley's release from the mission school faculty, appointed him clerk of their council, adopted him into the tribe, and gave him the name of In-go-nom-pi-she (One Who Can Not Be Put Down).[56]

In response to the determined resistance of the Quapaw home band, government officials followed two courses of action. On the one hand, Agent Jones sought to enhance the prestige of the leadership of the absentee band, assuming that it might then persuade the dissidents to join the majority. When Louis Angel visited the reservation in the midst of the Ponca crisis, therefore, Jones publicly declared him to be the principal chief of the tribe. Angel responded by encouraging the home band to return with him to the Osage country, an invitation that no more than four Quapaws accepted. For their part, John Hotel and his followers denied that Angel was chief because he had not been elected and had also abandoned the tribe, arguing instead that John Hunker had been the hereditary leader.[57] With Jones's approach so unfruitful, the new Central superintendent, William Nicholson, proposed an alternative—unilateral action on the part of the government. Congress should purchase the Quapaw reservation for the Poncas, place the proceeds of the sale to the credit of the Osages at 5 per cent interest, require that the home band join the absentees, and arrange for the Osages to adopt the Downstream People.[58] But Nicholson's ploy was just as unsuccessful. Whether Secretary of the Interior Carl Schurz "put his foot on it," as Hadley later said, or Ponca dissatisfaction with the reserve negated it, the proposal was never presented to Congress. In July, 1878, the Poncas were relocated on other, more suitable lands beyond the jurisdiction of the Quapaw Agency.[59] For Mrs. Tuttle the turn of events ended her hopes for a full complement of scholars at the mission school. After another disappointing term she and her husband retired from their work.

Yet attempts to persuade the home band to abandon the reserve did not cease. In September, 1878, when Agent Jones asked for authority to recall the absentees, the Bureau of Indian Affairs replied that, on the contrary, the minority should be advised "to join their brethren and be incorporated with the Osages."[60] Indeed, the agent of the larger tribe was informed the following spring that "the policy of the office has been to consolidate all the Quapaws with the Osages."[61] Encouraged by this attitude, a delegation of the absentee band headed by Bushyhead in July, 1882, tried to persuade those on the reserve to join the majority. But the home band, led now by Charley Quapaw, spurned the pleas of their kinsmen and insisted upon retaining the lands they presently occupied even if the remainder of the tribal domain was sold by the government.[62] Although Indian office policy in 1883 changed to the point that the absentees were deemed to have "abandoned their right [to be] . . . consulted in any matters . . . affecting the reservation," the commissioner did recommend in 1884 that the Tonkawas be settled on the Quapaw reserve.[63] Home band opposition, though, aborted these plans as well. Finally, as late as 1889 the government's persistent desire for the amalgamation of the Downstream People with the Osages resulted in a proposal by the resident minority either to sell the treaty lands for $5.00 per acre, with merger following, or to allot 320 acres to each member of the home band with the balance leased to either Indians or non-Indians.[64] Such terms were hardly realistic, for both the price and the allotment acreage were too high. Charley Quapaw and his followers must have known as much and framed the proposal only because of fifteen years of unrelenting federal pressure. If the government earnestly desired some solution to the Quapaw problem, they concluded, it would have to pay dearly. When the Bureau of Indian Affairs ignored the proposition, the resident tribesmen were hardly displeased.

That the home band of the Downstream People should cherish the retention of their lands and the perpetuation of a separate identity was not just a sociological or anthropological phenomenon. There was a good deal of hardheaded realism involved, for their reserve had value beyond that as just a place of residence. The presence of sub-surface minerals had long been recognized, although it was not until late 1865 that there was any interest in commercial exploitation.[65] The Bureau of Indian Affairs, however, refused to permit any mining operations at that time, or even later, in the 1870's and 1880's, when a rich lead and zinc district was discovered in adjacent southwestern Missouri.[66] The Indian office believed that mining was antithetical to its civilization program, but discerning Quapaws knew that their reserve was potentially valuable in terms of mineral resources. Such knowledge undoubtedly steeled their resolve to remain on the treaty lands.

Just as important was the intrinsic worth of the domain for agricultural purposes. Following the abandonment of the Ponca resettlement scheme, white farmers from across the border in Missouri and Kansas ventured onto the Quapaw reservation and established homesteads. In Baxter Springs, Kansas, a "Claim League" was even organized to promote the settlement of tribal lands upon the erroneous assumption that they had been purchased by the government and, deserted by the Poncas, were open to entry under the homestead laws. Only the arrival in May, 1879, of a company of the United States Army under Captain G. F. Towle prevented the consummation of this early "boomer" movement.[67] Yet, situated at "Camp Quapaw" until November, 1880, the army could not completely restrict the entrance of white agriculturalists. Given the presence of the intruder, members of the Quapaw home band saw no reason not to take advantage of his enterprise, and after 1875 many of them adopted the practice of renting or leasing land to non-Indians in return for one-third of the crop. Since Agent Jones registered no objection, by 1879 some 600 acres were cultivated under such an arrangement, a remarkable sum considering that the thirty-eight members of the home band themselves planted less than one acre per person. If the renters were honest, the resident Quapaws received the harvest from approximately 200 acres of land, or five times what they had in production themselves.[68] No wonder they refused to abandon their reserve and amalgamate with the Osages!

As in the case of mineral exploitation, the Indian office deemed the use of renters as subversive to its policy objectives. A "civilized" Indian would not emerge unless the Indian had lessons in the school of individual toil. The renter system, it was reported, gave the Quapaws, as "Lords of the Soil," an opportunity for "elegant leisure" and their reservation the appearance of a white man's country.[69] To correct this situation the secretary of the interior at first ordered that all renters be expelled from the Quapaw agency by December 1, 1879, but after concerted protests from Indians and non-Indians alike he modified his directive to permit a continuation of renting agreements if they were necessary to the welfare of tribal members.[70] By 1881 only sixty such instruments were operative throughout the agency, but all, according to Agent D. B. Dyer, were "a mutual advantage" to the parties involved.[71] The rent system, Dyer believed, enabled the Indians to have improved farms and to live independent of the government.[72]

Despite the agent's view, policy planners in Washington continued to judge the renting practice as an evil that deprived the Indians of character-building lessons. In June, 1882, therefore, the secretary of the interior ordered that the system must cease upon the expiration of existing contracts. When Dyer registered a persuasive counterargument, this directive, too, was modified to permit the continued use of renters by widows, orphans, minor children, the sick, aged, crippled, and infirm.[73] Although the secretary later refused to amend the regulations further, by 1887 it was apparent that many Indians not of the approved classes still relied upon unauthorized personnel to conduct farming operations.[74] This fact and the decision of the Indian office to substitute labor permits for the old renter contracts prompted Agent J. V. Summers in April to order those whites not properly engaged to remove from the agency within ten days. A protest by Senator F. M. Cockrell of Missouri succeeded in staying the implementation of this new directive until December, but thereafter those white men not holding labor permits issued by the agent and approved by the secretary of the interior were declared illegal intruders.[75] Moreover, holders of such permits had to be employed by Indians previously adjudged as belonging to the approved classes, a regulation that restricted white agricultural laborers to only twenty-two Quapaws.[76] If Washington officials were to have their way, the home band of the Downstream People would not escape the civilizing benefits of individual toil.

The government's fifteen-year struggle to make the rent system

Charley Quapaw, chief of the home band of the Quapaws before allotment. Courtesy Robert Whitebird.

compatible with its civilization program had not prevented the reservation Quapaws from deriving significant economic advantages from their landed estate. The use of renters was only one of the benefits accruing from the white man's enterprise. Of even more importance were those emanating from the growth of the cattle kingdom. The tribal reserve was located on one of the earliest, post-war routes that Texas drovers used to trail their cattle to market in the north. Its well-watered and high prairie lands provided excellent pastures where trail-worn beeves could be fattened prior to sale in Kansas. Energetic tribesmen, consequently, were able to tax the cattlemen one average beef for each one hundred head per month, a practice that in 1868 provided the Indians with enough meat for the winter.[77] Revenue increased after 1870 when the Missouri River, Fort Scott, and Gulf Railroad reached Baxter Springs, Kansas, and established a railhead and loading pens just south of the border on the reservation. Wishing to avoid state laws prohibiting the importation of Texas cattle, officers of that company paid the Quapaws $200 a year for the use of 320 acres of land and five cents a head for all stock that had been driven through the reserve.[78] Incidentally, the railroad also generated a market for crossties that were cut from timber stands controlled by the tribe.[79] Sold for nine cents a tie, revenue from this source supplemented the growing receipts obtained from individual cattlemen and the railroad itself.

For ten years the expansion of the cattle kingdom on the reservation of the Downstream People was wholly unregulated by the government. The Indian office did assert its authority after 1879, but, unlike reaction to the renter system, proposed at first only procedural regulations designed to protect the interests of the Quapaws rather than advance a particular philosophy of civilization. Accordingly, it raised the grazing tax per head from ten cents a season to ten cents a month and gave responsibility for collection to the agent.[80] Moreover, to protect domestic cattle from the dreaded tick fever, the introduction of herds from Texas was prohibited.[81] The imposition of these regulations had mixed results. The incidence of Texas fever decreased, but so, too, did the number of cattle on the Quapaw range.[82] The collection activity of the agent insured an honest accounting, but the Downstream People thereafter had to look to him for funds that had once been paid directly to them.[83] And where they had once obtained cash, at the discretion of the agent they frequently received only provisions or merchandise.[84] That the new regulations were on balance more beneficial to the Quapaws became apparent in 1883. With Agent Dyer's consent, the Baxter Springs Live Stock Company moved onto the reserve, established its head-quarters on Tar Creek, built fences, and paid a grazing fee of approx-imately $100 a month. The money was regularly distributed in per capita payments to the fifty-five members of the home band.[85]

The most significant of all cattle enterprises began operations in 1884. On March 19, H. R. Crowell, former mayor of Baxter Springs and secretary-treasurer of the Baxter Springs Live Stock Company, obtained in his name a two-year lease for that part of the reserve west of the mission school, or more than half of the tribal estate. Signed by all but two Quapaw family heads, the lease committed the cattleman to pay $3,000 a year in quarterly installments, the first of which was distributed per capita immediately. Crowell later as-signed his rights to the Cherokee Live Stock Company, the succes-sor of the Baxter Springs outfit, financed in part by Chicago-based entrepreneurs, which promptly established a headquarters on the reservation, extended fence lines, and entered into sub-leases with other operators.[86] This activity spawned a number of protests from competing cattlemen who were forced off the Quapaw range, from Kansas farmers who were no longer able to graze their own livestock on the "free grass," and from some dissident Quapaws who had been recruited by anti-Crowell forces.[87] Addressed to the secretary of the interior, these complaints were of sufficient weight to cause an in-vestigation by Special Agent W. H. Robb in April, 1884. The result of this inquiry was only to confirm the lease with one major modifica-tion: compensation paid the Quapaws was increased to $4,000 a year, payable semi-annually in advance.[88]

Any money paid by the Cherokee Live Stock Company, though, was not distributed immediately to the tribe. In July, 1884, Congress had required the deposit of such funds into the United States Trea-sury but had made no provision for withdrawing them.[89] Not until late 1887 was the money—totaling nearly $3,500—made available, and then only if the agent applied it toward agricultural purposes.[90] In the meantime, the Indian office re-evaluated the whole question of ranching on the various reservations. This study was encouraged in some measure by the inauguration of President Grover Cleve-land's administration in March, 1885, and a United States Senate inquiry into the matter.[91] The result was a decision, in late 1885, to abrogate all existing range leases on the basis that they tended to impede the Indian's formation of agricultural habits.[92] Rather than rely on funds from the Cherokee Live Stock Company, the Downstream People were admonished to feed themselves through individual labor.

Whatever the policy of the government with regard to cattle leases, renter agreements, or mineral exploitation, the Quapaws on the reserve had learned that the tribal estate offered more than just a place to build a house. Put differently, it was an economic resource of immense value, far more valuable than the regular annuity payment once so highly prized. This, no doubt, explained in part why the home band refused to follow their brethren to the Osage country or to approve the transfer of their domain to others. Moreover, the realization of the worth of the land was a testimony to the wisdom and statecraft of the leadership—John Hotel in the 1870's and Charley Quapaw in the 1880's. Their achievement was even more remarkable because the members of the home band were so few. In 1882, for example, they numbered less than fifty, or only one-fifth of the whole tribe.[93]

Without question the Bureau of Indian Affairs would have been happier had the Quapaws not found the reservation quite so fruitful. The use of white laborers and the collection of grazing fees, it believed, had thwarted not only the policy of amalgamation with the Osages but also the whole civilizing program. The Indian could never learn to be self-sustaining and to develop character if he did not have to work—and work alone, declared Agent Dyer, opened "the golden gates of human possibilities." Denied such an opportunity, Dyer said, Indians were "generally worthless," not from any natural deficiency but "because in many cases their faculties have been denied development."[94] According to the agent, the Quapaw home band illustrated what could happen when Indians were not compelled to work. "The greatest ambition of many," he reported, "is to ride about vestured in garments of barbaric tint, with paint and feathers. The majority are indolent, and . . . you can find them almost any day standing around their cabins or leaning around drowsily like animals who have been hired to personate men and are tired of the job. . . . If they manifest any energy at intervals, you soon discover it to be a mistake."[95]

Despite Dyer's pessimistic assessment, the government's civilizing program had not been a total failure. Many of the Downstream People on the reservation had acquired, at least externally, some of the cultural patterns of the white man. They wore comparable clothes, lived in similar houses, ate the same foods, and coveted identical creature comforts. And judging from reports about the fondness of the Quapaws for whiskey, their vices were identical. Economic attitudes also reflected those of white society. Although saving or deferred gratification remained an alien concept, the home band fully appreciated the value of money. As a consequence, it abandoned the chase and looked to the tribal estate as its source of sustenance. Religious beliefs of many of the Quapaws also paralleled those of the white man, thanks to the efforts of Jesuit fathers who maintained their mission despite Quaker disapproval. And because of Quaker benevolence, educational interest among some Indian families matched that of their white counterparts. Finally, the political patterns of the home band corresponded to those of the white man. With Louis Angel, their hereditary chief, among the Osages, the reservation Quapaws elected their leadership and conducted business in open council.[96] Taken together, then, these many and profound accommodations to alien cultural patterns suggested that the government's civilization programs had been more successful than some tribal agents apparently recognized. The transformation was not complete, but the home band bore at least a superficial resemblance to white men. This fact was particularly evident after the Downstream People regathered on the tribal reservation.

CHAPTER VII
ACCEPTING ALLOTMENT
1888-96

After 1880 the forty or so members of the Quapaw home band were increasingly aware of the unusual value of their reservation. Above all else, this had steeled them to resist the resettlement of other Indians on their domain. Yet the ability of the resident band to continue to preserve the vested interests of the Downstream People in their landed estate was contingent upon its survival as an independent unit of the tribe. In the decade of the 1880's, therefore, the Quapaw minority initiated the practice of adopting different Indian peoples as long as they established homes on the reservation. Happily, these wholesale adoptions and the pecuniary benefits enjoyed by the home band prompted the majority of the tribe who were absent in the Osage country to awaken to the value of Quapaw citizenship and return to the reserve. But this remarkable event occurred just as Congress passed the so-called Dawes Allotment Act, a measure that threatened to destroy the very magnet that had drawn the Downstream People together again—the economic potential of the land. To preserve to themselves alone the benefit of their national estate, the Quapaws took an unprecedented step and, without government approval, divided their domain among themselves. This action insured that no surplus lands would be available for non-Indian settlement and fully demonstrated how well the tribe had accommodated itself to the white man's ways. Put differently, the reservation system had worked beyond official expectations.

Although the practice of adopting non-Quapaws was eventually rationalized as a means of perpetuating control of the reserve, the procedure in its origin was of a different design. In February, 1880, for example, Paschal Fish, his son, Leander J., and his daughter-in-law, Julia, persuaded the home band to adopt them into the tribe. Of

Cherokee-Shawnee extraction, the Fishes built a house which they permitted Kansas cattlemen to use as headquarters for a ranching operation that thereby had access to the whole Quapaw reservation. Informed that the family was no more than a cover for an illegal operation, the commissioner of Indian affairs refused to recognize the adoption.[1] With so much grassland at stake, the cattlemen persuaded Senator P. B. Plumb of Kansas to represent them, and the Fishes employed a Washington attorney to intervene in the matter. Ultimately, in April, 1883, the secretary of the interior ruled in favor of the adoptions so long as the family resided on the reservation.[2] Although the issue would not be finally settled until 1890, the admission of the Fishes into the tribe represented the initial experience of the Quapaws with a practice that seemed to have potential beyond being just a front for designing white men.

According to the Treaty of 1833, the United States was bound to recognize the title of the Downstream People to their reservation only "as long as they shall exist as a nation or continue to reside thereon."[3] Since so few families comprised the home band, many government officials legitimately questioned whether the Quapaws truly did "exist as a nation" and "reside thereon." Fully aware of these doubts and believing their title to the land in jeopardy, the leadership of the tribal minority seized upon the adoption procedure as a way of increasing their ranks. In July, 1883, therefore, Chief Charley Quapaw directed Alphonsus Vallier, first councilman, to travel to the old tribal homeland in Arkansas in order to locate any Quapaw descendants and invite them to join their kinsmen in Indian Territory.

In accordance with these instructions, Vallier and Lewis F. Hadley, the latter perhaps having suggested the plan, canoed down Spring and Grand rivers to the Arkansas and, then turning east, reached Pine Bluff in mid-August. The community's oldest white settler, probably I. W. Bocage, directed Vallier to Abraham Dardenne, a mixed-blood Indian, to whom he explained the purpose of his mission. Other families of Quapaw-French ancestry, including the Rays, Imbeaus, and Hunts, were also visited and invited to remove to the reservation. Determined to take advantage of the unique opportunity, some three years later Dardenne and Abraham Ray settled their families on the tribal estate. They were an advance party of a small migration that soon included other Quapaw-French families as well. Agent J. V. Summers, however, questioned the right of the emigrants to remain on the reserve unless they had been properly adopted by the chief and council and the adoption papers approved by the government. At the local level this formality was accomplished forthwith. The appropriate documents were then forwarded to Washington, where Congressman C. R. Breckenridge of Arkansas arranged for their early consideration by the secretary of the interior, who in March, 1887, approved them.[4] Significantly, this action officially sanctioned the procedure by which the number of Quapaw families living on the reservation was nearly doubled.

Motivated by a strong desire to strengthen their control of the tribal estate even further, the home band now began the systematic adoption of members of other Indian groups. Unlike the Arkansas Quapaws, there were many who without any solicitation whatsoever volunteered to be incorporated into the tribe. The most notable of this group included John Smith, James Matthews, Anna Wright and her two children (Charles and Laura), Alex Rakestraw and his wife, and Mrs. Helen Wade and her three daughters (Florence, Isa, and Kitty).[5] In the fourteen months between September, 1886, and October, 1887, a host of other so-called "homeless Indians" were also adopted. Among these, the biggest contingent was made up of members of the Miami tribe, and as in earlier cases, most of them were the children or wives of white men. Included in this group— eighteen in all—were Francis Douthat and her two children, a brother, George Zahn, and a sister, Catherine Gordon, and her three children; Francis Washington; Ester A. Carden, her six children, and her mother, Mary Willhoite; and Louisa Washington.[6] Another equally large group of New York Indian extraction, in contrast to others, included some heads of families. Numbered in this party were the James Newman family; John Charters, his sister, Mrs. A. G. McKenzie, and her children, Charles and Clifford Geboe and Isabel Eichorne; and the A. W. Abrams family.[7] The admission to tribal citizenship in the fall of 1887 of Mary Portis and her three sons and Emma Hedges and her two sons, the latter Peoria Indians, brought an end to the flood of adoptions approved by the Quapaw home band.[8]

The initial reaction of the Bureau of Indian Affairs to the adoption of homeless Indians was wholly negative. On November 1, 1886, the commissioner declared that "The practice of adoption is an evil which will not be countenanced by this office."[9] Although he had supported the admission to tribal citizenship of the Arkansas Quapaws, Agent J. V. Summers agreed with his superior. In the first place, the adoptions had been made without the consent of the majority of the tribe then in the Osage country. In the second place, he was convinced that a well-organized conspiracy existed to secure control of the Quapaw reservation through the medium of numerous adoptions. Indeed, he said, "three syndicates had been organized for a common purpose—that of securing the future control of the mineral and grazing lands of the Quapaws." One of the combines, he reported, was led by A. G. McKenzie of Paola, Kansas, the kinsman of five of the New York Indians recently adopted by the home band. McKenzie and others had been successful thus far in implementing their schemes, Summers declared, because "The Quapaws are notoriously for sale."[10] Given this information, the commissioner of Indian affairs in March, 1888, specifically refused to sanction the adoption of McKenzie's wife and in-laws, the eighteen-member Miami group, Mrs. Hedges and her sons, and Helen Wade and her three daughters.[11] Although no action seems to have been taken in the other cases, the evidence makes it clear that the commissioner's decision was intended to be inclusive.

If government officials took a dim view of adoptions, so did the absentee band among the Osages. Since 1875 they had exhibited little if any interest in the activities on the reservation, although Louis Angel, as the hereditary chief, apparently did return on a regular basis, performing the traditional duties, such as child naming, that were his prerogative alone.[12] But by 1887 this general apathy gave way to active concern, apparently because the numerous adoptions carried out by the minority threatened to dilute the vested rights of the absentees in the landed estate of the tribe. Moreover, the home band had demonstrated that by capitalizing upon the enterprise of non-Indians, food and money were available on the reserve. It was also rumored that funds collected as grazing receipts would soon be distributed in a per capita payment. Finally, the mood of the Congress and the Bureau of Indian Affairs suggested that some form of allotment would doubtlessly be imposed, a fact that necessitated the presence of the absentees in order to protect their corporate interest in the land. As a consequence, many of the Quapaws in Osage country returned to the reservation, and some, especially Peter Clabber, Francis Quapaw, and John Beaver, took an increasingly active part in the tribal council. Among other things, they put a stop to any additional adoptions and, as their number increased, even wrested political control of the reservation away from the home band.

Although the new power structure opposed further adoptions of homeless Indians, it initially made no effort to impede attempts to win final confirmation of those already made. Thus, in June, 1888, Chief Charley Quapaw, Alphonsus Vallier, and Frank Vallier journeyed to Washington in the company of A. G. McKenzie to appeal the decision of the commissioner of Indian affairs that had nullified most of the adoptions made by the home band. In the capital city the delegation sent letters written by McKenzie to the secretary of the interior requesting that he reverse the action of the Indian office and admit to tribal citizenship McKenzie's wife and in-laws, the Newmans, the Abramses, and the entire Miami group save for Mrs. Willhoite. Since the latter was in good circumstances financially, the delegation indicated, her adoption petition need not be sanctioned, nor should those of the Mrs. Hedges, Wade, Wright and their children. The Quapaw delegates also opposed the admission to citizenship of James and Napoleon Robataille, Mrs. Susannah Benton, and Alfred Mudeater (Wyandott Indians), as well as Dr. G. G. Gregg, a white man, and Mrs. Douthat and her son, both of whom were to join the Senecas. No mention was made, though, of Mrs. Portis' family, John Smith, James Matthews, or Alex Rakestraw.[13]

If the delegation had wished for an immediate decision, it failed to obtain one. Instead the secretary directed that an official investigation of the entire adoption issue be made. Subsequently, in August, 1888, Frank Armstrong, a government inspector, visited the reservation and made a generally unfavorable report, although apparently he was inclined to support the admission to tribal citizenship of the Abramses, the Newmans, Mrs. Portis and her three sons, and Charles Bluejacket, the latter a Cherokee whose petition for adoption had heretofore elicited little attention.[14] Following this assessment, the secretary of the interior on February 2, 1889, ordered that a Quapaw roll be established on which would be listed those persons whose adoptions had been sanctioned. Also from this list, grazing receipts that had continued to accumulate in the treasury could be paid. Agent Summers, with the assistance of the tribe, prepared an official roll on March 15, 1889, enumerating 121 Quapaws who comprised not only the home band but many of the Osage absentees, Arkansas Quapaws (the Dardennes, Rays, Imbeaus, and Hunts), homeless

*The Vallier brothers, Frank (Quapaw interpreter),
George, and Amos. Courtesy Western History Collections,
University of Oklahoma.*

adoptees (the Abrams and Portis families), and two members of the Fish family.[15] Confusing comments made by Summers in forwarding the roll prompted some alterations in Washington, but on May 27 the secretary approved a listing of 116 enrolled members of the tribe.[16] The roll was then returned to the Quapaw agent, who in June supervised the payment of grazing receipts that totaled $4,500, with each member of the tribe receiving a per capita share of $38.79.[17]

The roll had been no more than completed when a concerted effort was made to "correct" it. Of all the others involved in these attempts, none was as important as Abner W. Abrams. Initially a member of the Stockbridge tribe, Abrams had been educated in Kansas and had worked as a head sawyer in Colorado and on the Pacific slope. He returned to Baxter Springs in 1887 and on July 6, at the age of forty, was adopted into the Quapaw tribe by the home band.[18] Intelligent, shrewd, and capable, he was soon employed by the tribal leadership as clerk of the council, conducting most of its correspondence and in time exerting a pervasive influence over its deliberations. As early as March, 1889, Abrams attempted to assure the confirmation of his own adoption by corresponding in behalf of the council with George W. Lockwood, a Washington attorney. He directed Lockwood, among other things, to press for recognition of the admission to Quapaw citizenship of the New York Indians (the Abrams and Newman families and the wife and in-laws of McKenzie), indicating at the same time that the eighteen Miami Indians should be expunged from the adoption list.[19] Although Abrams and his family were included on the role approved in May, the recommendation that still others be included and the receipt of information that at least four full bloods had been erroneously stricken from the list prompted the commissioner of Indian affairs to direct yet another investigation prior to the completion of a final enumeration.[20]

In accordance with his instructions, Special Agent Robert A. Gardner convened a council of the Quapaw Indians at the agency on July 8, 1889. In attendance were seventeen of the Downstream People, ten by blood and seven by adoption, the latter group including Abrams and two Arkansas Quapaws. The first action of the council was to confirm the citizenship of the four full bloods previously deleted from the roll. By close votes it then approved the inclusion of Mrs. Benjamin (Martha) Dardenne and Mrs. Louis (Melissa) Imbeau, but rejected Minnie Dardenne, the adopted daughter of Martha and, like the others, a white woman. By unanimous vote the adoption of the white husband of Jane Hunt, an Arkansas Quapaw, was also denied. By a similar decision the council rejected the petitions of Mrs. Ester A. Carden, Mrs. Francis A. Douthat, and Mrs. Catherine Gordon and their families, as well as those of George Zahn and Louisa Washington. Moreover, by a divided vote it refused to accept John Charters and the Geboe brothers. The applications of Mrs. McKenzie and Isabel Eichorne were unanimously rejected, although the adoption petitions of James A. Newman and his three sons were endorsed, as was that of Charles Bluejacket. Furthermore, the council denied citizenship for Mrs. Willhoite, Mrs. Emma Hedges and her children, Napoleon and James Robataille, the children of Mrs. Helen Wade, Mrs. Benton and her family, Alfred Mudeater, Mrs. Hailey Wright and her family, and Dr. G. G. Gregg. Finally, it refused to adopt William A. Douthat, the brother-in-law of Abrams, by a vote of nine to seven, the clerk of the council abstaining. Although Gardner did not support the admission to citizenship of the two white women (Martha Dardenne and Melissa Imbeau), he did recommend that the "actions at this Council should be respected, and made final in the cases brought before them [sic]."[21] His superiors did not disagree, and on October 18, 1889, the secretary of the interior approved a roll that conformed to the wishes of the council and enumerated 124 members of the tribe.[22]

Government officials no doubt believed that any increase in the population of the Downstream People would thereafter come as a consequence of natural rather than artificial means. But in December, 1889, Abner Abrams and Alphonsus Vallier appeared unexpectedly in Washington, presented a "revised and corrected list" containing 205 names to the commissioner of Indian affairs, and urged its immediate adoption. The new roll, certified by the chiefs and council, contained the names of thirteen individuals (Wm. A. Douthat, W. B. Hunt, Minnie Dardenne, Francis Douthat and her three children, John Charters, Paschal and Leander Fish, and Mrs. Emma Hedges and her two sons) who had been previously stricken from the roll or specifically rejected by order of the secretary of interior. Moreover, it included twenty-two Arkansas Quapaws, of whom three were white (Wm. Logan, Mack Adams, and Jack Hammitt) and who had never lived on the reservation. Forty-two of those on the revised list were living in the Osage country, four were newborns, and three were of a special class. Of this last group, Abraham Ray was a white man whose wife and children were Arkansas

Quapaws and had been previously adopted; James Newhouse was of Indian descent and had been adopted as a boy by Charley Quapaw; and Elizabeth H. Tousey was the mother-in-law of Abner Abrams. Altogether, then, there were eighty-six additions to the roll approved in October, 1889. Five had died since that date, so the Quapaw delegates sought confirmation of a list bearing 205 names.[23]

Several factors motivated this rather remarkable effort to expand the roll by more than one-third. Having previously failed, some persons sought another method by which the government might yet approve their adoption. Even more basic was the desire to share in an estate that was increasingly valuable, especially after it was learned that the Downstream People were due compensation for lands that should have been assigned to them, as stipulated in the Treaty of 1833. That document had granted the tribe 150 sections or 96,000 acres of land, but after ceding 26,122.82 as per the Treaty of 1867 only 56,685.41 acres remained, or some 13,191.77 less than what the Quapaws should actually have retained had the initial grant been accurate.[24] Equally important was the certain knowledge that allotment of the reservation was inevitable. When that occurred, inclusion on the tribal roll would assure one of having a portion of the divided domain.[25] Many of the Downstream People belatedly concluded, therefore, that citizenship was a matter of considerable consequence and anxiously sought to have their names added to the "revised and corrected list."

Given previous policy and the two investigations made prior to the approval of the earlier roll, it might have been expected that the Bureau of Indian Affairs would have hesitated to endorse the roll submitted by Abrams and his colleagues. Strangely enough, it did not. Instead, Commissioner T. J. Morgan recommended certification of the entire list save for the Fishes, John Charters, the Hedgeses, Sallie Cousatte who had died, and the intermarried white men, Hunt, Logan, Adams, Hammitt, and Ray. The final roll as approved on February 8, 1890, by Secretary of the Interior John W. Noble, included 193 names.[26] Altogether only forty-eight days had passed from the time of the submission of the new list until its confirmation. For the bureaucracy it must have been something of a record; for Abner Abrams it represented a major triumph in that both his mother-in-law and brother-in-law were included on the approved roll.

The completion of a new roll was just one of the issues that occupied the Quapaw delegation in the winter of 1889–90. Of equal concern was the matter of compensation for the land authorized in the Treaty of 1833 but never assigned. For assistance in presenting the claim before the government, the delegates turned to the former governor of Kansas, Samuel J. Crawford, then practicing law in Washington. Assuming that litigation would be required, Crawford persuaded Congressman Bishop W. Perkins of Oswego, Kansas, to introduce legislation that would enable the Downstream People to bring suit in the United States Court of Claims. Although the measure was favorably reported to the House of Representatives on March 1, 1890, the fifty-first Congress during its first session took no specific action.[27] In the meantime, Crawford altered his approach and, with the assistance of another Quapaw delegation headed by Abrams, lobbied for a direct appropriation that would compensate the tribe for the deficiency.[28] A man of considerable influence, the former governor eventually succeeded in attaching a rider to the Indian Appropriation Act passed on March 3, 1891, whereby $39,575.31 was allocated for the purpose desired. Representing a payment of $3.00 an acre, $30,000 of this sum was to be distributed per capita under the supervision of the secretary of the interior, while $9,575.31 was to be paid to the treasurer of the tribe and disbursed under the direction of the council.[29]

The council promptly appointed John M. Cooper of Baxter Springs, Kansas, as the bonded treasurer and directed him to receive the funds allocated for its use.[30] From these monies the leadership later donated $1,000 to construct a new building at the Quapaw Boarding School and erected a fence along the entire western and most of the northern border of the reserve.[31] In January, 1892, moreover, Cooper paid Samuel Crawford $2,770.27 for services rendered during the second session of the fifty-first Congress, which, if it was all that he received, was a modest enough retainer.[32] And in May, the treasurer was directed to distribute the balance of the funds still in his account in per capita payments to those listed on the 1890 roll.[33] In the meantime, early in 1892, a similar payment of more than $150 was made by the tribal agent, which in the aggregate was the balance of the congressional appropriation.[34]

The receipt and distribution of the money fostered a good deal of activity on the reservation. In addition to the fences, at least fifteen frame houses were erected and some 5,000 acres of land were broken for cultivation.[35] The financial windfall also revived the issue of adoptions. Most of the applicants whose petitions had been previously rejected by the secretary of the interior sought to have the decision reversed, either through congressional pressure or the intervention of attorneys.[36] Throughout 1891 the Quapaw council had consistently opposed the confirmation of any further adoptions, but once the $39,575 was paid its attitude became considerably more flexible. In May, for example, it had petitioned the commissioner of Indian affairs not to approve any more adoptions and in its meeting the following month refused to reinstate the Carden and Gordon families.[37] Yet one year later, on June 8, 1892, twenty of the Downstream People, ten of whom were adopted, signed a typewritten document indicating their desire to admit to the tribe not only the five Gordons and seven Cardens, but also Mary Willhoite, John Charters, Isabel McKenzie, Charles Geboe, and Louisa Washington. Abrams evidently took the document to the capital and submitted it to the commissioner, who in turn recommended its approval to the secretary of the interior. Despite the fact that the applications of the seventeen parties had been denied on numerous occasions, government officials had so much confidence in Abrams that on June 29 the secretary consented to the adoptions.[38] This confirmation, of course, was limited in scope and did not affect other parties seeking enrollment. But to make the turnabout complete, on July 19, 1892, when the Quapaws assembled to select a new chief, John Medicine, they adopted a resolution whereby they withdrew all previous protests to the approval of adoptions.[39]

For some reason, perhaps the receipt of reports that the change of attitude in the Quapaw council was induced by bribery, the Bureau of Indian Affairs suspended implementation of the order recognizing the adoptions of the Gordons, Cardens, and others. Instead, Robert A. Gardner was directed to visit the agency again and review the situation. Gardner conducted his investigation in October, 1892, and found that the action of the council removing objections to the enrollment of the seventeen was not a matter of record in Abrams' book of council proceedings. Moreover, the typewritten document had been prepared in Washington and submitted for signature by Samuel W. Smith, a Baxter Springs attorney, through Abrams. Advised that the Quapaws did not know what they had signed, Gardner had another council assembled in order to get a true expression of sentiment. Thirty-one members of the tribe gathered, and, after having the issue carefully explained, only eight of them voted in favor of approving the adoptions, while twenty-three voted against it. The inspector failed to find that bribery had been involved in the previous action, but believing that "the Quapaws have been very generous, in fact too much so, for their own good" he recommended that the seventeen names not be added to the tribal role.[40] But it was all in vain. Notwithstanding the vote of the council, the secretary of the interior on February 24, 1893, lifted the suspension and admitted the seventeen "homeless" Indians to Quapaw citizenship.[41] Only Abrams' earlier testimony to the inspector that a majority of the tribe desired the adoptions despite the action of the council can explain this remarkable reversal of policy. [42] When the secretary also approved the adoption of the Wade children in August, the final number on the tribal roll became 215 names.[43]

Gardner was probably technically correct in finding that bribery was not responsible for the Quapaws' withdrawal of objections to adoptions. Yet it was true that Abrams frequently called upon those whose petitions were pending to contribute or loan money to meet expenses of delegations traveling to Washington.[44] Indeed, John Charters reported that candidates for adoption were expected to pay a fee of $50.[45] Although Charters' testimony was discounted at the time, it proved to be accurate. In December before the secretary of the interior lifted the suspension, the council called upon members of the tribe previously adopted to pay their fees.[46] And on at least two occasions, in 1894 and 1896, Abrams receipted individuals for money paid for the same purposes.[47]

Fundamental to the whole issue of adoptions was the matter of allotment. Ever since the passage of the Dawes Allotment Act in 1887, the division of the Quapaw domain among enrolled members of the tribe had been only a matter of time. That act was the culmination of the tireless efforts of so-called "friends of the Indians," members of Congress, and government officials. By its provisions reservations were to be allotted at the discretion of the president in 160-acre tracts to heads of families and 80-acre tracts to single persons over eighteen and orphan children under eighteen.[48] Although allotment was inevitable, the Downstream People, and particularly Abrams, found the language of the act wholly unsatisfactory, particularly that which limited individual parcels to 160 acres. In November, 1889, therefore, the council selected Abrams and Alphonsus Vallier to go to Washington and seek a special act from Congress that would authorize 200 acres to each member of the tribe. After having submitted their "revised and corrected" roll, the delegates with the assistance of Samuel Crawford prevailed upon Senator P. B. Plumb and Congressman Perkins to introduce the desired legislation during the fifty-first Congress. Although the Senate eventually passed the measure on January 31, 1891, the House failed to concur, even though two different versions of the bill were reported favorably by its Committee on Indian Affairs.[49]

When the first session of the fifty-second Congress convened in December, 1891, Abrams and Vallier went back to the capital to make another attempt. Four different bills were introduced into each of the congressional houses, and in March, 1892, the delegates appeared before the Senate Committee on Indian Affairs. Abrams gave thorough testimony as to the situation of the Downstream People and urged adoption of the bill that would allot 200 acres to each enrolled member, organize the Quapaw agency into a county (Cayuga) of the Territory of Oklahoma, and declare the Quapaws and other Indians to be citizens of the United States. They preferred to be joined to distant and predominately white Oklahoma instead of to the proposed Indian Territory because the tribe did not trust the Cherokees, whom the leadership believed would control any governmental unit coextensive with the borders of the Five Civilized Tribes. As to why the Quapaws opposed allotment under terms of the Dawes Act, Abrams responded pointedly: "We have been led to believe that we would be forced into this general allotment of 80 acres to each individual . . . we have even been taught to believe that the balance of our land would be taken from us anyway and sold at some price arbitrarily."[50] To obtain the most land possible for each Quapaw and, obviously, also for himself was Abrams' paramount objective. The members of the committee were not critical of this goal and in May reported the bill favorably.[51] When the House acted similarly two months later, the Quapaws were confident that final approval of the legislation would come in the second session of Congress.[52]

Despite these rising expectations, the allotment bill endorsed by the Downstream People was not passed by the national legislature. Several factors accounted for this failure. For one thing, some Senecas whose tribe would be affected by the legislation objected to the proposed county of Cayuga being attached to Oklahoma Territory and sent a delegation to Washington to lobby against the measure. In light of this unexpected opposition, Abrams wrote to

Senator John T. Morgan of Alabama in January, 1893, that the Downstream People were willing to forego every feature of the desired legislation save for the 200-acre allotment provision. "[G]ive us that," he said, "and we will be satisfied.... "[53] By this time, though, Morgan was convinced that the bill could not pass.[54] Too many powerful interests opposed it, not only because there would be little if any surplus land available for white exploitation but also because the tax base for local and state government would be limited by the provisions restricting each allotment against alienation.[55] The Senator from Alabama, then, was inclined to let the measure die a natural death. Abrams did succeed in getting the House Committee on Indian Affairs to rewrite the pending legislation, but this effort, too, was in vain. The fifty-second Congress adjourned without further action.[56]

Abrams and the tribal council were bitterly disappointed. Four years of work and the expense of four delegations to Washington had seemingly accomplished nothing. Moreover, believing that legislative approval was certain, many Quapaws had gone ahead and selected a 200-acre allotment, fenced it, built houses, and broken the prairie sod for cultivation. Indeed, Abrams himself had planted 500 acres, nearly half of which was in wheat. In accordance with new regulations of the Bureau of Indian Affairs, others had rented or leased "their" land to white farmers, a practice that brought at least seventy-two families to the reservation. With 42,000 acres under fence and 10,000 acres in cultivation, therefore, the Downstream People stood to suffer immense economic dislocation because of congressional intransigency.[57] To protect their vested interests, they reasoned, dramatic and innovative—even unprecedented—action was required. Accordingly, at a council meeting on March 23, 1893, attended by every adult member of the tribe but four, the Quapaws unanimously agreed to allot their tribal estate without prior government approval. Signed by Chief John Medicine and sixty-seven others, the measure adopted authorized a committee composed of Abrams, Frank Buck, and Ben Dardenne to allot 200 acres to each enrolled member of the tribe. Heads of families were directed to select the tract desired. If disputes arose over boundaries, they were to be adjudicated by the council, subject to the approval of the secretary of the interior. The measure also set apart 400 acres for school purposes and ten acres (later increased to forty) for the use of the Catholic church. Finally, while the expenses of allotment were to be borne by the tribe, the act provided that the allotment of lands should be subject to rules and regulations that might later be prescribed by the secretary of the interior and the Congress so long as the number of acres allotted was not decreased or diminished.[58]

On April 6, Abrams and his colleagues on the allotment committee forwarded a copy of the act approved by the council to the Bureau of Indian Affairs. They related the reason the measure had been adopted and their hope that it would be approved in Washington, and they requested three tract books that would facilitate their work.[59] In a covering letter Agent T. J. Moore endorsed the "good efforts of the Quapaws," and later in his annual report he renewed his appeal that the act be ratified. "A grateful nation," he wrote, "can not refuse the just demands of its wards."[60] In the meantime, the allotment committee was hard at work. Having been furnished the desired supplies, it carefully entered the description of the 200-acre tracts selected by or for each of the enrolled members of the tribe according to a survey previously completed by the government. The land was generally selected in one location (a 160-acre segment plus an adjacent 40 acres), and no attempt was made to grade it according to value, a realistic approach in that the quality of the land varied little from place to place.[61] Many simply selected the 200 acres that they had already fenced and improved, and a few family heads located the allotments of their children adjacent to their own. Abrams, for example, obtained in this way a block of 1,200 acres. Few objections were raised to the practice, and, for that matter, the whole selection process was accomplished, reported the agent, "without friction or wrangling." By August, 1893, moreover, it was nearly completed.[62]

Two hundred acres to each of the Downstream People left at least 12,000 acres of the tribal estate undivided. When Abrams was doing his congressional lobbying, he had assured senators and representatives alike that the Quapaws expected that this surplus land should be sold to the best advantage.[63] But inasmuch as Congress had ignored his pleas and the tribe was now acting on its own, he did not consider previous promises binding. Henry L. Dawes and M. H. Kidd, commissioners then in Muskogee to negotiate the allotment of the reservations of the Five Civilized Tribes, shared this same opinion and in February, 1894, suggested that the surplus land be divided among the Quapaws. Accordingly, the next month the tribal council authorized the allotment of an additional forty-acre tract to each enrolled member, a distribution speedily accomplished by Abrams and his committee.[64] By the end of 1894, therefore, the entire tribal domain had been apportioned on the basis of the roll previously established and approved by the secretary of the interior. There were nineteen newborns before the completion of the first allotment and two more before the end of the second, so 234 Quapaws altogether received one 200-acre as well as one 40-acre tract, while two received only a 40-acre tract.[65]

After allotment had occurred, another contingent of twenty-five Arkansas Quapaws residing in the Pine Bluff vicinity recalled their heritage and petitioned to be added to the roll.[66] In August, 1893, Congressman C. R. Breckenridge of Arkansas forwarded to the secretary of the interior letters relative to their rights in the tribe, a claim that had been officially denied for at least nine of these Quapaws as early as March, 1892.[67] More than a year passed before the matter was referred to Agent George S. Doane, who was instructed to convene the organized council of the Downstream People in order to ascertain its sentiments in the case of each applicant. After the council had acted, the agent was to present the matter again to a general council composed of at least a majority of all the adult males. Doane was advised, moreover, that the basic assumption underlying all deliberations should be that Quapaws who had never resided on the reservation or who had removed from it had abandoned their rights.[68] Given the fact that some Arkansas Quapaws had been previously added to the roll with the consent of the government and that other adoptions had at one time been disapproved because the absentee or Osage band had not been consulted, such a prescription for discussions was a remarkable reversal of policy. Furthermore, it made the action of the council predictable.

Other factors also predetermined how the Downstream People would react to any expansion of the roll. On the one hand, in 1894 the nature and composition of the leadership had changed. Peter Clabber, long absent in the Osage country, was elected as principal chief, while John Quapaw, a member of the home band, had been selected as second chief. The latter office had been created two years earlier for Charley Quapaw when John Medicine had been elevated to the chieftainship, but now was used to disguise or to make more palatable the actual shift of the power base to the absentees, a shift that was also reflected in the four positions of councillor.[69] On the other hand, the allotment of the tribal domain was nearly com-

*Abner W. Abrams, adopted Quapaw and
influential tribal leader, about 1920.*

pleted, and any expansion of the roll would mean that the size of the tract already granted to each individual would have to be reduced. Therefore, on January 7, 1895, when Agent Doane submitted to the organized council the matter of admitting the Arkansas Quapaws to membership, he found no sentiment for such a course.

As a matter of fact, the leadership of the Downstream People was adamant in their opposition to any additional adoptions. Said Councillor John Beaver: "We are here to look after the interests of our tribe, and if we were to take in more adoptions we would soon have no more land for our children or other members of the tribe, and if anyone was to offer me $1,000 I would not take him into the tribe." And Chief Clabber added: "In regard to these Arkansas applicants for admission here, I feel that they have forfeited their rights. . . . They have had 61 years to apply or prove up their blood . . . " and are now "out-lawed by lapse of time. . . . " Forgetting that he himself had once abandoned the reserve, the chief concluded the discussion by declaring: "We have resided on the reservation and existed as a nation and preserved our rights. We have obeyed our treaty with the United States. These applicants have not, and we do not consider that they have any inherent rights to membership in our tribe." So pervasive was this view that the council also opposed the adoption of the white wife of Alphonsus Vallier, an irony of major proportions, because no one had contributed more than Vallier to the preservation of the tribal estate.[70] Five days later a general council of the Downstream People, also attended by hereditary chief Louis Angel, endorsed the sentiment of the leadership. Eighty adults—male and female and Quapaws by blood or adoption—signed or put their marks to a document that declared with finality: "Now [that] we have allotted our lands we will take in no more adoptions of any kind, for any pretext or for any purpose."[71] When Agent Doane forwarded the transcripts of the various deliberations of the tribe to Washington, the Bureau of Indian Affairs took cognizance of the sentiment therein expressed and rejected the applications of those seeking to establish long forgotten "rights."

In denying the claims of the Arkansas Quapaws, the Downstream People were seeking to preserve the work of Abrams and his allotment committee. But because the division of the tribal estate had never been officially sanctioned by congressional action, that effort itself was really no more than tentative. To win favorable and final consideration in Washington, the tribe continued to rely on the assistance of Samuel Crawford and other friends, especially Dennis Flynn, the territorial delegate from Oklahoma. As early as the second session of the fifty-third Congress that convened in December, 1893, Flynn introduced legislation that sought to confirm the division of the Quapaw reservation. For at least two reasons this measure was greeted with little enthusiasm by the commissioner of Indian affairs. For one thing, he opposed the allotment of lands in such large quantities to Indians; for another, he deemed unwise any legislation that would exempt so many acres from public taxation for twenty-five years, the period of time during which titles to individual portions were made inalienable and nontaxable by local and state government. It would be more desirable, the commissioner believed, if the Quapaws were authorized to sell up to 120 acres of their 200-acre allotment, leaving 80 acres to be held in trust for the full period.[72] Given such reluctance, the House Committee on Indian Affairs allowed the Flynn bill to languish on its agenda.

Interest in the measure, however, did not die. On January 22, 1895, in the midst of floor debate in the House, Representative Thomas Lynch of Wisconsin successfully attached a rider to the Indian Appropriations Bill that embodied the legislative objectives of the Downstream People.[73] The effect of the amendment was to ratify the act of the council dated March 23, 1893, and to confirm the work of the Quapaw allotment committee "subject to revision, correction and approval by the Secretary of the Interior." The measure stipulated as well that any Indian dissatisfied with his allotment could appeal to the secretary, who also had the authority to issue a patent for the land received. Allotments, moreover, were to be inalienable for twenty-five years from the date of the patent, and surplus lands, if any, were to be allotted from time to time by the tribe to its members.[74] The amended appropriations bill was forwarded to the Senate, but rather than accept it uncritically, the Upper Body made several additions and deletions. For example, the language inserted by Representative Lynch was deleted without debate on February 21, 1895.[75] In the conference committee, fortunately, House delegates insisted on retaining that part of the bill that pertained to the Downstream People. Simultaneously, Abrams and other Quapaw delegates arrived from the reservation to lobby their case with the Senate.[76] The visit proved timely, and on March

2 both bodies of Congress accepted a compromise version of the appropriations bill that, among other things, ratified the unilateral allotment of the tribal domain.[77]

Because the act relegated a supervisory role to the secretary of the interior, in May, 1895, the Bureau of Indian Affairs directed Special Agent W. H. Able to thoroughly investigate the procedure by which the allotments had been made.[78] Throughout the latter part of that month and into July, Able conducted extensive hearings at the agency. He found some discontent with the allotments received, as in the case of Amos Vallier, and believed that a good deal more would have surfaced had the chiefs and council been willing to cooperate. He also took testimony relating to individuals whose petitions for adoption had been previously denied by the secretary of the interior and who had not shared in the division of the tribal estate. During the course of this part of his examination, Able concluded that bribery and special favor had marked the adoption process; that some who had been included on the rolls, such as the Carden family, were undeserving; and that others, like the Hedgeses and the Wrights, had been excluded without sufficient cause. Behind all the corruption, he believed, was A. W. Abrams, who had gained control over the Quapaws but was nonetheless "an unfit person to be among them." Sure evidence of the clerk's guilt, according to the special agent, was Abrams' efforts, through the influence of Congressional Delegate Dennis Flynn, to have his investigation prematurely terminated.[79] Able may have over-reacted to what he found on the reservation, yet the fact remained that Flynn did protest the continuation of the inquiry and that the special agent was first reprimanded and then recalled by the commissioner of Indian affairs.[80]

Ironically, the termination of the Able investigation only intensified the controversy it had spawned. The Hedges family and Alphonsus Vallier, who continued to press for his wife's adoption, retained George H. Larmar, a Washington attorney, to argue their cases before the secretary of the interior. Drawing on the testimony obtained by the special agent, Larmar sought to prove that the Hedgeses had been excluded from the roll because they had failed to deliver $250 to Abrams and that the land which should have been allotted to them was awarded to members of the Carden family because they had previously agreed to lease it to Abrams.[81] With reference to the adoption of Mrs. Vallier, the attorney argued that justice had been denied her also because of the pervasive influence of the chairman of the allotment committee.[82] So damning and potentially disruptive were Larmar's oral and written communications that the commissioner of Indian affairs labored to counteract them. Lengthy rebuttals were prepared that attempted to justify not only the government's policy with regard to adoption but also to restore Abrams' tarnished reputation. "This office knows personally," Commissioner D. M. Browning wrote to the secretary of the interior, "that the said A. W. Abrams has been of great good to these Indians, and has done much toward improving their condition and preventing unscrupulous white men and others from defrauding them and getting control of much of their property."[83]

Such testimony, plus the receipt of correspondence from both the Quapaw council and Samuel Crawford urging approval of the schedule of allotments as made by the tribe, successfully combatted the doubts instilled by the Able investigation and Larmar's intervention.[84] On March 28, 1896, the acting secretary of the interior ruled that the charges of fraud had not been sustained, that further adoptions should be denied, and that the schedule of allotments should be approved.[85] Accordingly, on September 26, he issued 234 restricted fee patents to 200-acre tracts and on October 19, another 236 identical patents to 40-acre tracts. Delivered in February, 1897, the receipt of these titles concluded the allotment process on the Quapaw reservation.[86]

In the long history of the Downstream People few eras were as formative as that which led up to and concluded with the division of the tribal domain. In one way or another every facet of Quapaw life was touched. The readmission of their kinsmen so long absent in Arkansas and the adoption of others unfamiliar with ancient traditions made the perpetuation of unique cultural characteristics difficult at best. The return of the majority of the tribe from the Osage country undoubtedly retarded the disintegration process, but it certainly did not arrest it. The political complexion of tribal life was also affected by the many adoptions and the issue of allotment. A. W. Abrams, for example, came to control the organized council before and after the return of the Osage band, and much, if not all, that the leadership proposed or accomplished reflected his pervading influence. While it was true that Abrams at times participated in questionable transactions, on the whole his role was more honorable than dishonorable. Realizing that the Downstream People had no alternative to allotment, he so directed their affairs that despite immense pressure the entirety of the tribal estate was preserved for their benefit alone. Given the policy of the Bureau of Indian Affairs that no Indian needed more than 80 acres of agricultural land, the patenting of 240 acres to all but two members of the tribe was a coup of major proportions. Abrams enriched himself in that he secured the adoption of his own family, his mother-in-law, and his brother-in-law, but it was not at the expense of the Downstream People. From the point of view of the majority of the tribe, whatever the clerk of the council gained was just compensation for valuable services rendered.

For the Quapaws to offer no criticism of Abrams' increasing prosperity reflected just how much their economic attitudes had been influenced by developments on the reservation. The use of the tribal estate by white cattlemen and agriculturalists had schooled the Indians in the advantages of capitalism and private property. This, of course, was a lesson that government officials had hoped the Indians would learn and was one objective of the reservation policy. The officials must have been surprised by the extent of the tribe's commitment to these alien abstractions. With absolutely no encouragement from Washington, the Quapaws had selected individual allotments, improved them, and then conveyed the same to themselves. Even after discounting the influence of Abrams, such remarkable action could only be explained by the growing vested interests that most members of the tribe had in particular tracts of land. It also illustrated why the Downstream People were at pains to make the size of individual allotments large enough to encompass the whole domain, preventing thereby the allocation of any surplus lands to other than tribal members. Allotment, therefore, was no more than the logical extension of economic patterns previously adopted by the Quapaws—the abandonment of common ownership in order to obtain individual ownership. In light of events which occurred after the turn of the century, this development proved for many to be a prudent one.

CHAPTER VIII
ON THE WHITE MAN'S
ROAD, 1896-1921

The allotment of the landed estate of the Downstream People was presumably the next to last step in the process whereby the tribe would sever its unique ties with the federal government. All that remained was to guide the Indians through the twenty-five year transitional period during which alienation of title was forbidden. But for the Quapaws these plans never materialized. Following the division of the reservation, valuable mineral deposits were found on many of the allotments, the exploitation of which made some members of the tribe among the richest people in the world. Legitimate businessmen, swindlers, and hucksters descended upon the reserve in the wake of the bonanza, and unaccustomed to both the attention and the prosperity, the Indians were left bewildered at best and defrauded at worst. At first inclined to ignore the situation, the Bureau of Indian Affairs in time moved to assist the Quapaws in the management of their newly acquired wealth. Thus, despite the intent of the allotment program, the twenty-five-year transitional period witnessed a dramatic increase in the guardianship role of the government rather than a decrease.

Although it had not been publicized, the discovery of rich quantities of lead and zinc ore adjacent to the reservation was a powerful factor motivating the Quapaws to divide their lands in severalty. Mining for these minerals in southwestern Missouri had begun well before the Civil War, but it was not until the early 1870's that the extent of the ore was fully determined. By 1874, Joplin, the center of the mining activity, had a population of some 5,000 persons and was as boisterous as the better-known boom towns in the gold fields farther west.[1] From this focus, prospectors, schemers, and miners sought ore west into Kansas and southwest into Indian Territory. By

1891, commercial lead and zinc was being mined near present-day Peoria, Oklahoma, and hauled by wagon to railheads in Joplin and Baxter Springs, Kansas. In 1897, one year after the Quapaws had received restricted fee patents for their allotments, lead deposits were discovered in the western portion of their reservation by a farmer excavating for a water well. Lincolnville was immediately established and by 1903 had a population of 1,200. Prospecting demonstrated that ore extended westward for about two miles, at the western edge of which, near present Quapaw, mining operations began in 1904. Within ten years ore valued at more than one million dollars was extracted from this deposit. In 1907, the rich Commerce field was discovered, in the wake of which forty to fifty thousand miners rushed to Quapaw lands. By 1914 nearly five million dollars of lead and zinc concentrates had been recovered. So fabulously wealthy were these and other mines that within twenty years 79 per cent of the total value of the mineral output of the so-called Tri-State District came from the reserve of the Downstream People.[2]

Before lead and zinc production could occur, of course, the mining operators had to secure the permission of the Quapaws to whom the land had been allotted. It was no accident that the right of the Indian to lease his land for such purposes was established largely through the efforts and foresight of A. W. Abrams. As early as September, 1895, more than six months before approval of the schedule of allotments by the secretary of the interior, Abrams and others had secured mineral leases from individual allottees and submitted them to the government for confirmation according to the procedure stipulated in amendments to the Dawes Allotment Act. When these instruments were rejected by the Indian office on the basis that they were premature and did not stipulate a sufficient rate of royalty, Abrams and his colleagues took another approach. Following the final approval of the allotment schedule and assuming that new legislation did not make the consent of the secretary of the interior mandatory, they simply negotiated new agreements and neglected to send them on to Washington.[3] The Indian office, however, took strong exception to such conduct and directed Agent George Doane in October, 1896, to remove from the reserve all persons who were exploiting leases not properly approved.[4]

Abrams, who had parlayed his influence among the Quapaws into valuable first leases, saw his favored position jeopardized by this edict and hastened to the capital to protest. On November 30, he and Samuel Crawford appeared before the secretary of the interior to argue that by statute the Downstream People could lease their lands without reference to governmental authority.[5] When the secretary refused to accept their interpretation of the law, Abrams and Crawford took their case to the Congress. As on previous occasions, the two proved to be consummate lobbyists. On June 7, 1897, the national legislature empowered the Indians of the Quapaw Agency to lease their allotments for periods of three years for agricultural purposes and ten years for business purposes, as long as the lessor was not incapacitated "by reason of age or disability."[6] As the latter clause was interpreted by the Indian office to include only "the very old, idiots, imbeciles [and] insane persons," the legislation was a significant coup for Abrams and meant that leases in the Quapaw domain, unlike elsewhere in Indian Territory, could be negotiated without government supervision.[7] As a consequence, within months of the passage of the act most of the reservation was placed under some kind of lease agreement, the parties to which were only individual allottees and hopeful speculators.

Presumably, according to one Indian office inspector, the privilege to lease was "avowedly for the purpose of teaching [the Quapaws] business methods and preparing them for the control of their land without any restrictions upon them." Yet after the turn of the century the opposite had seemingly occurred. Instead of proper training, the inspector was convinced, it had "led them into profligacy, and into a condition in which a large per cent . . . [received] but very little for the use of their lands."[8] And in actual fact, the Downstream People seldom did realize the full value of their landed inheritance. The large fortunes to be wrested from the mineral district were the root of the problem. All kinds of immoral and frequently illegal schemes were perpetrated upon the Indians in efforts to divest them of the wealth that should have accrued to them alone.

The leasing system itself provided the most flagrant opportunities for illicit gain. Following the passage of the 1897 act, for example, the Quapaw Mining and Milling Company and the Iowa and Oklahoma Mining Company took advantage of the influence of Abrams, an officer of both concerns, to win control of potentially valuable allotments. For their leases the two corporations offered only a

5 per cent royalty on all ores mined—a sum once deemed wholly insufficient by the government—or ten cents an acre if they made no profits.[9]

In his own name Abrams also negotiated a host of agricultural leases, a number of which were obtained for him by William C. Renfrow, the late governor of Oklahoma Territory, and Dennis T. Flynn, recently defeated in his bid for re-election as territorial delegate. For these agricultural leases he and his associates generally paid five dollars a year for each forty-acre tract.[10] And as if the meager rate of royalty was not enough, Abrams and other speculators prevailed upon some Quapaws to give leases well in excess of the statutory limit. One agricultural lease ran for twenty-five years, while one for mining was executed for ninety-nine years.[11]

Other Indians were prevailed upon to execute "over-lapping" leases whereby a second instrument without significant alteration of consideration would become effective well before the expiration of the first. Still others signed agreements that did not bind the lessee to undertake mining operations. As a result, the lessee had control of the land with no requirement for capital expenditure, and the Indian had no royalty or penalty income.[12] The practical effect of these different leasing practices was to extend the control of the speculator over the various allotments and to prevent the Quapaw allottee from receiving a full measure from his landed inheritance.

An even more pernicious procedure designed to divest the Quapaws of just compensation for their allotments was that of buying royalty assignments made in the leasing agreements. Mrs. Francis Goodeagle, to illustrate, leased her allotment for the usual 5 per cent but then sold half of her interest to James K. Moore, a Baxter Springs resident, for $500. This investment eventually paid Moore at least $40,000.[13] Another famous case involved the purchase of Charley Quapaw's royalties to a 200-acre lease for only $100. Charles Noble and John Cooper, both of Baxter Springs and the latter once the bonded treasurer of the tribe, made the initial purchase; but when Vern E. Thompson and A. Scott Thompson, Miami attorneys, threatened suit in the allottee's behalf, Noble and Cooper endorsed one-fourth of the royalty assignment over to the attorneys and another one-fourth back to the venerable old leader. This transaction netted the four white men thousands of dollars in unearned royalty payments.[14] Unfortunately, the Goodeagle and Quapaw cases were not unique. By 1908, according to one observer, 90 per cent of all the Indians in the Quapaw Agency who had leased their lands had then sold their royalties at sums ranging from $50 to several hundred dollars.[15]

Of all the schemes designed to deprive the Downstream People of the fruits of their landed estate none was as successful as the practice of "pyramiding royalties." Once commercial quantities of ore were proven to exist, speculators holding the original 5 per cent lease would then sublease the tract for an additional royalty of 10 to 15 per cent. On occasion the sublease holder also assigned his rights to another party at an even higher percentage. As a consequence, the actual operator of the mine frequently paid royalties as high as 25 per cent of the value of all ores produced, only a fraction of which went to the original Indian lessor, especially if he had also sold his royalty rights.

The role of the middleman was best personified, predictably, by A. W. Abrams and his associate, Edward T. McCarthy. On the basis of leases they held jointly, most of which were overlapping and had been assigned to other parties, they were able to form the Baxter Royalty Company with a capital stock of ten million dollars. Had the sublessees paid to the Quapaw owners the full amount of the pyramided royalties claimed by Abrams and McCarthy, these assets would have accrued to the allottee. The Indian's income at the very least should have tripled and might very well have quadrupled. Not only did this practice restrict royalty receipts but it also measurably reduced the life of the mine. Burdened with payments to middlemen, the actual operator was forced to mine only the most valuable ores, leaving unextracted minerals that once marketed might have sustained payments to the allottee. Moreover, the operator frequently never encountered deposits of sufficient quality to permit him to meet his royalty obligations. In those instances the mine closed, and the Quapaws received no income at all.[16]

The inequitable leasing system was nothing more than an unabashed effort to divert the wealth of the Downstream People into the hands of others. But it was not the only technique used. Some Quapaws, James Xavier and his wife, for example, were even induced to sell their landed allotments despite restrictions against alienation.[17] Although the titles to the lands of some original allottees were clouded in this manner, the practice was usually confined to tracts inherited by the Quapaws. William M. Springer, judge of the United States Court for the Northern District of Indian Territory, had held as early as 1897 that restrictions against alienation of allotments were personal to the allottee and did not run with the land after it passed into the hands of heirs. Furthermore, when it was found that partition of the estate among the different heirs was impracticable, the court directed that the land be sold by the United States Marshal. In some instances one of the heirs would purchase the interests of the others and then claim the property for two-thirds of its assessed value. More often, white speculators would buy the interests of one or all of the heirs and apply to the court for partition, at which time the adequacy of purchase price was not deemed to be of issue.

In this way W. E. Rowsey (who was once the clerk of the district court and who recently had joined the First National Bank of Miami, Oklahoma), Rowsey's wife, H. C. Brandon, and C. D. Goodrum (both of Lamar, Missouri,) obtained what was known as a "Marshal Deed" to four-hundred acres of land left to the heirs of Mary and Meh-ska-nah-ban-nah Grand Eagle. Although valued at $4,000, the tract was purchased by Rowsey and his associates for only $200. In a similar transaction, Rowsey bought from Joe Buffalo for $250 the allotments which the Indian had inherited from Thomas Buffalo and Buffalo Calf and which had been appraised by the Indian office as worth $6,600. By such transactions Mr. and Mrs. Rowsey, Brandon, and Goodrum secured between four and five thousand acres of mineral lands.[18]

Although the local federal court approved of this disposition of heirship lands, the legality of the practice remained in question. In October, 1899, Assistant Attorney General Willis Van Devanter, later a Justice of the Supreme Court, wrote an opinion that questioned the right of Peoria and Miami Indians to dispose of inherited lands that had been restricted from alienation, unless previously approved by the secretary of the interior.[19] Upon learning of this decision, Rowsey immediately wrote ex-judge William Springer, his old boss then practicing law in Washington, asking for help in getting approval of the Marshal Deeds. "Could you 'tack on' an amendment allowing the sales of heirship land in the Quapaw Agency," he asked in January, 1900, "and if so, how much money must I demand from the parties desiring such legislation?"[20] This, he wrote the next month in a classic understatement, "will be by far more satisfactory to us than having to send our deeds to the Department for approval."[21] He suggested that Springer make contact with Dennis Flynn, then still in Congress, who "has told me often that he would assist in getting through anything I might desire."[22] Although Rowsey was never successful in his quest for congressional approval of his purchase of inherited lands, the practice continued unabated after the turn of the century and clouded the title to thousands of acres of allotted property.

That the Downstream People were being deprived of the full value of their original allotments and just compensation for inherited estates was so obvious that the Bureau of Indian Affairs was forced to reassess its role in at least the leasing process. To precipitate this decision, though, required still another instance of premeditated fraud: Widow Crawfish sold a royalty of some $270 a month for a consideration of $20 a month.[23] Presented with the facts of the case, the United States attorney general ruled in June, 1906, that the government could intervene because the widow was clearly incapable of conducting her own business affairs. As authority, he cited the statute of 1897 that had empowered the Quapaws to lease their lands so long as they were not impaired by reason of age or disability. If they fell into the latter class, interpreted by the Indian office as consisting of only the very aged, idiots, imbeciles, and the insane, their leases were to be consummated under the supervision of the secretary of the interior only.[24]

Given the attorney general's ruling, on October 22, 1906, the commissioner of Indian affairs directed the superintendent of the Quapaw Agency, Horace B. Durant, to submit a list of Indians within his jurisdiction who, because of their age or disability, required governmental assistance in the negotiation of leasing agreements. The next month Durant forwarded such a list enumerating 113 adult Indians in his agency, 43 of whom were Quapaws, that in his judgment could not manage their allotments with benefit to themselves. At the same time the superintendent made clear that his assessment extended only to mineral leases, for while the Indians were not "getting *all* which might be derived" from agricultural leases, they were "receiving fair or adequate rentals" and "fast learning to better their conditions."[25] Durant's report had some impact, and the matter of regulating farming leases was dropped by the Indian office. But given the general view that action elsewhere was required, on January 24, 1907, the secretary of the interior promulgated regulations that would extend government supervision to mining transactions negotiated by forty-three adult as well as twenty-two minor Quapaws, including Chief Peter Clabber.[26]

The new regulations were met by vigorous protests. Abrams rushed to Washington and, with Samuel Crawford, demanded that the rules be revoked. Since the Quapaws held their lands in fee rather than by trust patents, they insisted that the government had no right to intervene in leasing practices. Moreover, despite the ruling in the Widow Crawfish case, they argued that leases did not constitute an alienation of title, citing as evidence a 1904 decision of the Court of Appeals for the Indian Territory.[27] And the Quapaws themselves objected to the new regulations. Labeling them a "ukase" in disguise and as having designated the allottees "as fit subjects for a Lunatic Asylum," Chief Peter Clabber inquired who had judged the Indians to be imbeciles. If it was the secretary of the interior, the chief declared, then "he instead of the Quapaws hath need of a guardian."[28] These obviously were not Clabber's own words, but the point of view was certainly his own as well as that of other members of the tribe.[29] Still, the opposition of the chief and the council was unquestionably motivated by the business community in the mining district, whose own vested interests were threatened by the regulations.[30]

Regardless of their origins, the different protests caused the Bureau of Indian Affairs to reassess its decision to intervene in the leasing procedure. If the Quapaws had no objections to the order of things on their reservation, why should the government be unduly concerned? Moreover, inasmuch as thousands of dollars had been invested in the region, could the Indian office risk disturbing the status quo? Obviously, additional thought and information were required. Commissioner of Indian Affairs Francis Leupp, therefore, requested the secretary of the interior to seek another opinion from the attorney general about the responsibilities of the government in supervising business leases.[31] He also directed his personal secretary, R. G. Valentine, to go to the Quapaw Agency and interview those Indians affected by the regulations of January 24. More precisely, Valentine was to determine whether or not government supervision was absolutely necessary.

For five days in May, 1907, the commissioner's secretary visited with and in the homes of as many of those adjudged incompetent as he could. Particularly impressed with the ability and intelligence of

Chief Peter Clabber and Tallchief, the last ancestral leader of the Quapaws, about 1912.
Courtesy Charles Banks Wilson.

Peter Clabber, he came to use the principal chief as the standard by which he assessed the business acumen of others. It was an imprecise measure at best, but Valentine reported that "down to the most ignorant fullblood" the Indians of the Quapaw Agency were "ready to be freed from the guardianship of the Government." Indeed, "as fast as the law permits or can be made to permit," he reported, "I think these Indians should be thrown wholly on their own feet." If they were victimized in the process, they were only learning what they "ought to be learning at the cost of the experience." As Valentine saw it, only twenty-five Indians within the jurisdiction of the agency, none of whom were Quapaws, would come to actual pauperism if "the Government set them entirely free." Even these, he concluded, should not be subjected to direct supervision—a backward step—but only placed under the protection of legal guardians appointed by the county court.[32]

On the strength of these recommendations and philosophically committed to less rather than more government control, Commissioner Leupp recommended to the secretary of the interior that the regulations promulgated on January 24, 1907 be rescinded. At the same time, he proposed that the Quapaw superintendent be authorized to request the local courts to appoint guardians for the twenty-five Indians or their heirs whom Valentine assumed might be reduced to poverty without some kind of assistance. Unwilling to depart so radically from his intended course, the secretary on November 16, 1907, consented only to amend his regulations. Assuming the validity of Valentine's revised list, he insisted that the twenty-five enumerated therein or their heirs be subject to the rules previously published until other provisions were made for the management of their estates.[33] His reluctance to accept all of the recommendation of the commissioner stemmed, no doubt, from the disposition of his office to recognize the attorney general's opinion upholding the right of the government to exercise supervision in the matter of mining leases. Indeed, the secretary even refused to request a review of that opinion as earlier urged by Leupp.[34]

Given these amended regulations, the new superintendent of the agency, Ira C. Deaver, sought to have those Quapaws involved made wards of the court. In April, 1908, he petitioned the Ottawa County Court to appoint Horace B. Durant, recently retired from the government service to enter the private practice of law, as legal guardian for at least seven of the nine. But when the matter came up for a hearing, Abrams and his attorneys appeared in order to argue that the allottees in question were competent to attend to their own business affairs. To permit the government to designate guardians, obviously, was to recognize the authority of the secretary of the interior in at least one facet of Quapaw affairs, a principle Abrams had long denied. Although the court ignored this issue, on a technicality it did refuse to appoint guardians.[35] When advised of this decision, the Indian office directed Deaver to abandon his effort and to consider the Quapaws involved to be fully capable of negotiating whatever business leases they desired.[36] Despite the obvious inequities of the leasing system, then, the government in May, 1908, determined not to insist upon supervision but to permit the Downstream People to lease their lands, whatever the results.

However progressive a policy of "Let the Indian Beware" may have been, it was damaging and unrealistic. Too much evidence existed that fraud was a common occurrence in the Quapaw mining district. While government intervention in the leasing process was deemed imprudent, an attempt to enforce observance of the law was not. Accordingly, with the approval of the Indian office, the attorney general assigned a special assistant, Paul Ewert, to take whatever measures were necessary to insure that all business transactions involving the Quapaw allottees were fully legal. Establishing his office in Miami on December 1, 1908, Ewert proceeded to examine all relevant records and after a year of exhaustive research concluded that "the leading businessmen of this community... have been guilty of... unlawful and fraudulent and conscienceless transactions."[37] To correct the situation, his methods ranged from jawboning—"I have got through fooling with you," he declared—to threatening legal action—"I will trifle with you no longer," he wrote—and to instituting suit.[38] Although the special assistant infuriated practically everyone with whom he came into contact,[39] he achieved spectacular results. During his first fifteen months in office, he forced the grafters "to disgorge" something like 9,000 acres of mineral lands secured by fraudulent deed and to cancel unlawful agricultural and mining leases on nearly 30,000 acres.[40]

Much that Ewert accomplished did not require court action, but he was never adverse to full-fledged prosecution. When such action was appropriate, his suits generally focused on one of three issues— the sale of inherited lands, overlapping leases, or the assignment of royalties. With regard to the former, Ewert's task was considerably facilitated by a July, 1908, decision of the Eighth Circuit Court of Appeals in the case of C. D. Goodrum v. Buffalo, whereby the court held that restrictions ran with the land and disqualified heirs from alienation or sale.[41] Despite this decision, Goodrum and W. E. Rowsey had retained some of the property they had obtained by means of the so-called Marshal Deeds, a fact that caused Ewert to initiate prosecution which ultimately forced the two speculators to file quitclaims to the land.[42] In the matter of overlapping leases, the special assistant was particularly concerned with those procured by A. W. Abrams. Describing the controversial adopted Quapaw as treacherous, he sued in the federal courts to annul all but the first of Abrams' leases on the Minnie Redeagle allotment. The original instrument had been executed in March, 1902, for ten years, the second in May, 1905, another in September, 1906, and a fourth in March, 1920. The practical effect of all these leases was that Abrams and his Iowa and Oklahoma Mining Company had control of the Redeagle allotment until March, 1920, or until the expiration of the restricted period lacking one year. But Ewert lost his case in the District Court as well as on appeal to the Circuit Court, the latter decision coming in March, 1912.[44]

In the meantime, the special assistant to the attorney general raised the overlapping issue and the issue of the assignment of royalties in still another case, the United States v. Charles Noble, John M. Cooper, A. Scott Thompson, and Vern E. Thompson. This particular suit related to the purchase of Charley Quapaw's royalties and, after decisions unfavorable to the government in the lower courts, was appealed to the Supreme Court of the United States. In April, 1915, the high court ruled in an opinion delivered by Mr. Justice Hughes that the secretary of the interior had general supervision over the leasing of allotted Quapaw land, that mineral leases could not exceed ten years, that overlapping leases were illegal, and that the Indians could not assign future royalties to another party.[45] Put differently, the decision, although it came three years after he had resigned his position, sustained Ewert in every contention and became the basis of much of the policy promulgated in the Quapaw district.

It was a significant judicial victory, and Ewert believed that the government never fully capitalized on it. Although Noble and Cooper's estate returned to Charley Quapaw the full amount of royalties they received in the fraudulent transaction, Scott

Thompson and Vern Thompson prevailed upon the old chief to settle in full all sums owed by them for the consideration of five dollars.[46] Prodded by Ewert, the secretary of the interior requested the attorney general's office to seek a more complete restitution from the attorneys, but because Vern Thompson was at that time County Judge of Ottawa County, the United States attorney for the Eastern District of Oklahoma in March, 1917, advised against initiating any legal action.[47] Two years later a case was filed against James K. Moore which the government won on appeal in 1922, but because Moore had dissipated his illgotten wealth, the heirs of Mrs. Francis Goodeagle never recovered the money due them.[48] If some of the fruits of the Noble decision were lost to the Downstream People, it was largely the fault of government agencies other than the Bureau of Indian Affairs. The Department of Justice, for example, was reluctant to pursue the issue and, when it did proceed, so constructed its bills of complaint that full restitution was made virtually impossible.[49]

Although the eventual result of Ewert's four-year tenure in the Quapaw district was to expand the supervisory role of the government, during the actual course of it he and the Indian office initiated and supported proposals designed to terminate the federal guardianship for some, if not all, of the Indians. Several considerations prompted this course. For one thing, many of the more fortunate Quapaws were of very little Indian blood and were members of the tribe by adoption. Yet because titles to their allotments were restricted against alienation for twenty-five years these so-called "White Quapaws" were exempt from taxation, particularly property taxes. Also, Oklahoma's admission into the union in 1907 had increased the pressure for white acquisition of Indian lands. the law allowed mentally or physically disabled Indians to dispose of their allotments,[50] but the application of this measure was necessarily so limited among the Downstream People that relatively few acres passed into white ownership or became taxable.[51] Encouraged by Ewert and convinced that the general guardianship role of the government should be speedily abandoned, Secretary of the Interior J. R. Garfield endorsed pending legislation that would remove restrictions on and permit the sale of all but forty acres of each Quapaw allotment. Being "moral, sober, progressive and self-supporting," he said, the Indians as a whole were "fully competent to manage their own affairs."[52] Congress passed the measure on

March 3, 1909, stipulating, however, that restrictions would be raised only upon the *application* of adult allottees.[53] At the time this exclusion was not deemed of much significance, probably because similar language, adopted in 1902, governing the disposition of heirship land had not retarded sales to non-Indians.[54]

The Bureau of Indian Affairs published its regulations governing the removal of restrictions on March 15, 1909. It was required that Quapaws who wanted to take advantage of the statute and sell portions of their allotment make application to the superintendent of the agency. That official would then conduct an investigation, on the basis of which the secretary of the interior could remove restrictions from the land either "unconditionally" or "conditionally." If the latter designation was made, then the secretary would prescribe the terms of sale and the disposition of the proceeds. If the former, sale could be made without reference to the government.[55] It was also the presumption that unconditional removal would place the property, whether sold or not, on the tax rolls of the county.[56] Anticipating a plethora of applications, in August, 1910, the commissioner of Indian affairs also appointed a three-member commission to visit the Quapaw agency and evaluate the Indians as to the extent of their competence to take advantage of the regulations.[57] After some twenty days in the field, the following January the commission reported that sixty-nine of the Downstream People were competent and qualified to have restrictions removed from their allotment, that fifty-five were not qualified but were nonetheless capable of conducting business affairs, and that twenty-one were wholly incapable of carrying out any economic transactions.[58] Presumably, upon the basis of this information the Indian office could prudently assess applications for removal of restrictions.

Few applications materialized, however.[59] Even before the competency commission had been created, A. W. Abrams urged the Quapaws to employ counsel to oppose its appointment and work. He was motivated by the fear that if allottees were denominated "incompetent," they would be deemed incapable not only of selling but also of leasing their own lands.[60] Although there was some logic in his position, he failed to perceive until later that the real objective of the government was to decrease rather than increase its guardianship role. When Abrams finally did come to a full appreciation of the situation, his course and that of the tribal council dramatically altered. Once at pains to demonstrate the competence of the

Quapaws in order to retain their leasing rights, he and the tribal leadership now sought to preserve their "incompetent" status in order to prevent the lifting of restrictions and the necessity of paying taxes. Therefore, when young Victor Griffin and others circulated a petition that endorsed the removal of restrictions and the sale of allotments in order that a new tribal home might be purchased in Mexico, Chiefs Peter Clabber and John Quapaw denounced the effort as unrepresentative of the will of the majority of the Downstream People.[61] In this instance, the law worked to the advantage of Abrams and the chiefs. A voluntary application from the allottees was required before restrictions could be raised. Moreover, legislation passed by Congress in June, 1910, which equated a certificate of designation of competency with removal of restrictions specifically excluded Oklahoma Indians.[62]

Because so few of the allottees initiated applications and the wealthy, adopted Quapaws continued to "hide" behind restrictions to avoid payment of taxes, the Indian office sought another procedure whereby allotments could be either sold to whites or placed on the tax rolls. In 1912 it supported legislation that would have given the secretary of the interior authority to remove restrictions from the land of adult allottees whether they agreed or not.[63] But Congress proved reluctant to take such a drastic step and, instead, in February, 1913, made the Oklahoma tribes subject to the statute that made a declaration of competency and the lifting of restrictions one and the same thing.[64] Yet this action failed to accomplish the objectives of the Indian office. On the one hand, allottees were required by the legislation to make application before a certificate of competency could be issued. On the other, the United States Supreme Court ruled on May 13, 1912, in the case of Choate v. W. E. Trapp, that removal of restrictions and or declaration of competency did not place property on the tax rolls during the period of inalienability so long as the land was retained by the original allottee or his heirs.[65] The decision of the court was a disappointment, although not nearly as disappointing as the powerlessness of the government to force the adopted Quapaws to bear the full responsibilities of citizenship. The secretary of the interior, as a consequence, tried again in 1916 to secure legislation that would enable him to unilaterally remove restrictions, but this effort, too, failed.[66]

The 1916 attempt came as a result of a new policy instituted by Commissioner of Indian Affairs Cato Sells, an appointee of Wood-

*John Quapaw, long-time councillor and later
chief of the tribe.
Courtesy Western History Collections,
University of Oklahoma.*

row Wilson. Since entering office in 1913, Sells had encouraged the practice of removing restrictions from Indian lands whenever the law would permit. Yet not until April 17, 1917, did he give a full expression to this disposition in his "new declaration of policy." Separating full bloods and mixed bloods into two distinct classes, he asserted that all able-bodied Indians of less than half Indian blood should be given full and complete control of all their property. At the same time, those of more than half Indian blood should have restrictions against alienation removed from all of their land save for a forty-acre homestead.[67] As far-reaching as the declaration may have been for some tribes, its impact on the Downstream People was minimal. Specific statutes required that they must voluntarily apply to have restrictions removed or certificates of competency issued. Only a few Quapaws took advantage of the opportunity,[68] a circumstance that prompted Sells to direct Superintendent Carl Mayer to invite the Indians of his agency who were twenty-one years of age or over to make applications which he "would be pleased to favorably consider. . . . "[69] In September, 1919, Mayer did circulate such an invitation, but after eight months just two applications were received, and those involved only inherited land.[70] Obviously, the allotted Quapaws were aware of their favored position and were not inclined to abandon it. Indeed, by 1920 only thirty-six living allottees had had restrictions entirely removed from the lands initially assigned them, only a part of which had passed into the possession of non-Indian owners.[71]

While Commissioner Sells was addressing himself to the so-called competent Quapaw, he was not unconcerned about those of the Downstream People who seemed incapable of understanding the subtleties of the American economic system. That inequities existed in the mining district was a basic assumption of his policy as it affected the tribe. Of particular concern to him was the case of Benjamin and See-sah Quapaw. Using a pretended power of attorney, Charles Goodeagle, a talented, Haskell-educated young full blood, had taken control of Benjamin's and See-sah's royalties from mining leases covering their allotments and applied them to questionable, even fraudulent, schemes in Baxter Springs. Twenty thousand dollars was invested in the Goodeagle Oil Refinery; some $80,000 was used to begin construction of the Goodeagle Hotel; undetermined sums were invested in a Goodeagle Garage; $12,000 went to underwrite the Goodeagle-Nichols Drugstore; lots were purchased in Goodeagle's name; and two white men, W. T. Apple and Edward E. Sapp, were retained as financial and legal advisors for fees of $5,000 and $2,400 per year respectively. Altogether, Goodeagle and his associates within two years expended more than $120,000 of the royalties paid Mr. and Mrs. Quapaw and indebted them for $50,000 more.[72]

In light of such practices and the revelations previously made by Paul Ewert, Sells acted to bring both the underaged and the uneducated Quapaws of more than half Indian blood under the close supervision of the government. For authority the commissioner relied on the "hitherto unrecognized provision of the Act of 1897" that authorized the secretary of the interior to supervise leases when the Indian was incapacitated by "age or disability."[73] Previously, of course, the clause had been interpreted as relating to physical or mental infirmities rather than to blood quantum or business abilities. Regulations that would implement the new policy were published on April 7, 1917, although orders of incompetency had been issued in some individual cases as early as the previous May.[74] In these and later instances the Indian found that once he was so designated his allotment could be leased for agricultural and mining purposes only with the approval of the secretary of the interior and that royalty income from the property was paid directly to the superintendent. Significantly, if restrictions had already been or might be removed from a part of his allotment, he could continue to manage that portion of his estate without governmental supervision, an obvious attempt to encourage some voluntary applications. Yet even here the Indian office made a distinction, refusing all requests to lift restrictions if the allotment in question lay in the mineral district.[75] The criteria upon which orders of incompetency were issued, then, included amount of Indian blood, business capacity, age (as in the case of minors), and whether the allotment was valuable for mining purposes. These conditions were paramount even if the Quapaw in question had been classed as competent to negotiate leases by the commission of 1910.

As might be expected, the declarations of incompetency had important ramifications. Assuming "once incompetent always incompetent," leases made previously with allottees and heirs so declared were reviewed according to the authority assumed in April, 1917.[76] Much to the chagrin of the mining community, the leases were then either accepted as written, amended, or canceled as fraudulent or inequitable. Apparently, two considerations governed these reviews. One was protection of the interests of the Indian owners; the other, recognition of the heavy investments made by different mining companies. As a consequence, the results were varied, and at times perplexingly inconsistent. The leases held by the Welsh Mining Company on the Thomas Buffalo, Buffalo Calf, and Mary J. Calf allotments, for example, were voided in June, 1920, on the grounds that the lessors were minor heirs and thus incompetent by themselves or by guardians to execute leases. Moreover, the 5 per cent royalty paid to the Indian owners was considered an inadequate consideration. New leases with different corporations were then approved, in one of which the Skelton Lead and Zinc Company agreed to pay at least a 10 per cent royalty to the Quapaw lessors.[77]

But not all reviews of existing leases resulted in such favorable terms for the Indians. In March, 1918, the secretary of the interior approved the one held by the Commerce Mining and Royalty Company on the allotments of Benjamin and See-sah Quapaw even though it stipulated a royalty rate less than that proposed by a competing firm. In October, 1915, the officers of the Commerce organization canceled their pre-existing 5 per cent lease and executed a new one at 6 per cent. Considering the second instrument invalid, Walter T. Apple and Harry N. Harris waited until the original lease was scheduled to expire and then negotiated an entirely different one with Mr. and Mrs. Quapaw, authorizing a royalty payment of 10 per cent. The secretary considered the latter firm a mere claim-jumper, without any substantial equity in the property, and affirmed the 6 per cent lease of the Commerce company. That the Indians would have 4 per cent less in royalty income made little difference.[78] Yet on another occasion the secretary approved a similar 10 per cent lease taken by Harry H. Hawkins on the Minnie Ball Dawes allotment, primarily because the pre-existing lease stipulated a lower rate of royalty. The holder of the original lease, he also adjudged, had not made substantial investments.[79]

In addition to the review of leases, the declarations of incompetency engendered a serious controversy with the Ottawa County Court sitting at Miami, Oklahoma. At least two issues were involved: the probate of the estates of deceased Quapaws and the authority of guardians appointed by the court for minors and incompetents. Before Oklahoma's statehood the heirs of an allottee and the disposition of estates were determined by the United States

District Court according to the laws of Arkansas; after statehood in 1907 these matters fell within the jurisdiction of the appropriate county court.[80] The law that equated certificates of competency with the raising of restrictions and which was applied to the Quapaws in 1913, however, limited the authority of the local court in that the secretary of the interior was made responsible for determining heirs when no will existed.[81] As a practical matter, though, the secretary did not intervene in the probate process if he was informed of the proceedings and no attempt was made to dispose of restricted land without his prior approval. If an heir to an estate was a minor or an incompetent, then the county court generally appointed a guardian who was responsible for administering the inheritance. As more and more of the original Quapaw allottees died, therefore, the court, through its guardian appointees, became increasingly involved in complicated transactions ranging from the negotiation of leases to the expenditure of royalty receipts. Perhaps it was because he saw his power threatened that Ottawa County Court Judge C. S. Wortman reacted so negatively to Commissioner Sells's orders of incompetency.

Entering office in January, 1919, Judge Wortman challenged the right of the Indian office to exercise any control over the property of the Downstream People other than to restrict the sale of their lands. Declarations of incompetency notwithstanding, he insisted that all royalties accruing from the allotments and personal property of deceased Indians were subject to his jurisdiction. After James J. Whitebird died, for example, Wortman appointed an administrator for his estate, who then demanded that Whitebird's guardian and Superintendent Carl Mayer pay to him any funds they held to the deceased's credit. The guardian complied with the demand, but Mayer, who upon the death of Whitebird had directed that royalties be paid to his office pending the determination of heirs, refused. The judge promptly cited the superintendent into his court and ordered him to give a full and true account of all funds held by him. Moreover, the royalty company was enjoined from making further payments to Mayer.[82] Wortman also launched a campaign to appoint guardians for living Quapaws, particularly those recently declared incompetent by Commissioner Sells. In other instances he directed administrators to make mining leases on lands in which deceased allottees or heirs had an interest, and, on still other occasions, he ordered lease holders to pay royalties over to administrators even though they held the lease by virtue of the approval of the secretary of the interior.[83] In sum, the county judge was determined to subvert the efforts of the Indian office to expand its supervisory role among certain classes of the Downstream People.

But Commissioner Sells refused to have his policy annulled by the antics of so minor a county official. He directed the superintendent not to pay out funds entrusted to him and recommended that the United States attorney general intercede in the state and federal courts. And when Judge Wortman prevailed upon the Oklahoma senatorial delegation to make inquiries in his behalf, Sells vigorously defended the position of the Indian office, insisting that the court was without jurisdiction in regard to funds deposited with the superintendent. The judge's action, he declared, was "an interference with a government function and policy."[84] The commissioner stood upon firm legal ground, for federal law did empower the secretary of the interior to make the final determination of heirs and it did restrict allotments from alienation of title. Moreover, the 1897 leasing statute, if broadly interpreted, authorized the secretary to supervise the negotiation of leases for incompetents, a view strengthened by the decision of the Supreme Court in the Noble case. Although Sells was anxious to test his position, his contest with Wortman never came to an actual showdown. In late 1920 the judge was defeated in his bid for re-election to a second term.

Other legal questions raised by the declarations of incompetency required judicial action. Perhaps none was so significant as that involving the financial affairs and allotments of Benjamin and Seesah Quapaw. The full dimensions of the fraud that had been perpetrated on them in Baxter Springs was not revealed until after an extensive investigation conducted in January, 1918, by E. B. Linnen and J. W. Howell, two Indian office inspectors. On the strength of the evidence they accumulated, the following May, Commissioner Sells recommended that the government institute suit against the guilty parties. Not only did he seek redress for the injured Indians, but he also sought a decision on the right of his office to assume responsibility for the affairs of Mr. and Mrs. Quapaw.[85] Accordingly, in January, 1919, the attorney general caused a fifty-one-page printed bill of complaint to be filed in the case of United States v. Walter T. Apple, et al., in the federal district court of Kansas.[86] Because the issues were complicated, all parties to the suit agreed that it should be referred to a special master. Taking evidence and testimony that comprised 1,941 typewritten pages, this special officer of the court reached a conclusion that was most disappointing to the government. In almost every instance he ruled that the debts contracted by Charles Goodeagle in the name of the Quapaw family were valid and binding. Approving the findings of the special master in June, 1923, the federal district judge also ruled that Benjamin Quapaw had been competent to deal with his property rights and had, in fact, been so determined by the government in 1910.[87]

The case was taken on appeal to the circuit court, but in September, 1923, the greater part of the decision was affirmed by that tribunal as well.[88] Although the Indian office recommended that a further appeal be made to the Supreme Court, the attorney general decided against it. As a consequence, Benjamin Quapaw was required to pay to creditors some $24,698 in satisfaction of judgments against him and his deceased wife.[89] Moreover, the assumption that a declaration of incompetency denoted prior incompetence, a theory fundamental to the government's assertion of authority in 1917, had to be re-evaluated as an underpinning of federal Indian policy.

Although the courts failed to sustain the Bureau of Indian Affairs in its contention that fraud had been perpetrated on Benjamin and See-sah Quapaw, in another case they upheld the right of the secretary of the interior to supervise leases negotiated by the two Indians. When the secretary approved the mining lease of the Commerce Mining and Royalty Company upon the couple's allotments, he did so despite another existing lease stipulating a higher royalty held by Apple and Harris.[90] The two speculators then brought a suit against the royalty company, the purpose of which was to challenge the right of the secretary to declare leases made by allottees designated incompetent as null and void. At Commissioner Sells's request, the Department of Justice intervened in the suit, which was tried in May, 1920, in the District Court for the Eastern District of Oklahoma. Although the trial judge did not rule specifically on the authority of the secretary in the leasing process, in an oral decision he indirectly endorsed that position by denying the complaint of Apple and Harris and directing that their lease be canceled.[91] In sum, it was a vindication of the legality of the government's guardianship role in the Quapaw district.

Of all the litigation stemming from declarations of incompetency, none was as lengthy or as sensational as that involving leases covering the Mary J. Calf allotment. Initially held by the Welsh Mining

Company, the lease to this allotment, later assigned to the Skelton Lead and Zinc Company, had been canceled by the secretary of the interior in June, 1920. An entirely new lease proposed by the Skelton company was subsequently approved by the secretary on behalf of the heirs of Mary J. Calf.[92] But Paul Ewert, who upon resigning from government service had engaged in the mining business, held an interest in the cancelled lease, and he sued the Skelton firm on the grounds that a prior, valid lease existed, an action that also challenged the right of the secretary to intervene in the matter. Given this issue, the attorneys for the Skelton company, Vern E. Thompson and M. A. Whipple, proposed to the Indian office that the government become a party to the suit.[93] Although the commissioner of Indian affairs did recommend such action, the matter was finally resolved out of court. In 1924 the Skelton interests settled with Ewert for $20,000.[94]

The supervisory role of the government in these negotiations was also at issue in another legal case involving the original lease of the Welsh Mining Company. The lease in question, negotiated in 1914, was cancelled in part because of inadequate royalty compensation, leading the heirs of Mary J. Calf to bring suit against the company in 1923 to recover funds they believed had been improperly denied them. As their attorney they chose Joseph W. Howell, who as an Indian office employee had investigated the Benjamin Quapaw frauds, and who had been responsible for the rationale underlying the declarations of incompetency promulgated in 1917. Central to Howell's case was the fact that Mary J. Calf had been listed as incompetent in 1907 and again in 1910, and that her minor and incompetent heirs were therefore without authority to enter into a lease with the Welsh Mining Company. This being the case, the 1914 instrument was without effect, and the heirs were entitled to compensation for all ores mined. That guardians had negotiated the lease was beside the point, for that power lay with the secretary of the interior. In 1925 the District Court for the Eastern District of Oklahoma denied the complaint, but upon appeal the Eighth Circuit Court in 1927 reversed the lower court and ruled that the old leases were null and void, that the royalty rate was unconscionable, and that the defendants were liable for the proceeds of the ores sold by them.[95] When the Supreme Court refused to issue a writ of certiorari,[96] the Court of Appeals directed the District Court to determine the liabilities of the defendants. After additional petitions to the Circuit Court, Howell in 1929 finally settled for $360,000.[97] It was a sweet victory for the attorney, not only because it netted him a $50,000 fee but also because it vindicated his view, enunciated ten years previously, that the Quapaw leasing act of 1897 was designed only "to *admit* the *capable* and *able-bodied* Indian to the privilege of leasing his allotment."[98] All others, or those that were incompetent, were to negotiate leases under the supervision of the proper government officials.

That the government had special responsibilities toward those Quapaw wards deemed incapable of conducting their business affairs had been posited by Commissioner Sells well before Howell won his case. Such a conviction had motivated his declarations of incompetency, his challenge of Judge Wortman, and his requests that the government intervene in litigation testing established policy. No doubt it was this same concern that led him in 1920 to recommend an even more remarkable step—the extension of restrictions against alienation on allotments owned by the Downstream People deemed incompetent.[99] In order to provide evidence for the necessity of such action, in October Sells directed Superintendent Carl F. Mayer and Special Supervisor John R. Wise to form another competency commission that should evaluate the business capacity of Quapaws who held or inherited original allotments upon which restrictions expired in September and October, 1921.[100] Finishing its work in January, 1921, the commission found that of the 336 enrolled members of the tribe, 31 original allottees, including Chief Peter Clabber, and 37 unallotted heirs were incompetent to transact their own affairs. Restrictions on the lands owned by these sixty-eight Quapaws, it recommended, should be extended beyond the time they were originally scheduled to expire. On the other hand, fifty-six original allottees, most of whom were of little Indian blood and had heretofore refused to make application for removal of restrictions, were wholly competent and inalienability provisions on their land should be allowed to expire. Altogether, the commission recommended that restrictions be extended upon 17,225 acres of land, or less than one-third of the 56,685 acres originally allotted in 1893.[101]

The proposal to extend restrictions on lands owned by incompetent Quapaws was met by widely different reactions. The Downstream People had long since concluded that restrictions against inalienability of title were in and of themselves highly beneficial,

Chief Peter Clabber and family,
posed by their home with R. G. Valentine,
an Indian Office employee, about 1906.
Courtesy Oklahoma Historical Society.

especially because they shielded the land from taxation. As early as 1912, Chief Peter Clabber had registered objections to proposed legislation that would have deprived them of such benefits.[102] Indeed, in 1917 the tribal council in a petition witnessed by A. W. Abrams urged that "the restrictive period on all allotments made to full-blood, illiterate, and incompetent allottees" be extended.[103] Two years later the request was renewed by the council, only this time it contained the suggestion that restrictions continue for an additional twenty-five years.[104] Encouraged by Commissioner Sells's endorsement of the proposal, on May 13, 1920, delegates of the council appeared before a United States House of Representatives committee holding hearings at the Chilocco Indian School to press for an extension of restrictions.[105] Altogether, it was a remarkable demonstration of support for a course of action that could only result in a larger government role in the Quapaw district.

That the extension of restrictions would increase the authority of the federal guardian also accounted for much of the opposition to the proposal. Judge Wortman, in the last months of his two-year term on the bench and at the time seeking re-election, organized the so-called "Guardian Trust," a combine which realized that its favored position in probate matters would be annulled once the authority of the government was fully confirmed.[106] But rather than emphasize this threat to their vested interests, the trust focused attention on the taxation issue. Appearing before the same congressional committee that also heard representatives of the Downstream People, spokesmen for the trust argued that the extension of restrictions would deprive the county government of necessary revenues obtained from property taxes.[107] Styling itself the "Publicity Committee of Taxpayers," it also mailed a card to every county voter, urging opposition to the continuation of restrictions if citizens favored "taxes coming down . . . Indian land put on the tax list, Indian money deposited in banks in Ottawa County, and the state courts having jurisdiction [to] protect the Indian the same as others. . . . If these restrictions come off next year," the committee proclaimed, "it will mean millions of dollars saved for the taxpayers in this county."[108]

As was usually the case in charges of this type, the claims were highly exaggerated. Superintendent Mayer pointed out, for example, that the county contained more than 222,000 acres of unrestricted Indian land upon which taxes were assessed. Of the 35,357 acres of restricted Quapaw land, no more than 9,000 acres were producing lead and zinc ores. Only one-third of this restricted mineral land was owned by Indians declared incompetent whose funds were handled by the government. The owners of the other two-thirds drew their royalties directly and thus paid income and personal taxes.[109] Given these facts, it was obvious that the perpetuation of restrictions could hardly be as deleterious to the county as Wortman and the Guardian Trust insisted. Nevertheless, the question of taxation continued to be of importance, especially when Congress formally took up the proposal to extend restrictions on specified Quapaw allotments.

On January 15, 1921, Secretary of the Interior John Barton Payne submitted a draft of a bill to the Congress which he felt met the needs of the peculiar situation in northeastern Oklahoma. The measure would extend restrictions for twenty-five years on lands owned by thirty-one Quapaw allottees and thirty-one heirs, each of whom was named specifically—a significant departure from established precedent. It also gave the secretary of the interior the right to prescribe the terms and conditions of leases that might be negotiated, and it provided that the state of Oklahoma might tax minerals produced as if they were mined on unrestricted lands so long as the tax did not become a lien on the Indian property.[110] On January 22, when the House Committee on Indian Affairs held hearings on the legislation, the wisdom of including the latter provision was evident. Indeed, members of the committee were so pleased that they acknowledged the measure to be "one of the most liberal bills ... ever submitted by the department to Congress."[111] After brief statements by Benjamin Quapaw and Victor Griffin, the committee reported the bill favorably.[112] On March 3, 1921, both the House and the Senate passed the legislation, thereby confirming the guardianship role of the government and extending restrictions until 1946.[113]

Given the settled policy of the United States following the allotment of Indian reservations, the extension of restrictions on lands belonging to sixty-two Quapaws was an event of some magnitude. Prevented at the outset from alienating their allotments for twenty-five years, the Downstream People were expected to complete their transition into white society during that time span, at the conclusion of which they would manage their own affairs. Instead, because of circumstances unique to their situation—fraudulent and inequitable mining leases and the dissipation of sizeable fortunes—just the reverse had occurred. The majority of the enrolled members of the tribe, most of whom were of less than half Indian blood and Quapaw only by adoption, met the expectations of policy planners. For these, restrictions against alienation of title had been previously raised or were allowed to expire in 1921. Still, the fact remained that Quapaws by blood and tradition were, after twenty-five years, subject to more instead of less government supervision. Once authorized to lease their allotments independently, they found that privilege first curtailed and then eventually denied. Funds derived from royalty payments were initially expended without direction, but after declarations of incompetency, only with the approval of the Indian office. This circumstance was wholly unplanned; it arose without malice aforethought, and it was evolutionary instead of revolutionary. It meant, however, that instead of being released to manage their own affairs, most Quapaws of more than half Indian blood would, after 1921, have every facet of their lives subjected to some kind of bureaucratic scrutiny.

CHAPTER IX
THE POOR RICH
QUAPAWS

In 1924 the Indian Rights Association tion published an exposé of "legalized robbery" among the Five Civilized Tribes entitled *Oklahoma's Poor Rich Indians*. The report stirred the national conscience and resulted in a congressional investigation of Indian affairs in the Sooner State.[1] Although neither the publication itself nor the ensuing controversy dealt specifically with the Downstream People, they could have easily done so. Conditions among the Quapaws matched those existing among the other tribes. Unscrupulous white men preyed upon the wealthy Indians, corrupt agency officials conspired to dispossess them, and small fortunes were rapidly dissipated. Moreover, after 1921, when restrictions against alienation were extended, the rules and regulations of the Indian office made personal freedom something of an abstraction. Still, the sensational revelations of the report were based on a fundamental fallacy—that Oklahoma's Indians tenaciously resisted adoption of the cultural patterns of the predominant society. The fact was that they had already abandoned many of the characteristics that identified them as a distinctly different people. The Quapaws, for example, so pursued individual rather than corporate goals that during the 1930's they vigorously opposed reform programs that envisioned a restoration of traditional ideals and practices. Thus, if the Downstream People were "poor rich Indians," it was because their rights as individuals were abused. That they were anxious to preserve those rights illustrated the extent of their accommodation to alien economic and cultural patterns.

The decision of the Quapaws to allot their lands in 1893 was the most notable example of this accommodation. Yet in comparison with others, it may not have been the most significant. Support of formal education, for instance, had continued to have a profound, almost incalculable impact on the Downstream People. The allotment act had set aside a tract of 400 acres for school purposes, a part of which was occupied by the Quapaw Industrial Boarding School. When that institution closed in 1900, Congress authorized the tribe to dispose of 240 acres of this surplus land and retain 160 acres for the use of schools. Relying on their $1,000 educational stipend and anticipating rentals from the quarter-section of land, the tribal leadership in 1902 opened five day schools on the reservation, enrolling thirty-two Indians and more than two hundred white children. Unfortunately, these schools lasted only one year, primarily because the necessary revenues never materialized.[2] Just as important, perhaps, was another institution which promised to provide the tribe with even better educational opportunities—St. Mary's of the Quapaws.

The allotment act of 1893 had segregated forty acres of the domain of the Downstream People for the use of the Catholic church. In part responsible for the donation, Father William H. Ketcham, the first priest ordained in what is now Oklahoma, the next year constructed a small school building that accommodated three or four sisters and about thirty day pupils.[3] Financed in large measure by the generous gifts of Mother Katharine Drexel of Pennsylvania, this small institution was nurtured by the Sisters of St. Joseph from Muskogee and was operated in conjunction with St. Mary's mission until 1897, when insufficient student patronage dictated its closing.[4] But given the obvious interest of the Quapaws in education, in 1902 Father N. O. Dannis opened another day school and admitted twenty-seven Indian children ranging in age from five to twenty years. Within twelve months the number of students had increased to more than fifty. Anxious to support and even expand this undertaking, the tribal council in 1904 gave to St. Mary's a one-story frame building recently vacated by the government school and petitioned the Bureau of Indian Affairs to apply the $1,000 educational stipend toward the support of Quapaw students admitted to the institution. With enlarged facilities and additional income, the council felt, St. Mary's could board its pupils and become a worthy successor to the school abandoned by the Indian office. The commissioner of Indian affairs promptly approved the request, a decision that made the Catholic school the principal focus of educational activity in the Quapaw district for at least two decades.[5]

Unlike that of its successor, St. Mary's curriculum was heavily weighted toward academic subjects. The instruction which ex-tended through the ninth grade was, according to one inspector, "quite bookish ... [and] pretty thorough."[6] Heavy emphasis was also placed on musical education, the success of which was demonstrated when patron interest in student programs required two performances instead of one.[7] In this, as in all subjects, instruction was provided by the Sisters of Divine Providence of San Antonio, Texas. Mother Katharine Drexel continued her support of the boarding school through contributions to the Bureau of Catholic Missions in Washington, D. C., the administrative duties of which Father Ketcham had recently assumed.[8] Until 1927 the leadership of the Downstream People annually approved the payment of their $1,000 annuity to St. Mary's, an obvious endorsement of its administration and programs.[9] Following the death of Chief Peter Clabber in 1926 and the subsequent rise of anti-Catholic hostility, the tribal council changed its opinion and on May 11, 1927, refused to consent to further appropriations.[10] Although the $1,000 represented only a fraction of administrative costs, it was symbolic of the tribe's commitment to the school. As a consequence, but only with a good deal of regret, the Bureau of Catholic Missions closed St. Mary's later that month.[11]

Despite the rejection of the benevolent efforts of the Catholics, the Downstream People did not abandon their interest in formal education. Their youngsters entered the public schools of Quapaw and Lincolnville, following the example of Elnora Quapaw Hampton who in 1926 was the first member of the tribe to graduate from a local high school. Others enrolled in the Sacred Heart Catholic Institute at Vinita, Oklahoma; Chilocco Indian School near Ponca City, Oklahoma; Haskell Institute in Lawrence, Kansas; and Carlisle Indian School in Pennsylvania. For higher education older Quapaw students attended Bacone College in Muskogee, Oklahoma; Northeastern Oklahoma Junior College in Miami; Tulsa University; and other regionally located institutions, including the University of Arkansas. These students generally adapted well to the various facets of college life, including sports. Johnny McKibben, the "Gray Ghost," captained the 1938–39 football team at Tulsa University, and during the early 1970's Russell Garber was an outstanding tailback at the University of Arkansas. That McKibben and Garber should excel in football was no accident. The Quapaws had a long tradition of annual gatherings devoted to recreational activities

St. Mary's of the Quapaws. Courtesy Oklahoma Historical Society.

that included ball games of different varieties. Perhaps it was this tradition that also motivated some of the wealthy members of the tribe during the 1920's to contribute thousands of dollars to the construction of an athletic stadium at Haskell Institute.[12]

Commitment to an alien educational system was only one of the accommodations which the Downstream People made to the white man's way. Another of equal significance was in religious practices. Catholic influence, predating the Civil War, had been particularly strong among the Quapaw home band during the 1870's, with priests from the Osage Mission in Kansas saying mass regularly at the house of Charley Quapaw.[13] Members of this group, no doubt, were responsible for sending a petition to the bishop of Indian Territory in 1891 which declared: "If you will send us a priest, the Quapaw reservation will become a beautiful garden of the church."[14] The next year Father Ketcham was assigned to visit the reserve at least monthly. So favorably was he received that in 1893 the tribe allotted the Catholics forty acres for school and church purposes. "I do not care much for the white man's religion," Buffalo Calf was reported to have said, but, he added, "I am willing to give

land to that Church because it is our Church."[15] Confirmation of
the pervasiveness of Catholicism among the Quapaws came from
Ketcham the following year. "With the possible exception of 5 or 6,"
he reported to the Indian agent, "all the Quapaws by blood are
Catholic."[16] Erecting a church building near the school, Ketcham
and succeeding priests continued the tradition of devotion and service that characterized earlier "Black Robes," to the extent that
even Chief Peter Clabber was converted in 1924.[17] But as suggested
by the failure of the tribal council to reaffirm the appropriation for
the mission school, Catholic influence began to wane during the
mid-1920's. An interest in other denominations and the rise of
peyoteism undoubtedly accounted for this phenomenon. Yet even
after the mission church and school closed in 1927, members of the
tribe retained an affection for Catholicism. Thirteen years later one
observer reported: "All Quapaws are Catholics at heart."[18]

Although the Downstream People seemingly abandoned the Christian tradition, they continued to be influenced by strong spiritual
values. As a matter of fact they had only transferred their allegiances
to another religious fellowship—the peyote cult. Introduced by John
"Moonhead" Wilson, an Indian of Delaware-Caddo-French extraction, peyoteism appealed to the Quapaws because it represented a
method by which old cultural patterns could be more easily accommodated along with new ones. According to the doctrine of the
peyote cult, the "Messiah," or Wilson, had been translated to the
upper world by the consumption of a non-habit-forming narcotic
found in the buttons of a type of cactus. "Father Peyote" had then
shown him the empty grave of Christ and taught him that the
"Great Ruler" worked his will on earth through the sun, moon,
stars, lightning, and thunder. He was also shown the "Road" which
led from the grave of Christ to the moon, the one the suffering
Savior had taken in his ascent, and was told to follow it until the end
of his life, when he would come into the actual presence of Christ.
In his visit to the sky realm, Wilson was also instructed in how to
build an altar, or "Moon," that should be the focus of true worship,
how to paint faces and to dress hair for worship services, and what
songs to sing. Sometime after this revelation, about 1895, the Messiah took his gospel to the Downstream People, where Victor Griffin
became one of his first converts and foremost disciple.[19]

Among the Quapaws the focus of peyote worship was the Big
Moon. A permanent structure, the altar was constructed of a con-

Round House of the Peyote cult, about 1955.
Courtesy Charles Banks Wilson.

crete slab with an outer apron raised to resemble a horseshoe or
half-moon that opened to the west. A straight west-east line through
the middle of the central depression, representing the road that
Moonhead had followed when transported by Father Peyote, pierced
three cement hearts: the "Heart of the World," the "Sacred Heart of
Christ," and "the Heart of Goodness." A north-south line intersec-
ted with the former near the middle of the depression, or grave, to
form the Cross, and on the apron other lines were drawn to sym-
bolize the days of the week and the months of the year. Two ash
mounds near the top of the altar were the "graves" of Christ and
John Wilson, while at its open end lines emanating from the "Heart
of the World" which formed either M's or W's signified "Moonhead"
or "Wilson." This Big Moon altar was enclosed by a circular building, or "round house," that opened to the west. To this structure the
faithful repaired for services that began in the evening and continued until noon the following day. Generally preceded by sweat
baths, worship was conducted by eight men and consisted of songs
accompanied by the drum and rattle, prayers, the use of peyote as a

sacrament, and the sharing of candies and fruits. Tobacco, eagle feathers, and a staff were used in each service as well.[20]

The theology of the "Peyote Road," despite its external trappings, was distinctly different from traditional native American beliefs. Not only did it recognize the power of a single God and emphasize the person of Christ, but it stressed the individual rather than the communal nature of the relationship with the Supreme Deity. Believers were to be honest, truthful, and generous; they were to preserve family bonds and earn their own livings; and they were to avoid alcohol. Put differently, it was a religion that, to a degree, accommodated and conformed to prevailing standards of white conduct.[21] As a consequence, peyoteism enabled the Quapaws, and particularly the full bloods, to make internal adjustments to alien cultural patterns, especially economic, which had theretofore been accepted only externally. It was thus possible to rationalize the great wealth that accrued to individual members of the tribe without doing violence to traditional religious beliefs. At the same time, the fortunate Quapaw had a responsibility to share his wealth with others, a duty symbolically expressed at the climax of peyote worship itself. In essence a method of accommodation, then, "Father Peyote" grew in influence as individual Quapaws grew in wealth, peaking in the late 1920's when St. Mary's mission was abandoned.

Following John Wilson's death, young Victor Griffin served as the high priest of the cult and, in view of the large incomes of the faithful, ultimately presumed to speak for all of the Downstream People. It followed that in the late 1940's, once lead and zinc mining ceased to be so profitable and after many of the wealthy Quapaws had died, that Griffin's leadership of the tribe would be challenged.

If religious life reflected a growing accommodation to white society, so did the work of the tribal council. Composed of a first and second chief and three councilmen, under the influence of Abner Abrams it had taken the lead in allotting the tribal reservation. Somewhat later, the council also permitted the Kansas City, Fort Scott, and Memphis Railroad to extend its line across the reservation. For its right-of-way the company paid the tribe $356.25, a sum disbursed per capita ($1.52 to each) in 1896, even though only specific allotments were affected.[22] Authorized by Congress to dispose of the 400 acres of land initially set aside for educational purposes,[23] the chiefs and council sold 240 acres in 1901 to pay tribal debts,[24] while the remaining 160 acres were marketed in 1906 to Walter T.

Apple for $20,000. After considerable controversy, the proceeds of the latter plus some accumulated rents and royalties were distributed per capita in May, 1908, with 310 Quapaws receiving $70.23 each.[25] In addition to selling the last portion of the tribal estate, the council also met annually to approve the contract with St. Mary's mission school and, of course, spearheaded the movement to extend restrictions on mineral-rich allotments in 1921.

The concern demonstrated by the Quapaw leadership over the extension of restrictions illustrated a basic change in its role in tribal affairs. With some exceptions, the council had traditionally reflected the will of the majority of the Downstream People, especially after they had regathered on the reservation in the late 1880's. Yet following allotment and the general tendency of enrolled members of less than half Indian blood to forsake their tribal ties, the council increasingly mirrored the special interests of the full blood minority. That a large percentage of this element of the tribe shared in the profits of lead and zinc mining only contributed to this particular perspective. Thus first Chiefs Peter Clabber (1893–1926), John Quapaw (1927–28), and Victor Griffin (1929–58), all of whom were full bloods, tended to speak in support of the wealthy few. The fact that Quapaw and Griffin were also leaders of the peyote cult further illustrated the oneness of the leadership with the royalty-rich members of the tribe. Most of this group followed the "Peyote Road" as well.

Although significant, the educational, religious, and governmental accommodations to non-traditional patterns of life and thought were not nearly as dramatic as those resulting from the large and sustained incomes received by the wealthy Quapaws. Between 1923 and 1943, royalties derived from lead and zinc mines on restricted allotments totaled $14,689,599, peaking at $1,679,863 in 1926, dropping to $83,466 in 1933, and rising again to $969,901 in 1943.[26] The number of individuals receiving royalties varied from year to year and tended to increase as the estates of original allottees were divided among heirs. In 1925, for example, some forty-five Quapaws shared in the payment, while ten years later the number of recipients had increased to ninety.[27] Yet because some mines were more valuable than others, no more than ten families received the bulk of the royalty income. Among the most notable of these were the Benjamin Quapaws, the John Beavers, the Antoine Greenbacks, the Harry Crawfishes, and the family of Flora Y. G. Whitebird. In

1926 at least 96 per cent of the monies deposited in the Quapaw agency was placed to the credit of members of these fortunate families.[28] As a consequence, some had astonishingly large cash balances—many in excess of $200,000 and at least two approaching $500,000. By 1941, one account exceeded $1,000,000.[29]

Because these funds were royalty payments derived from government approved leases on restricted allotments held by allottees and heirs designated incompetent in 1921, they had been paid to the federal guardian and placed to the credit of the different owners at the agency. Given the large balances which by 1930 aggregated more than $4,000,000,[30] the Indian office found itself in the unexpected situation of having responsibility for large sums of money beyond that immediately required by individual Indians. No policy existed for such a contingency, and all manner of suggestions were received about how to use these funds. These ideas ranged from loans to church groups and business organizations to purchases of real estate and state and municipal bonds.[31] Although the commissioner of Indian affairs did not doubt his authority to apply the money toward such investments, he did question the wisdom of such a practice.[32] To engage in a general loan business or to invest in business and agricultural properties would not only involve considerable risk but also increase the administrative responsibilities of the federal guardian. Excepting the purchase of homes and farms for the use of individual Indians, therefore, the Indian office determined to limit the investment of surplus funds to government bonds, treasury certificates, and interest-bearing deposits in local banks.[33] The rate of return for the Quapaws would be significantly less, but so would the risk of financial loss and the cost of administration.

Although the balances carried by the agency were large in 1932, they represented just more than one-third of the total royalty payments received since 1923. Put differently, during the 1920's and even into the 1930's, the wealthy Quapaws engaged in an orgy of spending that consumed nearly two-thirds of an income that totaled more than $8.5 million. Ironically, the administrative system aided and abetted this dissolution of funds. In some instances, royalty income from restricted allotments was paid immediately to those Indians deemed competent by the superintendent. The individuals receiving such funds were then at liberty to spend the income as they saw fit.[34] Most of the money, however, was placed in separate accounts and disbursed according to regulations governing indi-

*Young Victor Griffin, at this time leader
of the Peyote cult and later chief of the
tribe, about 1905.
Courtesy Charles Banks Wilson.*

vidual Indian money. Quapaws to whom the money was credited, therefore, were forced to look to the superintendent for whatever funds they desired to spend. As a rule, each was given a monthly cash allowance to meet day to day expenses, but large expenditures for such things as appliances, repairs, vacations, and clothing required a purchase order from the agency. Major outlays for cars, houses, or agricultural properties generally necessitated the prior approval of the Indian office in Washington. The weakness of the system was the discretionary authority given the superintendent at the local level to disburse funds and the tendency of the Bureau of Indian Affairs to rely on his judgment. For the Quapaws this resulted in the rapid dissipation of accounts. Between 1924 and 1929, Superintendent J. L. Suffecool not only acquiesced in but seemingly encouraged the spendthrift propensities of the wealthy Indians. "I have studied this question thoroughly," he once wrote, "and have long since arrived at the conclusion that there is nothing to be gained and everything to lose by not permitting them to have that which they desire."[35]

Given the disposition of Suffecool, the Quapaws became enthusiastic spenders. Harry Crawfish, for example, during 1927 expended more than $74,000, or about five-sixths of his annual income. For the same period, Mrs. John Beaver spent nearly $40,000, or approximately half of her income; while her husband had expenditures of more than $33,000, a sum representing a third of his income.[36] At the same time Mollie Greenback disbursed $25,000 from her account, more than she received during the year, and Mrs. Flora Y. G. Whitebird spent over $20,000, or half of her income.[37] In 1929, Alex Beaver spent $30,811, although he received in income less than $23,000.[38] But none of these matched the expenses of Mrs. Anna Beaver Bear Hallam. During 1927 she spent more than $77,000 or about one-third of the royalties paid to her; in the next fifteen months her expenditures exceeded $108,000, an amount nearly equal to that inherited from her father.[39] If these individual outlays were large, then collectively they were gigantic. In the year preceding October 1, 1929, Superintendent Suffecool authorized disbursals of $1.3 million from the accounts of thirty to thirty-five Quapaws.[40]

The purposes for which the money was spent ranged from legitimate to frivolous. Some of it was used to purchase homes and farms, to construct barns and sheds, to buy blooded stock, and, on one occasion, to finance a business opportunity.[41] Yet most went for less substantial purposes. During Suffecool's superintendency (1924–29), the Quapaws paid out more than $262,000 for automobiles, with at least forty-four cars purchased in one fifteen-month period alone.[42] Additional large appropriations were made to underwrite extended vacations. In the last six months of 1928, for example, Harry Crawfish drew $4,530 for this purpose. He also expended other significant sums for clothing, on occasion as much as $3,000 to $5,000 a year.[43] Expensive tombstones were also purchased, ranging in cost from $1,800 to $3,800.[44] Despite expenditures of this kind that were duplicated time and time again and the disbursement of large monthly allowances of which no accounting was made, the wealthy Quapaws were frequently unable to meet many of their financial obligations. Indeed, in September, 1929, it was estimated that they had outstanding and unauthorized debts that totaled as much as $40,000.[45]

If this unrestrained spending had accrued to the permanent benefit of the Indians, few if any objections would have been raised. The fact of the matter was that most went for pleasure and personal gratification. As a consequence, the Quapaws had little to show for their money. Willie Buffalo, for example, after spending $35,000 in twenty-four months had assets of only two used cars and real estate valued at $1,250.[46] The $77,000 spent by Mrs. Hallam in 1927 resulted in nothing more permanent than $10,000 in automobiles and $3,400 in furniture and household equipment.[47] Harry Crawfish had $10,000 worth of buildings and repairs as well as $8,400 in cars to show for expenditures of $74,000.[48] Indeed, of the small fortune disbursed by Crawfish between 1927 and 1929, at least 24 per cent went for automobiles and their upkeep.[49]

That the wealthy Quapaws were deriving little from their good fortune eventually became apparent to the Bureau of Indian Affairs. In the spring of 1929 the commissioner detailed inspectors to investigate the situation at the agency. Submitted in October, the report of the investigators contained allegations of fraud and collusion against the superintendent and his staff. It detailed evidence that Suffecool had misappropriated authorized funds, had shown partiality to particular automobile and insurance agencies, and had owned an interest in a firm that did business with the Indians. Moreover, it hinted that kickbacks had been received in some of the transactions involving the purchase of automobiles.[50] Although Suffecool at-

tempted to exonerate himself of these charges, he was first suspended from office and, along with his chief clerk, eventually dismissed from the Indian service.[51]

Although the dissipation of funds argued to the contrary, the
Bureau of Indian Affairs had sought to curb the spending habits of
the wealthy Quapaws. As early as 1922, Superintendent O. K. Chandler, Suffecool's predecessor, had been encouraged to set up budgets
for his charges.[52] During Suffecool's tenure, financial restraint was
theoretically encouraged by the issuance of monthly allowances.
Unfortunately, the use of purchase orders and the granting of special
authority made this practice a fiction. In late 1927, the Indian office
determined to get away from the obvious weaknesses of the purchase order system and directed Suffecool to draw up budgets for
individual Quapaws. These budgets would enable the Quapaws to
meet most of their obligations without reference to the agency. By
encouraging the Indians to live within their means, it was presumed
that their large balances could be preserved and valuable business
experience gained.[53] That this effort proved a failure was evidenced
by the unremitted spending the following year and the tendency of
local businessmen to grant credit to the Quapaws on the assumption
that, although unauthorized, the bills would eventually be paid by
the agency.

Following Suffecool's dismissal in 1929, Superintendent H. A.
Andrews instituted additional procedures designed to prevent the
rapid liquidation of accounts. Pressured by the tribal council, in
1934 he and the Washington office agreed to compromise all unauthorized debts that remained outstanding at seventy-five cents on
the dollar. The agency made this concession, though, with the distinct understanding that local merchants would grant the Quapaws
no further credit.[54] Yet this solution was only of momentary effectiveness, for unpaid bills continued to accumulate.[55] Despite the
inability of the Quapaws to live within the financial limits prescribed by the Indian office, Andrews sought throughout the 1930's
to curtail expenditures further by reducing monthly and even
Christmas allowances.[56] At first he required that his charges meet
only their day to day expenses with their allowances, but over the
decade he insisted that they stretch them to include car expenses,
livestock food, housing upkeep, medical care, taxes, insurance, and
purchases of furniture, dishes, bedding, and linens.[57] Andrews also
initiated the practice of preparing monthly statements for the Indi-

ans showing receipts and disbursements, assuming that such an accounting would encourage some fiscal responsibility.[58]

Although the superintendent established precedents that were followed into the 1960's,[59] his efforts were seldom applauded by the Quapaws. Deprived of their abundant funds, they resented reductions in allowances at the very time they were expected to pay for goods and services previously billed directly to the agency. Finding themselves short of cash, they were forced to swallow their pride and beg the superintendent for more money. Andrews had the discretionary authority to make contingency payments and frequently did, but more times than not the person soliciting additional funds had his request denied.[60]

Despite the controls instituted by the Indian Office and the curbing of the spending spree characteristic of the 1920's, the depletion of individual accounts at the agency continued. At least two factors contributed to this condition. On the one hand, income from royalty payments all but ceased during the early years of the depression. The price of lead and zinc ore fell to such an extent that many of the mines had to discontinue operations. On the other hand, some Quapaws refused to limit their expenditures. In 1933, for example, Harry Crawfish disbursed from his account $47,500, although his income totaled just more than $25,000.[61] Between December 1, 1928, and November 30, 1938, Helen W. Romick spent $233,543, an amount that exceeded her income by more than $82,000.[62] Although Mrs. Romick's case was undoubtedly exceptional, the dramatic reduction of her account was not. By 1963 only seven Quapaws had balances at the agency in excess of $45,000, although it was true that two of these surpassed $500,000.[63]

Assuming that the liquidation of small fortunes was regrettable, who then was responsible? Without doubt the superintendent of the Quapaw agency and other Indian office personnel must bear part of the blame. Suffecool, especially, aided and abetted the process, and Andrews, despite budgets and the elimination of purchase orders, did not always insist on strict observance of the regulations. Moreover, Washington officials occasionally succumbed to pressure and permitted large expenditures that contradicted the spirit, if not the letter, of previously stated instructions. Policies that restricted investment opportunities to government bonds and securities also contributed to the reduction of accounts. For one thing, the rate of return was minimal; for another, very little of the royalty income was ever so invested. Instead the agency carried relatively large, nonproducing cash balances, which on the surface were seemingly inexhaustible.

If the federal guardian was shortsighted in the administration of Indian moneys, so too were the Downstream People. With a history of abject poverty and a culture that had little concept of saving, or "deferred gratification," they valued money only for its ability to satisfy immediate desires. Those, of course, were many, and with funds at the agency available to supply them, they were unwilling to have their desires stifled. After all, they reasoned, the money did belong to them. Moreover, as a people who had accommodated themselves to the customs and habits of white society, why should they be deprived of their wealth when non-Indians had unlimited access to theirs? That automobiles, travel, clothing, appliances, and expenditures for similar purposes would in the long run decrease rather than increase their net worth was of no significance. Given this perspective, the Quapaws spent without thought for the future. But they did not always spend selfishly, a fact that the Indian office never fully appreciated. Wealthy families hosted the entire tribe at annual powwows, funerals, memorial gatherings, and holiday celebrations, paying for all the food, prizes, and other incidental expenses. On these occasions as many as 3,000 people would be entertained at a cost of perhaps $10,000. The requests of less fortunate Quapaws for "loans," food, or clothing were never turned down if funds were available. Furthermore, the homes of the wealthy were always open to visitors in need of a place to stay or a meal to eat. And this generosity was not limited to members of the tribe. Large donations were also made to educational institutions such as Bacone and Haskell and to the county for road work. Charity, then, as much as personal gratification contributed to the rapid reduction of individual Quapaw fortunes.[64]

While it was true that wealth for the Downstream People proved ephemeral, it nevertheless resulted in profound and apparently permanent alterations in many traditional cultural patterns. The payment of royalties and the disbursal of funds to individual Quapaws tended to set them apart from the rest of the tribe. With the integrity of the group so undermined, accommodations to the standards of an egocentric white society became less difficult. The wealthy families easily accepted the teachings of "Father Peyote" and the doctrines of

Christianity. And in financial matters, they came to pursue personal rather than common goals.

A growing sense of individualism was not the only implication of unanticipated riches. Family relationships were also affected. Throughout their history the Downstream People had revered the family unit with its tradition of marital fidelity as their basic social unit. This institution was retained relatively inviolate by the first generation of wealthy Quapaws, but the second wholly abandoned it. For the younger generation, divorce became the rule rather than the exception. Indeed, it was not uncommon for some to marry as many as six or seven different times. Bigamous relationships occasionally occurred, one married the ex-husband of her sister, a father married the ex-wife of his son, and couples would divorce and remarry, at times more than once.[65] Aside from the expense of attorney fees and financial settlements, this kind of activity left the family unit in shambles. More to the point, it contributed the final *coup d' état* to traditional Indian society. Without the family, the clan system and other social customs became meaningless and mere vestiges of a bygone day. Hence for the Downstream People wealth undermined both family and community, eliminating thereby most of the obstacles that had prevented a more complete accommodation to white society.

That a total integration was not achieved resulted in large measure, ironically, from policy implemented by the federal guardian. The basic objective of the government at the time of allotment had been assimilation, a goal that had been actively pursued among the Downstream People until at least 1918. Yet evidence of incompetence had forced officials to re-examine this time-honored policy which in 1921 occasioned the extension of restrictions on certain valuable allotments. Such action not only effectively reversed a traditional policy but also increased rather than decreased the guardianship role of the government in the Quapaw district. A majority of those enrolled in the tribe were not affected, yet the rest—most of whom were of more than half Indian blood—found themselves confronted by a host of regulations that envisioned new and seemingly contradictory goals. Individualism, for example, had been extolled as the cornerstone of civilization, but after 1921 independence of action, the very essence of individualism, was curtailed and frequently even denied. Especially apparent in the rules governing the investment and expenditure of royalty income, the curbing of independence tended to characterize other facets of the federal guardianship as well. In sum, government policy slowed the process of accommodation at least until the 1950's, when the wealth that had once distinguished the Downstream People was all but dissipated.

Directly responsible for implementing the federal will in the Quapaw district was the Indian agency situated at Miami, Oklahoma. Located at the Seneca Indian School at Wyandott after the close of the Civil War, it had been transferred in 1921 to Miami, the county seat, in order to facilitate the large volume of business arising from mining activity on restricted lands. Seven years later, when 90 per cent of the work related to Quapaw affairs, the agency was staffed by a superintendent and seven employees, including a farmer. Also stationed at Miami, although not directly attached to the Indian office, was an engineer of the United States Bureau of Mines, who after 1923 assisted the superintendent in collecting and interpreting technical data relative to the extraction of lead and zinc ores. In the 1930's a physician and nurse joined the agency force, opening a clinic at Miami in 1935. A social worker was also added during the early 1940's. Although seldom less than 50 per cent, the amount of time the agency staff devoted to the wealthy Indians decreased after the 1920's, primarily because the economic depression curtailed mining activity. As a consequence, the superintendent and his associates were able to devote more attention to the condition of the less fortunate Quapaws as well as to members of the other tribes residing within the jurisdiction of the agency. But even then, the principal concern of the federal guardian in northeastern Oklahoma continued to focus upon the affairs of the wealthy Indian.[66]

After 1921 the question of mineral leases covering restricted Indian allotments required the most attention of administrators both in Miami and Washington. Many of those negotiated by individual Quapaws prior to Commissioner Sells's declarations of incompetency had been approved or canceled according to new regulations adopted in December, 1920. Others, however, were not reviewed in light of the fact they were due to expire within a year or two. In the latter category were leases controlled by the Eagle-Picher Company on seven different Quapaw allotments covering 1,043 acres. Anxious to continue their profitable operations, in February, 1921, Eagle-Picher submitted a proposal for new leases that would provide

*Benjamin Quapaw, perhaps the wealthiest member
of the tribe, about 1910.
Courtesy Kenneth Spencer Library, University of Kansas.*

a royalty of 7½ per cent to the Indian owners.[67] When action on this
proposal was deferred, it carried over to the Harding administration
and became a matter for the consideration of Secretary of the Interior Albert B. Fall and Commissioner of Indian Affairs Charles H.
Burke. Advised that the actual operators on the tract, all of whom
held subleases from Eagle-Picher, were paying a total royalty of 17½
per cent, of which less than one-third went to the Indian, Fall and

Burke rejected the pending proposal on the grounds that the rate of royalty to be paid the Quapaw owners was wholly insufficient and that no provisions for a bonus were made. At the same time they directed that new regulations governing the approval of leases be prepared.[68] The Eagle-Picher Company, fearing that a $2,000,000 investment was in jeopardy, protested the decision as shortsighted, resulting from a new administration not "thoroughly conversant" with its position. Yet their concern was allayed somewhat by the oral assurances of long-time assistant commissioner of Indian affairs, E. B. Meritt, "That the Picher Company would be properly taken care of. . . . "[69]

Following the adoption of new regulations in December, 1921, new proposals for leases on the seven allotments in question were submitted to the Bureau of Indian Affairs. But on this occasion bids were made by both Eagle-Picher and a combine of investors already active in the district and composed of George W. Beck, Jr., S. C. Fullerton, and W. W. Dobson. The latter group offered a 10 per cent royalty and a $50,000 bonus to the Quapaw owners, while the former renewed its proposal of only a 7½ per cent royalty.[70] Following a hearing in Commissioner Burke's office attended by representatives of the parties involved, these bids were also rejected in March, 1922, on the basis that the actual operators of the mines should have an opportunity to contest for the leases as well.[71]

To provide the Indian office with more information about the special interests of those seeking the lease, Burke appointed a three-member commission to hold hearings at Miami. Meeting on May 26, the commissioners heard testimony from representatives of the mining companies and, for the first time, of the Indian owners. The tribal council had retained W. W. Hastings, lately a member of Congress from Oklahoma, and H. B. Durant, once the Quapaw agent, to appear for the tribe on the premise that action taken in the pending case would be a precedent for others. During the course of the proceedings, Hastings argued that no lease should be approved that did not eliminate the middleman, pay the Indians the highest possible rate of royalty, or provide for a bonus. To act otherwise would be unconscionable, he insisted, because the present operators paid a royalty of 17½ per cent and had paid an aggregate of $478,000 in bonuses in order to obtain the rights to the sublease they currently exploited. Hastings recommended, therefore, that the interests of the Indians could best be served if the government would put those leases soon to be renewed up for public auction.[72]

As a consequence of the Miami hearing, Commissioner Burke determined to seek new bids on the six Quapaw allotments. In June his staff prepared detailed specifications that were to govern all applications.[73] The following month, proposals were received from Eagle-Picher, the Beck organization, and individual operators. A comparison of these bids reflected that Beck and his associates had offered more than their rivals by some $185,000 in the aggregate.[74] Yet because the higher bidders had applied for leases on individual allotments rather than on the entire tract and were considered "johnny-come-lately" speculators, their proposal was rejected in favor of the one from Eagle-Picher. The latter application provided for a rate of royalty to the Quapaw owners of 10 per cent, for prospecting and experimental funds, and a 2½ per cent administrative charge to the sublessees operating on the tract.[75] Although royalty rates paid to the Indians were increased by 100 per cent and the government was relieved from administration of six separate leases, the fact remained that the Picher Company's bid was lower than that submitted by the Beck group. Obviously, as Meritt had previously promised, the vested interests of the corporation were "properly taken care of" by the Bureau of Indian Affairs.

The news that Commissioner Burke and Secretary Fall had awarded the lease to Eagle-Picher elicited considerable criticism, charges of fraud, and lengthy litigation. On the advice of Hastings and Durant, the Quapaw owners of the six tracts refused to sign the legal documents that formalized the transaction and pointed out that the Beck organization had increased its bid by raising the rate of royalty to 12½ per cent.[76]. Thereafter the two attorneys rushed to Washington to personally protest the decision.[77] Yet their effort was for naught. In accordance with instructions he received from Washington, Superintendent O. K. Chandler on August 19, 1922, reluctantly signed the instruments on behalf of the Indians. The following month Secretary Fall declared the leases operative.[78] His decision was criticized by both mining operators and Indians, and after Hastings was re-elected to Congress in 1923 he spearheaded an unsuccessful legislative effort to require the secretary of the interior to award leases to the highest bidder.[79] Moreover, the Quapaws later traveled to Rapid City, South Dakota, to present their grievances to

President Calvin Coolidge, who had come to the Black Hills to dedicate Mount Rushmore.[80]

It was not until Fall's role in the infamous Elk Hills and Teapot Dome scandals became public knowledge that his approval of the Eagle-Picher lease was labeled as wholly fraudulent. O. K. Chandler, recently dismissed from his own office because of administrative irregularities, persuaded the Indians to bring suit against the company on the assumption that its leases were illegal because they had not been properly executed (since they were signed over the protests of the owners) nor honestly secured.[81] The resulting case, Whitebird, et al., v. Eagle-Picher Company, was tried in the United States District Court in Oklahoma City, where on September 10, 1928, the judge ruled against the Quapaw plaintiffs. The court found neither evidence of fraud nor that the secretary of the interior had exceeded his authority in executing the leases despite the nonconsent of the Indians. In 1920 the Circuit Court of Appeals and the Supreme Court, the latter by denying a writ of certiorari, affirmed the original decision.[82] Of importance to Eagle-Picher, the judicial action was of even more significance for the Quapaws. Not only had it confirmed the authority of the federal guardian to act contrary to the wishes of its wards, but it also illustrated the impotence of the Indians in shaping specific policy. In other words, independence of action, presumably the hallmark of civilization, was declared by the court as being beyond the prerogative of restricted Quapaws.

That the government considered the administration of Indian allotments within its purview alone was further illustrated in 1930. In that year the lease of the Skelton Lead and Zinc Company on the Buffalo Calf allotment was scheduled to expire. Persuaded by the company attorney, Vern Thompson of Joplin, Missouri, that his clients deserved special consideration, the Indian office wrote specifications that required any new lease on the tract to compensate the Skelton firm some $200,000 for its improvements. As a consequence, only the Skelton company submitted a proposal for a new lease, all other firms considering the $200,000 requirement an impossible condition. A new lease was then prepared on the basis of the single bid received and submitted to the Indian owners for signature. They, however, refused to sign, whereupon, as in the Eagle-Picher case, the superintendent of the agency signed for them. The Quapaws protested vigorously and even presented their grievances to a United States Senate committee in November, 1930, but the decision of the court in the Whitebird case undercut their efforts. Accordingly, the lease to the Skelton company stood as executed by the Bureau of Indian Affairs.[83]

Although the federal guardian was pre-emptory in the awarding of mining leases, it always assumed that it was acting in the best interests of its Indian wards. The Quapaws, for example, could not expect a large and sustained income from their property if royalties were fixed at a rate so high that mining activities could not be profitably continued. Conceding that much to the industry, it did not follow that the government would fail to insist upon full compliance with leasing agreements. Indeed, just the reverse was true, although action was sometimes belated. In 1939 evidence was discovered which seemed to indicate that considerable lead and zinc was being sold without royalty payments to the Indian owners. Moreover, it appeared that the mining companies were utilizing sulphur content in the ores without compensating the Quapaw lessors. Three years later the Indian office approved a contract between two Indians and the accounting firm headed by Merton H. Cooper of Joplin, Missouri, whereby the latter was to conduct an audit of the appropriate records and seek restitution of all unpaid royalties.[84] On the basis of Cooper's findings, the Bureau of Indian Affairs persuaded the Department of Justice to file two suits against the Eagle-Picher Lead Company in the United States District Court in Kansas City seeking a total judgment of more than $1,000,000. Representatives of the company promptly obtained a hearing before the attorney general's office in Washington, in the wake of which in May, 1934, the suits were dismissed and further prosecution abandoned.[85] Although the secretary of the interior urged the attorney general to reconsider the decision, the Department of Justice refused to re-enter the case, recommending instead that any further litigation be pursued by private attorneys.[86]

Still impressed by the evidence amassed by Cooper, in May, 1935, the Indian office approved a contract whereby the auditor, for a fee not to exceed 25 per cent of the recovery, was empowered to bring legal action against Eagle-Picher.[87] Thereafter, Cooper associated himself with another accountant, Stanley Spurrier of Wichita, Kansas, and two attorneys, Vernon Lowrey and Ross Collings of Washington, D. C. After more than a year of additional investigation, Cooper and his colleagues reported that the Quapaw owners of the allotments leased by the Picher Company were due more than

Quapaw, Oklahoma, at t
mining boo
Courte

$15,000,000.[88] Still another year passed before they were ready to go to court. Finally, in August, 1937, a petition in the case of Crawfish v. Eagle-Picher Lead Company was filed in the United States District Court in Cincinnati, Ohio, the location of the home office of the company. The firm of Taft, Stettinus, and Hollister was retained as local counsel, a strategic selection in that two of the partners were prominent Ohio politicians.[89] There followed a series of legal maneuvers on both sides, all of which delayed an actual trial of the case on its merits. Yet because the suit affected the financial standing and credit of the company, in the summer of 1939 the vice-president of the firm indicated a willingness to make a compromise settlement.[90] At the same time, ironically, the Quapaws who were parties to the suit had refused to advance funds to the attorneys so that final briefs could be prepared, a decision they later reversed on learning of the possible compromise.[91] After careful consideration, the Indian office determined not to subvert the judicial process and advised the company that any proposed settlement of the case should originate with the counsel of record. Moreover, given the new development, it also requested the Department of Justice to consider intervening in the case.[92]

Despite the fact that the attorney general's office had abandoned similar litigation five years before, in early 1940 it decided to file a

ght of the lead and zinc
out 1925.
tional Archives.

bill of intervention in the pending suit as urged by the Indian office.[93] But before doing so, it reviewed the data accumulated by Cooper, only to find that it was not as impressive as the government had been led to believe.[94] In the meantime, learning of the intention of the Department of Justice to intervene, Eagle-Picher renewed in the fall of 1941 its offer to make an out of court settlement. After numerous conferences in Washington, all parties agreed on a payment of $253,150 by the defendant in satisfaction of all claims made in the suit.[95] Once the money was paid, the Indian office allocated $50,000 to the auditors and attorneys involved and deposited the remainder in the agency accounts of twenty-four different Quapaws.[96] For the Indians, the income represented a payday that would not have been possible without the sustained interest of the Bureau of Indian Affairs.

The federal guardian was equally supportive in other facets of Quapaw affairs. It frequently exacted bonus payments from lessees, the largest—$105,000 for a sixty-acre tract—being paid in 1926.[97] The Indian office, moreover, strenuously objected to attempts on the part of the Internal Revenue Service after 1922 to tax the royalty income received from restricted Quapaw allotments. Making payment of the tax under protest, it appealed the matter to the attorney general, who ruled in March, 1925, that such income was exempt from federal tax laws.[98] There followed a seven-year effort to get the $161,344 in taxes previously paid refunded to the Indians, the principal burden of which was carried by O. K. Chandler, who acted under private contract with the heirs to the estate of one of the claimants. By 1932 all the income taxes paid prior to 1925 had been refunded.[99]

In the long run, though, the campaign to avoid federal taxes on income was for naught. In 1934 the Internal Revenue Service levied taxes on monies derived from interest on bank accounts, liberty bonds, and tax refunds.[100] In 1935, when the United States Supreme Court ruled that such reinvestment income, as well as income received from initial royalty payments, was indeed taxable, the Indian office was forced to reverse its course and on January 1, 1939, began the practice of filing annual tax returns on all sources of income received by the owners of restricted property.[101] Another landmark judicial decision in November, 1941, also necessitated the payment of federal taxes on the estates of all restricted Quapaws who had died after 1925.[102] Granting that some taxes were due, the Indian office contested the valuation of the estates as determined by the Internal Revenue Service. In 1939 the legal firm of Bright, Thompson, and Mast of Washington, D. C., was employed, apparently without the knowledge of the Indians, to seek a reduction of the assessed valuation, especially as it related to the worth of mining properties. The attorneys made a remarkable contribution, securing a tax saving of more than $68,000 on some nine different estates. For their efforts in these cases they were paid almost $8,000.[103]

As with federal taxes, the Indian office could not long shield its wards from those levied by the state of Oklahoma. One of the objections to the extension of restrictions in 1921 had been that such an action would reduce the tax base of the state. To overcome this concern, Congress provided that a gross production tax of one-half of 1 per cent on all ores mined be paid over to Oklahoma's treasury. Nevertheless, in 1927 the state auditor sought to collect an income tax, an effort he soon abandoned after encountering stiff resistance from the commissioner of Indian affairs.[104] Following the Supreme Court's decision in 1935 that restricted income was not exempt from federal taxation, the attempt was renewed, but the Indian office again insisted that the payment of the gross production tax to the state excluded any further taxation.[105] In the meantime, the Quapaw council, seeking to avoid a confrontation with the state, sent Chief Griffin and Vern Thompson to Washington, where in 1937 they proposed to raise the gross production tax to three-fourths of 1 per cent.[106] Congress passed legislation to that effect the same year, an action that only partially satisfied state officials, for not until 1942 did they forget about collecting taxes on income derived from restricted sources.[107]

Taxes on the estates of deceased Quapaws, however, were another matter. Although in 1926 the Supreme Court had sustained a lower court's ruling that specifically prohibited collection of state taxes from two Quapaw heirs,[108] the Oklahoma Tax Commission brought suit against the federal government in an effort to force Five Tribes Indians to pay inheritance taxes. Hearing this case on appeal in 1943, the high court reversed its earlier position and in a split decision upheld the right of the state to collect taxes on the totality of an Indian's estate save for lands expressly exempt from taxation.[109] Although the courts in this and other instances ruled against the Indian office in its attempts to shield the Quapaws from paying different taxes, they responded more favorably when it came to county assessments. In May, 1939, in the case of United States v. Board of County Commissioners of Ottawa County, the Federal District Court for the Northern District of Oklahoma decreed that property purchased by restricted Indians from restricted funds be stricken from the tax rolls.[110] Considered in light of other decisions that reversed the historic relationship between the Downstream People and the United States, it could hardly be considered a significant judicial victory.

The same was true in disputes involving town lots. Following the discovery of lead and zinc deposits in the Quapaw district, as many as 50,000 miners moved onto Indian lands. Both temporary and permanent buildings accommodated their need for shelter and commercial establishments. Occupying restricted allotments, these facilities were erected on lots leased as businesses according to the act of 1897.[111] Yet residents of the mining communities considered such an arrangement wholly unsatisfactory, for it was impossible to make adequate provision for the maintenance of streets and other services. In response, in 1919 Senator Robert L. Owens of Oklahoma pushed through Congress legislation that authorized the sale of inherited and unpartitioned allotments for townsite purposes.[112] Although a townsite commission was appointed, no land was ever sold, because lease rights and huge chat piles—a common feature of the lead and zinc mining industry—made it virtually impossible.[113] As a consequence, the *ad hoc* condition remained, with those owning improvements paying permit fees or rent to the agency. The amount of income from this source reached a peak in 1927 when more than $44,000 was collected.[114] The ensuing national depression and the closing of some of the mines reduced this amount to less than $3,400 five years later.[115] Attempts by the superintendent to collect past due rentals were wholly unsuccessful, even from those who were fully capable of paying.[116] To strengthen his hand, the Department of Justice successfully prosecuted some of the "squatters," including one local school district, and the tribe contracted with Vern Thompson to institute action against others.[117] Yet on the whole the problem remained unsolved, perhaps even worsened, through World War II and eased somewhat with the general economic recovery thereafter.[118]

The objective of the Indian office in its leasing regulations, its opposition to federal, state and local taxes, its encouragement of litigation, and even its administration of personal finances was to conserve the wealth of individual Quapaws. Yet for the Indians themselves, the result frequently was dependence on rather than independence of the federal guardian, seemingly a contradiction of the policy that envisioned a tribal population unsupported and integrated into white society. But as stifling as it may have appeared, the government's administration of Quapaw affairs was not entirely suffocating. There were too many pressures, both economic and social, that broke down traditional patterns and nurtured an emerging sense of individualism and identification with the predominant society. The reaction of the tribal council to the so-called Indian New Deal of the 1930's illustrated just how far the Quapaws had walked on the white man's road.

Following his inauguration in 1933, President Franklin D. Roosevelt appointed John Collier as commissioner of Indian affairs. A trained sociologist who had worked among the southwestern Indians, Collier admired the group orientation of tribal life and considered attacks on it by his predecessors as regrettable. The objective of his administration became, therefore, the preservation of the elements of traditional society that remained and the restoration of those that had been abandoned. He sought to create a reservation-based "Red Atlantis" that could instruct white America in the advantages of the common life, leading it from a morass of economic and social decay. To implement his program Collier prevailed upon Senator Burton K. Wheeler of Montana and Representative Edgar Howard of Nebraska to introduce legislation that would end further allotment of Indian land, return to tribal control unallotted as well as allotted acres, gather landless Indians on consolidated reserves, establish tribal governments with corporate privileges, instill appreciation for native cultures, and create a tribunal to deal specifically with Indian legal affairs. Following the introduction of the Wheeler-Howard bill, the commissioner scheduled a series of "congresses," three of them in Oklahoma, to test the reaction of the Indians themselves. What he learned on his tour must have surprised him.[119]

For their part, the Quapaws were openly hostile to the proposed legislation. In fact, on March 10, 1934, the tribal council formally rejected the bill and directed its attorney, Vern Thompson, to appear before Congress and make known its objections.[120] Two days later the Quapaws endorsed a resolution of the Miami-based Association of Indian Tribes that labeled the measure "as a flagrant slap at Indian intelligence."[121] And on March 14, at a Muskogee, Oklahoma, meeting of the Indian National Confederacy, they joined in the general condemnation of the Red Man's New Deal.[122] In the meantime, on the thirteenth, Vern Thompson had specified the Quapaw objections before the House Committee on Indian Affairs. Not only was the bill unconstitutional because it infringed upon fee simple titles, he said, but it would deprive the Indians of heirship rights by insisting that previously allotted land be returned to common ownership. The formation of tribal communities, he asserted, would force the Indians to withdraw from the citizenship body of which they had been a part for more than forty years. Finally, Thompson noted that the legislation would deprive the wealthy full bloods of their mining royalties and distribute them instead to prodigal and profligate mixed bloods.[123] Obviously, the Quapaws were more concerned about the individual sacrifice demanded by the measure than its communal advantages.

The tribe, therefore, was highly critical when John Collier arrived at Miami on March 24 to preside over the ninth of his celebrated congresses. With 550 Indians gathered in the auditorium of the local junior college, Thompson, just home from Washington, reiterated the objections of his clients to the bill. The commissioner responded with patience and good humor, yet on occasion his answers and

attitude doubtlessly offended his hearers. By emphasizing the erosion of the Indian land base, he left the unmistakable impression
that the native Americans had proved to be incapable of managing
their own affairs. His explanation of what would happen if the
Wheeler-Howard bill was rejected sounded more like a threat than a
warning. And his earnestness in advocating a white-liberal reform
program suggested that skeptical, conservative Indians did not always know what was best for themselves.[124] As a consequence,
Collier failed to make many converts. Indeed, three days after his
visit the Quapaw tribal council resolved to continue its resistance.
And on April 9, Thompson presented a formal expression of opposition to the House Committee on Indian Affairs and introduced the
draft of an amendment that would exempt the Quapaws from the
provisions of the measure.[125] For the wealthy full bloods the individual sacrifices envisioned by the Collier program were inordi-
nately high. Moreover, it would force them to "retreat" from civilization, a concept they had learned to identify with individual ownership of land, and to return to "supervised barbarism." Rather than
conserve the best of the present, the Wheeler-Howard bill appeared
to call for a gigantic leap backward.[126]

This attitude, expressed by other tribes as well, had a telling impact on Congress. Collier's proposed Indian Reorganization Act was
emasculated nearly beyond recognition, with those provisions calling for the mandatory return of allotted land and the establishment
of new reservations deleted. In addition, the Oklahoma Indians were
exempted from most of the provisions of the measure as finally
passed. Two years later, however, the Oklahoma Indian Welfare Act
extended the major benefits of the Indian Reorganization Act to the
various tribes in the Sooner State.[127] Yet even this measure was met
with little enthusiasm.[128] The Downstream People, for example,
ignored it, refused to organize under its provisions, and preferred
instead to continue with the traditional chief and council system
that had come to embody the hopes and aspirations of the wealthy.[129] The rejection of Collier's "Red Atlantis" clearly reflected
that the nineteenth-century policy of individualism and private
property had triumphed among the Quapaws.

Yet if no personal sacrifices were required, the tribe was not adverse to taking advantage of other New Deal programs. Throughout
the 1930's many of the Downstream People were employed on road
improvement projects sponsored by the Indian office.[130] Others were

assisted directly or indirectly by the relief programs of the Federal
Emergency Relief Administration, the Civil Works Administration,
the Public Works Administration, and the Civilian Conservation
Corps.[131] Still others took advantage of lands made available for
educational and other purposes.[132] And in 1937 the Indian office
purchased in the name of the tribe a 528-acre tract of land to be used
to provide homes for landless Indians. Known as the Quapaw-
Grandeagle project, the tract was situated two miles south of Picher
and cost the government nearly $19,000.[133] The following year,
moreover, the council itself purchased forty acres of the old John
Beaver allotment for use as a campground and site for the annual
powwow.[134]

With the possible exception of land purchases, the various relief
projects of the New Deal threatened neither the individualistic
orientation of the Downstream People nor private property. The real
threat, or so it seemed to the tribe, came from adverse judicial decisions that resulted in both federal and state taxes, from private parties who laughed at Indian ownership by refusing to pay rentals, and
from mining corporations who failed to make honest accountings.
Just as ominous was the fact that many federal agencies no longer
considered the Indian as subject to special consideration. Attorney
General Homer Cummings, for example, ruled in May, 1933, that
property issuing from commercial leases was "clearly unrestricted
and therefore subject to the jurisdiction of the state court in appropriate proceedings."[135] The decision raised the specter of local
judges seizing control of individual estates and remanding them to
the custody of court-appointed guardians. Although they chafed
under its rules regulating the disbursal of royalty income, the
Quapaws nonetheless realized that the Indian office alone stood
between them and an even greater and perhaps more successful
attack on their vested interests. As a consequence, they were anxious to retain the protection provided by the Bureau of Indian Affairs
and to extend further the restrictions against alienation of titles due
to expire in 1946. As early as 1931 Chief Victor Griffin had asked for
the passage of legislation that would accomplish this goal, but it was
not until 1939 that Congress was persuaded to act.[136] Attended by
Griffin and Vern Thompson, hearings were held in June on a bill
extending restriction on eighty-nine Quapaw tracts of allotted land
for an additional twenty-five years.[137] By July the measure had been
adopted by Congress and approved by President Roosevelt, assuring

*Victor Griffin, chief of the Quapaws,
1929–58, about 1954. Courtesy Charles Banks Wilson.*

the continuation of the federal guardianship until 1971.[138]

The decision of the tribal council to seek another extension of restrictions was but one more indication of accommodation to the white man's way. Although it necessitated some sacrifice of independent action, it assured the retention of vested property rights and the continued recognition of individual interests. Those considerations, of course, were hardly traditional. They were instead non-Indian characteristics learned as a result of persistent white contact, government policy, and unexpected wealth. Nonetheless, by the 1940's, these characteristics had been assumed by the Quapaws and reflected the extent of the tribe's assimilation. To perpetuate the federal guardianship, then, was to preserve individual rights and clearly indicated that the Downstream People had acquired a perspective identical to most of Oklahoma's citizens. They no longer matched the profile of "Oklahoma's Poor Rich Indians."

CHAPTER X
THE LAST THREE DECADES

The assimilative forces at work among the Downstream People during the fifty years following allotment continued virtually unchecked after 1946. Save for a handful of traditionalists, individual identification with the tribal unit rarely occurred, for most Quapaws pursued goals attainable only within the context of white society. The council, once a cohesive factor, was no longer influential in that those for whom it spoke had lost most of their wealth. After World War II, government policy was designed to encourage this drift toward tribal extinction. Indeed, it looked to the day when the federal guardian would finally be without any Quapaw wards and could retire from the "Indian business." Yet, as had been the case on earlier occasions, just the opposite of what was intended actually occurred. Rather than merge quietly into the body politic, the Quapaws reorganized their tribal government and sought to recapture some the the traditions that made them a unique people.

To enable the government to wind up its Indian business, in 1946 Congress created the Indian Claims Commission. Composed of three members, the Commission was to hear and adjudicate claims of the various tribes against the United States which had existed prior to formation of the Commission. In the following May, Vern Thompson, who for years had based his legal practice on Quapaw-related cases, secured a contract through parties acting for Chief Victor Griffin authorizing him and his associates to represent the tribe in litigation before the Commission. Although the selection of Thompson was protested on the grounds that it had been prearranged and not made in an open council of the tribe, the commissioner of Indian affairs duly approved the contract that called for a contingent fee of 10 per cent and reimbursement of expenses from any sums recovered.[1] In November, 1947, the attorneys for the plaintiffs filed an original petition before the Commission seeking recovery of the value of the land ceded by the tribe in 1818 and 1824. For the area relinquished in 1818, calculated as comprising 43,520,888.24 acres, they requested a judgment of $54,397,110.30 plus interest. For that ceded in 1824, stated as 1,163,604.75 acres, they asked for $1.25 per acre less any payments made under provisions of the treaty.[2] The exhibits filed in the case required hundreds of typewritten pages; the printed briefs were just as lengthy.

After hearing testimony from expert witnesses and complicated legal arguments, the Commission made its initial decision on March 14, 1951. On the premise that the tribe had not actually possessed the territory ceded, it ruled against the Quapaws on claims issuing out of the Treaty of 1818. At the same time, it accepted the contentions of the tribe with regard to the Treaty of 1824 and adjudged that the Downstream People should have received $987,092 for their Arkansas domain. Precedent to a final judgment, government attorneys presented a 434-page study prepared by the General Accounting Office listing all appropriations made for the benefit of the tribe under treaty provisions. On the basis of this detailed information, the United States then demanded offsets against the judgment in the amount of $344,907 plus the value of the land granted the Quapaws in Oklahoma. Although on December 6, the commission disallowed all but $75,638 of the offsets, Thompson appealed the ruling as well as the decision denying compensation under the Treaty of 1818 to the United States Court of Claims. The appellate court upheld the original opinion but directed a further reduction of the offsets.[3] At this point Thompson and his associates determined to make no further appeals. "We are anxious, after so many years," they wrote, "not only to terminate the litigation, but also to collect our fee."[4] As a consequence, the Indian Claims Commission on May 7, 1954, established $927,668.04 as the net amount due the Quapaws.[5] Congress promptly appropriated the money on August 26, just as promptly Thompson and his two associates were paid $107,643 for fees and expenses.[6]

No postwar event had more impact on the Downstream People than the Indian Claims Commission award. When Chief Griffin and his colleagues on the council, in December, 1954, attempted to restrict the distribution of the funds to those of one-sixty-fourth or more Quapaw blood, members of the tribe who had heretofore forgotten their Indian ancestry challenged their authority to act. Searching its archives and finding no written record of how the traditional leadership was selected or that it was empowered to speak for the tribe, the Bureau of Indian Affairs agreed that the Quapaws were without a recognized governing body. Accordingly, in August, 1956, Paul Fickinger, director of the Muskogee area office, assembled approximately a hundred of the Downstream People in general council at Miami and proposed that they adopt a formal resolution that would authorize a Business Committee to oversee tribal affairs. Previously prepared in Fickinger's office, the document provided for a chairman, vice-chairman, secretary-treasurer, and four councilmen who, elected for two-year terms by a general meeting of the tribe, would compose the Business Committee. Although many protested that the traditional chiefs should be retained either as the new officers or as ceremonial leaders, the administrative organization as proposed by Fickinger was adopted. Robert A. Whitebird, a full-blood Quapaw, was immediately elected chairman. Walter King, Jr., and Harry Gilmore were chosen as vice-chairman and secretary-treasurer, respectively.[7]

Under the new tribal organization and Whitebird's leadership, steps were taken that finally resulted in payment of the Indian Claims Commission's judgment. In 1957 the Business Committee drafted legislation for congressional action that would authorize per capita payment of the money to those listed on a specially prepared judgment fund roll. To be compiled under the direction of the Indian office, the roll would enumerate only those living members of the tribe who were Quapaw by blood rather than adoption and who could trace ancestry to the allotment roll completed in 1890.[8] Not until July, 1959, was Representative Ed Edmondson of Oklahoma able to shepherd the measure through Congress. Hearings the previous June attended by Chairman Whitebird and other members of the Business Committee had facilitated the final action.[9] The Bureau of Indian Affairs immediately distributed application forms to those who sought to be included on the judgment fund roll. Within the prescribed six-month limit some 1,387 were returned for consideration, of which 188 were eventually rejected. In April, 1961, the secretary of the interior approved a final roll listing 1,199 Quapaws eligible to participate in the Claims Commission award.[10] Shortly thereafter, and nearly seven years following the initial judgment, payments of $946.41 were made to each of the Downstream People.

Although the money was significant, the most noteworthy development associated with the Claims Commission decision was the formation of an elected Business Committee. Significantly, the million-dollar payment was more the occasion than the cause of this event, because other factors were more important. For one thing, Chief Victor Griffin was an invalid, remaining physically incapable of leadership until his death in 1958. Furthermore the source from which the traditional council had once derived its influence no longer existed. Royalty income from lead and zinc mines totaled only $280,972 in 1956. Three years later it plummeted to $12,424; in 1960 there was none.[11] With their money all but gone, the once wealthy Quapaws had no lever by which they could impede the creation of a new governmental structure that served the interests of others than the favored few. Demographic changes also facilitated tribal reorganization. Between 1895 and 1930 the population of the Downstream People increased some 32 per cent, from 236 to 350. By 1943 it had reached 600 and in 1961, of course, totaled more than 1,200, or almost a 350 per cent increase in thirty-one years. Of those listed on the judgment roll, moreover, probably no more than 20 per cent were of more than one-fourth Indian blood.[12] The dilution of the Quapaw strain meant that a growing population identified with the tribe in name only. With little reverence for traditional practices, the biologically assimilated welcomed the proposal to institute a governmental structure that would be more responsive to their particular interests. When the Bureau of Indian Affairs recommended tribal reorganization, therefore, the political climate among the Downstream People was conducive to the change.

Once properly constituted, the Quapaw Business Committee responded admirably to the challenges of leadership. In addition to assisting in the preparation of the judgment fund roll, it also assumed responsibility for the 528 acres purchased in the tribe's name in 1937. A Farm Committee appointed by the chairman promptly negotiated a new agricultural lease that increased the annual rental on the tract from $200 to $1,000 a year. The Business Committee used part of this money to improve the recreational facilities on the forty-acre tribal council ground; another part paid the tribe's membership dues to the National Congress of American Indians.[13] Annual meetings called by the chairman and attended by as many as a hundred members of the tribe heard formal reports from the secretary-treasurer, appointed committees, and provided a forum for both grievances and suggestions.

Receiving the support of the majority of the Quapaws and with its confidence increasing, the Business Committee was not adverse to challenging even government policy. When Fickinger had proposed tribal reorganization in 1956, he also had recommended that the Downstream People take advantage of "termination," a program by which the tribe would sever all ties with the United States and "go it alone."[14] Robert Whitebird and Walter King, Jr., however, had just attended a meeting of the National Congress of American Indians where they had come to question the value of such a policy. Profoundly skeptical, they persuaded the Business Committee to steer a course that avoided the implementation of termination among the Quapaws.[15] And as if that were not sufficient indication of independent action, Chairman Whitebird and his colleagues initiated a campaign that culminated in June, 1970, with Congress again extending restrictions on almost 12,500 acres until 1996.[16] Not only had termination been defeated but the Quapaws had won the protection of the federal guardian for another twenty-five years.

In addition to tribal reorganization, payment of the Claims Commission's judgment also occasioned a minor cultural renaissance. Young men and women of Quapaw ancestry for the first time exhibited some interest in those ancient traditions that had once distinguished the Downstream People. One of these youths, Alfred Skye, was anxious "to recapture some of the old splendor that the younger ones . . . never had the privilege of taking part in."[17] Unfortunately for the new converts to Quapaw ways, there was little that could be recaptured after centuries of acculturative forces had taken their toll. Still, a few traditions had survived, and these became the focus of the cultural revival. Heretofore sponsored by private parties, the annual powwow now became a tribal venture, organized and partly financed by the Business Committee.[18] More a social than ceremonial occasion, the dance nonetheless enabled many of the Downstream People to participate in ancient rituals that momentarily linked them with the past. Rites performed at the burial of the dead were more widely venerated following the renewal of interests in things traditional. Greater honor was bestowed upon the annual memorial feasts that families sponsored until the fourth anniversary of the death of a loved one. And parents became anxious that

The family of Maude Supernaw.
Although she was the daughter of Tallchief and
a spiritual leader of the Quapaws, Mrs. Supernaw
lived her life among the Osages.
Photographed about 1910.
Courtesy Charles Banks Wilson.

Quapaw leaders in native dress posed outdoors by tents.
Note the lamp hanging from a tree.
Front row: John Beaver, Victor Griffen, the granddaughter of
Tallchief, Tallchief, Peter Clabber.
Second row: Joe Whitebird, Silas Fire, Sigdah Track,
John Mohawk, Robert Lotson, John Crow, and Francis Goodeagle
and his grandson.
Courtesy Western History Collections,
University of Oklahoma.

children should receive Indian names from the lips of Mrs. Maud Supernaw, the elderly daughter of the last hereditary chief of the tribe, Tallchief.[19]

Although significant, the cultural revival experienced by the Quapaws after 1956 had run its course by the mid-1960's. Of the changes spawned by the Claims Commission award, the tribal reorganization was the most enduring. The Business Committee as an institution became the cohesive force in the life of the tribe, a symbol of viability with which the Downstream People could identify. Following Whitebird's retirement in 1968, leadership was provided by John McKibben (1968–70), Jake Whitecrow (1970–72), John Redeagle (1972–74), and Jess McKibben (1974–76). The magnitude of the programs they administered was a source of pride to the tribe, especially that which in 1975 resulted in the opening of an industrial park near Quapaw, Oklahoma. Thus despite government policy that had envisioned tribal extinction, accommodation to white cultural patterns, and biologic assimilation, in 1976 the Quapaws still retained separate identity. Much of that which had made them distinctive was, as La Flesche's informant had said early in the twentieth century, "gone, all gone." Still, although it was some 300 years since they had danced the calumet for Father Marquette, the Downstream People had survived—a rather remarkable accomplishment in itself.

APPENDIX I

List of members of the Quapaw tribe of Indians residing or being upon the Quapaw Reservation, Quapaw Agency, Indian Territory, upon 15th day of March, A.D., 1889.[1]

NO.	NAME		AGE	SEX
1	Charles Quapaw		53	M
2	Huldah Quapaw	wife	28	F
3	Grace Red Eagle	niece	15	F
4	John Medicine		51	M
5	James Medicine		21	M
6	Ollie Sects		21	F
7	James Silk		48	M
8	Frances Silk	wife	46	F
9	Paul Silk	son	10	M
10	Antoine Greenback		38	M
11	Betsy Greenback	wife	43	F
12	Isabella Greenback	daughter	11	F
13	Minnie Greenback	daughter	9	F
14	Joseph Greenback	son	3	M
15	Isaac Daylight Antoine Greenback, Guardian		15	M
16	Charles Bluejacket[2]			
17	John Quapaw		31	M
18	Red Sun Quapaw	wife	46	F
19	Frances Quapaw	daughter	3	F
20	Sinnie Brown John Quapaw, Guardian		17	F
21	Alice Brown John Quapaw, Guardian		13	F

22	Boston Brown		10	M
	John Quapaw, Guardian			
23	Joseph White Bird		31	M
24	Lena White Bird	wife	33	F
25	Harry White Bird	son	12	M
26	Julia White Bird	daughter	6	F
27	Eudora White Bird	daughter	4	F
28	Thomas Crawfish		28	M
29	George Lane		31	M
30	Annie Lane	daughter	3	F
31	Alphonsus Vallier		45	M
32	James Vallier	son	9	M
33	Frank Vallier		36	M
34	Alice Vallier	wife	21	F
35	Amos Vallier		18	M
36	Soloman Quapaw		21	M
37	Abraham Dardenne		63	M
38	Annie Dardenne	wife	39	F
39	Lula Dardenne	daughter	19	F
40	Edward Dardenne	son	17	M
41	Agnes Dardenne	daughter	13	F
42	Annie Dardenne	daughter	12	F
43	Benjamine Dardenne	son	9	M
44	Benjamine Dardenne		49	M
45	Martha Dardenne	wife	32	F
	Minnie Dardenne[3]	daughter	13	F
46	Elizabeth Ray		46	F
47	Abraham Ray	son	15	M
48	Frank Ray	son	16	M
49	Louis Ambeau		43	M
50	Melissa Ambeau	wife	4[1]	F
51	Effie Ambeau	daughter	9	F
52	Harvey Ambeau	son	8	M
53	Frank Ambeau	son	6	M
54	Lizzie Ambeau	daughter	4	F
55	James A. Newman[4]			
56	James L. Newman			
57	Minnie M. Newman			
58	Maude A. Newman			
59	Sig-deh or Track		36	M
60	Xavier		30	M
61	Louis Angel		48	M
62	Martha Angel,		18	F
	Louis Angel, Guardian			

63	John Beaver		31	M
64	Sha ka Stet tah	daughter	8	F
65	Benjamin Quapaw[5]		31	M
66	Ah sah ta[6]		8	M
67	Pious Quapaw		40	M
68	Mis com mon nin ny		17	F
69	Slim Jim		35	M
70	Dick Quapaw		25	M
71	Francis Quapaw[7]		34	M
72	Ho gom me Quapaw	wife	29	F
73	Cha dah squi Quapaw	daughter	15	F
74	Gab ne ton gah Quapaw	son	6	M
75	A ba ge zhe Quapaw	son	3	M
76	Greenback		26	M
77	Cletus		25	M
78	George Red Eagle		23	M
79	Kha dah ska kun ka[8]		30	M
80	Gen Harrison		20	M
81	John Quapaw		20	M
82	Ka zhe ka or Little Turtle		50	M
83	Mary Portis		44	F
84	John N. Portis	son	22	M
85	J. C. Portis	son	20	M
86	Charles B. Portis	son	16	M
87	John B. Derrenisseaux		76	M
88	Mary Derrenisseaux	wife	65	F
89	Abner W. Abrams		42	M
90	Maude E. Abrams	daughter	4	F
91	Samuel W. Abrams	son	2	M
92	Harrison Abrams	son	½	M
93	Melissa J. Abrams[9]	wife		
94	Jane Hunt		48	F
95	Meline Hunt	daughter	10	F
96	Joseph W. Hunt	son	6	M
	W. B. Hunt[10]			
97	Peter Clabber		41	M
98	Meh het ta Clabber	wife	41	F
99	John Thompson	son	17	M
100	Wm. Thompson	son	15	M
101	Nellie J. Ball		31	F
102	Samuel Ball	son	7	M
103	Minnie Ball	daughter	3	F
104	Buffalo Calf		58	M

105	Mary J. Calf	wife	50	F
106	Frank Calf	son	13	M
107	Thomas Calf	son	8	M
108	Joseph Calf		21	M
109	Mary Joseph		39	F
110	Infant Joseph	son	½	M
111	Caletus or Mud		33	M
112	Geo Vallier		13	M
113	James Young		25	M
114	Mrs. Crawfish		51	F
115	Fannie Crawfish	daughter	13	F
116	Harry Crawfish		27	M
117	Lizzie Cedar		46	F
118	Mrs. Stafford		88	F
119	Victor Griffin		12	M
	Mrs. Stafford, Guardian			
120	Julia Stafford		13	F
	Mrs. Stafford, Guardian			
121	Antoine Stafford		6	M
	Mrs. Stafford, Guardian			
122	John Crow		27	M
123	Frank Buck		22	M
	Pascal Fish[11]		88	M
124	Mary Poteau or Zah me[12]			
	L. J. Fish[13]		37	M

APPENDIX II

List of names of members of the Quapaw tribe as per roll recommended by Commissioner of Indian Affairs T. J. Morgan, Feb. 7, 1890, and approved by Secretary of the Interior J. W. Noble, Feb. 8, 1890.[1]

NO.	NAME		AGE	SEX
1	Charley Quapaw	husband	53	M
2	Huldah Quapaw	wife	28	F
3	Grace Red Eagle	niece	15	F
4	John Medicine		51	M
5	James Medicine		21	M
6	Joe Buffalo	husband	21	M
7	Ollie Buffalo	wife	21	F
8	Francis Silk	mother	46	F
9	Paul Silk	son	10	M
10	Antoine Greenback	father	38	M
11	Betsy Greenback	wife	43	F
12	Isabella Greenback	daughter	11	F
13	Minnie Greenback	daughter	9	F
14	Joseph Greenback	son	3	M
15	Isaac Daylight Antoine Greenback, guardian		15	M
16	Charles Bluejacket		49	M
17	John Quapaw	husband	31	M
18	Red Sun Quapaw	wife	46	F
19	Frances Quapaw	daughter	3	F
20	Sinnie Brown John Quapaw, guardian		17	F
21	Alice Brown John Quapaw, guardian		13	F

22	Boston Brown		10	M
	John Quapaw, guardian			
23	Joseph Whitebyrd	husband	31	M
24	Lena Whitebyrd	wife	33	F
25	Harry Whitebyrd	son	12	M
26	Julia Whitebyrd	daughter	6	F
27	Eudora Whitebyrd	daughter	4	F
28	Thomas Crawfish		28	M
29	George Lane		31	M
30	Alphonsus Vallier	father	45	M
31	James Vallier	son	9	M
32	Frank Vallier	husband	36	M
33	Alice Vallier	wife	21	F
34	Amos Vallier		18	M
35	Solomon Quapaw		21	M
36	Annie E. Dardenne	mother	39	F
37	Lulu Dardenne	daughter	19	F
38	Edward J. Dardenne	son	17	M
39	Agnes Dardenne	daughter	13	F
40	Annie Dardenne	daughter	12	F
41	Benjamin Dardenne	son	9	M
42	Benjamin Dardenne	husband	49	M
43	Martha A. Dardenne	wife	32	F
44	Minnie Dardenne	niece	13	F
45	Elizabeth Ray, wife of 131	mother	46	F
46	Abram Ray	son	15	M
47	Frank Ray	son	16	M
48	Louis Imbeau	husband	43	M
49	Melissa Imbeau	wife	41	F
50	Effie Imbeau	daughter	9	F
51	Harvey Imbeau	son	8	M
52	Frank Imbeau	son	6	M
53	Lizzie Imbeau	daughter	4	F
54	Catherine Imbeau	daughter	2 mo.	F
55	James A. Newman	father		M
56	James L. Newman	son		M
57	Minnie M. Newman	daughter		F
58	Maude A. Newman	daughter		F
59	Mary Portis	mother	44	F
60	John N. Portis	son	22	M
61	James C. Portis	son	20	M
62	Charles B. Portis	son	16	M
63	John B. Derrenisseaux	husband	76	M

64	Mary Derrenisseaux	wife	65	F
65	Abner Abrams	husband	42	M
66	Melissa J. Abrams	wife	29	F
67	Maude E. Abrams	daughter	5	F
68	Samuel W. Abrams	son	3	M
69	Harrison Abrams	son	1	M
70	Sarah J. Hunt	wife	48	F
71	Malina Hunt	daughter	10	F
72	Joseph W. Hunt	son	6	M
73	Peter Clabber	husband	41	M
74	Meh-het-ta Clabber	wife	41	F
75	John Thompson	son	17	M
76	Wm. Thompson	son	15	M
77	Nellie J. Ball	mother	31	F
78	Samuel Ball	son	7	M
79	Minnie Ball	daughter	3	F
80	Infant Ball	son	2 mo.	M
81	Buffalo Calf	husband	58	M
82	Mary J. Calf	wife	40	F
83	Frank Calf	son	13	M
84	Thomas Calf	son	8	M
85	Mary Joseph	mother	39	F
86	Robert Joseph	son	1	M
87	George Vallier		14	M
	Frank Vallier, guardian			
88	Mrs. Crawfish	mother	51	F
89	Fannie Crawfish	daughter	13	F
90	Harry Crawfish	son	21	M
91	Lizzie Cedar		46	F
92	Mrs. Stafford	grandma	88	F
93	Victor Griffin	grandson	12	M
94	Julia Stafford	granddaughter	17	F
	Mrs. Stafford, guardian			
95	Frank Buck		22	M
96	Felix Dardenne	brother	17	M
97	Dillie Dardenne	sister	12	F
98	Lawrence Dardenne	brother	28	M
99	Mary Dardenne	sister	24	F
100	Wm. A. Dauthat		32	M
101	Frances Dauthat	mother	28	F
102	Zahn A. Dauthat	son	8	M
103	Minnie E. Dauthat	daughter	3	F
104	Charles A. Dauthat	son	1	M
105	Amos Newhouse		42	M

106	Martha Logan	wife	61	F
107	George Logan	son	12	M
108	Katy Logan	daughter	20	F
109	Samuel Cousatte	husband	23	M
110	Mary Cousatte	daughter	4	F
111	Felicia Adams	wife	27	F
112	Emma Adams	daughter	13	F
113	Cora Adams	daughter	11	F
114	Carrie Adams	daughter	9	F
115	Ettie Hamitt	wife	22	F
116	Abram Dardenne, Jr.	husband	39	M
117	Margaret Dardenne	wife	38	F
118	Willie Dardenne	son	17	M
119	Irenee Dardenne	daughter	12	F
120	Abram Dardenne, Jr.	son	9	M
121	George Red Eagle	husband	23	M
122	O-gosh-shung Red Eagle	wife	18	F
123	Sophia Red Eagle	daughter	1	F
124	Sig-dah or Track	husband	36	M
125	Me-kah-tun-ka	wife, mother	18	F
126	Meh-ska-na-ba-nah	daughter	4	F
127	Tcha-ta, or Leak	son	4 mo.	M
128	Ha-dah-ska-tun-ka	brother to 136	9	M
129	Noh-tah-to, or Green Heart	brother to 136	8	M
130	Sin-tah-hah-hah	brother to 136	6	M
131	Xavier	husband	30	M
132	Mah-shing-tin-nah	wife	16	F
133	John Crow	husband	27	M
134	Mrs. Crow	wife	35	F
135	Benjamin Spada	husband	50	M
136	Meh-het-tah Spada	wife	50	F
137	Mah-sha-ska Spada	daughter	19	F
138	John Beaver	husband	31	M
139	Heh-dah-tah Beaver	wife	34	F
140	Paw-his-ka Beaver	son	9	M
141	A-no-meh-ta-ha Beaver	daughter	6	F
142	Anna Beaver	daughter	2	F
143	Meh-tah-heh-gee-gah	widow	40	F
144	Dick Quapaw	husband	25	M
145	Ta-gah Quapaw	wife	36	F
146	Pious Quapaw	husband	40	M
147	Ta-meh-heh Quapaw	wife	24	F
148	Ta-meh Quapaw	daughter	3	F
149	Benjamin Quapaw	husband	31	M

150	See-Sah Quapaw	mother	25	F
151	Hum-bah-wat-tah Quapaw	daughter	2	F
152	Cletus	husband	25	M
153	Mis-kah-det-tah	wife	40	F
154	Little Greenback	husband	25	M
155	Mrs. Greenback	wife	24	F
156	Wes-ah Greenback	daughter	5	F
157	John Greenback	son	1	M
158	Ba-shung-ge-ne-zeh, Little Greenback, guardian	brother to [154]	6	M
159	Kah-dah-ska-hum-ka	husband	30	M
160	Kah-daah	mother	31	F
161	Wah-zing-ka (or Bird)	son	8	M
162	Men-ska-nah-bah-nah	daughter	4	F
163	Infant not named	daughter	1	F
164	John Quapaw	husband	20	M
165	Wat-tah-nah-zhe	wife	17	F
166	Infant not named	son	4 mo.	M
167	Pah-ska (or White Nose)	orphan	5	F
168	Oh-sta-wet-tah	widow	45	F
169	Mrs. Bushy Head	widow	35	F
170	Mah-nah-wa-cont-tah, or Walking God	son	8	M
171	Meh-no-bah		24	F
172	Meh-tah-heh-zhe-gah	widow	30	F
173	Laura Meh-tah-heh-zhe-gah	daughter	8	F
174	Mary Meh-tah-heh-zhe-gah	daughter	6	F
175	Mish-ka	widow	50	F
176	Hah-win-nah-zhe	not married	25	M
177	James Young	not married	25	M
178	Louis Angell		48	M
179	Martha Angell Louis Angell, guardian		18	F
180	Ah-sah-ta		8	M
181	Mis-con-mon-nin-ny		17	F
182	Slim Jim		35	M
183	General Harrison		20	M
184	Ke-zhe-ka, or Little Turtle		50	M
185	Mary Choteau, or Zah-me		37	F
186	Coletus, or Mud		33	M
187	Francis Quapaw	husband	34	M
188	Ho-gom-me	wife	29	F
189	Cha-dah-squi	daughter	6	F

190	Gab-ne-ton-gah	son	3	M
191	A-bu-ge-zhe	son	3	M
192	Sha-mah	daughter	1 mo.	F
193	Elizabeth H. Tousey		51	F

The following names were added by the authority of the Secretary of the Interior:

194 Wm. W. Blakesly (Authority 25840)
195 Leander J. Fish (Authority 26141)
196 Catherine Gordon (Authority 31302)
197 Rosa Gordon (Authority 31302)
198 Harry A. Gordon (Authority 31302)
199 Harvey O. Gordon (Authority 31302)
200 Sarah E. Gordon (Authority 31302)
201 Mary M. Wilhoit (Authority 31302)
202 John Charters (Authority 31302)
203 Louisa Washington (Authority 31302)
204 Isabel McKenzie (Authority 31302)
205 Charles C. Geboe (Authority 31302)
206 Ester A. Carden (Authority 31302)
207 Atha J. Carden (Authority 31302)
208 Louis LaFontain Carden (Authority 31302)
209 William O. Carden (Authority 31302)
210 Felicia M. Carden (Authority 31302)
211 Sarah C. Carden (Authority 31302)
212 Alexander Carden (Authority 31302)
213 Florence A. Wade (Authority 36549)
214 Isa Wade (Authority 36549)
215 Kitty Wade (Authority 36549)

NOTES

Chapter I, The Downstream People

1. Alice C. Fletcher and Francis La Flesche, *The Omaha Tribe*, B.A.E. *27 Ann. Rept.*, 68.
2. Thomas Nuttall, *A Journal of Travels into the Arkansa Territory* (ed. and with notes by Reuben Gold Thwaites), 119; J. Owen Dorsey, "Migrations of Siouan Tribes," *The American Naturalist*, Vol. XX (Mar., 1886), 215; Francis La Flesche, "Omaha and Osage Traditions of Separation," *Proceedings of the Nineteenth International Congress of Americanists*, 459.
3. Joseph R. Caldwell and Robert L. Hall (eds.), *Hopewellian Studies, Illinois State Museum Scientific Papers*, Vol. XII, 82–83; James A. Ford, *Menard Site: The Quapaw Village of Osotouy on the Arkansas River, Anthropological Papers of The American Museum of Natural History*, XLVIII, Pt. 2, 182.
4. George E. Hyde, *Indians of the Woodlands: From Prehistoric Times to 1725*, 7–8, 18n.
5. *Ibid.*, 17–37; Shirley Gorenstein (ed.), *North America*, 86–88.
6. Hyde, *Indians of the Woodlands*, 36, 68–69. See also David I. Bushnell, Jr., *Native Villages and Village Sites East of the Mississippi*, B.A.E. *Bulletin No. 69*, 15–16.
7. Jacques Marquette, *Voyages of Marquette, in The Jesuit Relations*, 59, 155; Isaac Joslin Cox (ed.), *The Journeys of Rene Robert Cavelier Sieur de LaSalle*, I, 257; John G. Shea (ed.), *Early Voyages Up and Down the Mississippi*, 120; Hyde, *Indians of the Woodlands*, 156–57.
8. Hyde, *Indians of the Woodlands*, 54, 164.
9. La Flesche, "Omaha and Osage Traditions of Separation," 459–60.
10. See *ibid.*
11. Henri Joutel, *A Journal of the Last Voyage Perform'd by Monsr. de la Salle*, 159.

12. Notes of Governor George Izard respecting the Arkansas Territory, Jan., 1827, Izard MSS, American Philosophical Society. This same account, with some variations, was recorded eight years earlier by Thomas Nuttall. See Nuttall, *A Journal*, 119.

13. John R. Swanton, *The Indians of the Southeastern United States*, B.A.E. *Bulletin 137*, 197; Marquette, *Voyages*, 151.

14. For a discussion of this point see Philip Phillips, et al., *Archaeological Survey in the Lower Mississippi Alluvial Valley, 1940–1947, Papers of the Peabody Museum of American Archaeology and Ethnology*, Vol. XXV, 412.

15. Ford, *Menard Site*, 182.

16. The assertion that the grandfather of the principal chief participated in the Quapaw occupation of the Arkansas lands does not stand unsupported. Visiting the Downstream People in 1819, only eight years before Governor Izard made his notes, Nuttall observed: "From their own tradition it does not appear that they were visited by the whites previous to the arrival of La Salle; they say, that many years had elapsed before they had any interview with the whites, whom they had only heard of from their neighbours." Nuttall, *A Journal*, 118. For Douay's comment see Cox, *Journeys*, I, 258.

17. This theory was first advanced by Father Charlevoix in 1721. See Pierre de Charlevoix, *Journal of a Voyage to North America*, II, 246. For a later but similar view consult J. Owen Dorsey, "Kwapa Folk-Lore," *The Journal of American Folk Lore*, Vol. VIII (Jan.–Mar., 1895), 130. See also Thwaites's note in Nuttall, *A Journal*, 117.

18. Phillips, et al., *Archaeological Survey*, 420; *Final Report of De Soto Expedition*, in 76th Cong., 1st sess., *House. Ex. Doc. 71*, 52–ff., 228. In fairness to Phillips and his coauthors, it should be noted that they do not subscribe to a late seventeenth-century Quapaw penetration into the lower Mississippi. They would date the migration at just before or just after the DeSoto entry.

19. Joutel, *A Journal of the Last Voyage*, 162–63.

20. Marquette, *Voyages*, 157 and 159; Shea, *Early Voyages Up and Down the Mississippi*, 73, 77, and 127; Shea (ed.), *Discovery and Exploration of the Mississippi Valley*, 173; Pierre Margry, *Discoveries and Settlements of the French in Western and Southern North America, 1614–1754* (unpublished translation), II, 207, and III, 431, 442, and 450.

21. Marquette, *Voyages*, 157; Joutel, *A Journal of the Last Voyage*, 154–55; Margry, *Discoveries*, I, 595, and III, 443.

22. Phillips, et al., *Archaeological Survey*, 410, 414–18; Ford, *Menard Site*, 152–56; Joutel, *A Journal of the Last Voyage*, 155; Margry, *Discoveries*, III, 442.

23. Nuttall, *A Journal*, 290; Joutel, *A Journal of the Last Voyage*, 155;

Jean-Bernard Bossu, *Travels in the Interior of North America, 1751–1762* (trans. and ed. by Seymour Feiler), 62; Marquette, *Voyages*, 153–55.

24. Henri de Tonti, *Relation of Henri de Tonty Concerning the Explorations of LaSalle from 1678–1683* (trans. by Melville B. Anderson), 75; Shea, *Early Voyages Up and Down the Mississippi*, 173; Charlevoix, *Journal of a Voyage to North America*, II, 248.

25. Nuttall, *A Journal*, 126; Joutel, *A Journal of the Last Voyage*, 158; Shea, *Early Voyages Up and Down the Mississippi*, 73.

26. John Pope, *A Tour Through the Southern and Western Territories of the United States*, 26.

27. Nuttall, *A Journal*, 125, 127.

28. *Ibid.*, 124–25.

29. Quoted in Essie J. Avery, "The Social and Economic History of the Quapaw Indians since 1833" (M. A. thesis, Oklahoma State University, 1940), 63.

30. Dorsey, "Kwapa Folk-Lore," 131.

31. J. Owen Dorsey, "Siouan Sociology," B.A.E. *15 Ann. Rept.*, 229–30.

32. *Ibid.* The inference that there were no camping circles is drawn from J. Owen Dorsey, "Camping Circles of Siouan Tribes," *American Anthropologist*, Vol. II, o.s. (April, 1889), 175–77.

33. Joutel, *A Journal of the Last Voyage*, 156 and 185; Marquette, *Voyages*, 165; Bossu, *Travels*, 62; Shea, *Early Voyages Up and Down the Mississippi*, 72; Shea, *Discovery and Exploration of the Mississippi Valley*, 173.

34. Marquette, *Voyages*, 155; Tonti, *Relation of Henri de Tonty*, 75; Bossu, *Travels*, 62–63.

35. Bernard Romans, *A Concise Natural History of East and West Florida*, I, 100; Bossu, *Travels*, 63–64.

36. Bossu, *Travels*, 64–65.

37. Joutel, *A Journal of the Last Voyage*, 155; Swanton, *The Indians of the Southeastern United States*, 777; John Francis McDermott, *The Western Journals of Dr. George Hunter, 1796–1805, Transactions of the American Philosophical Society*, LIII, Pt. 4, 95; Marquette, *Voyages*, 155; Phillips, et al., *Archaeological Survey*, 397; Father Louis Hennepin, *A Description of Louisiana* (trans. by John G. Shea), 82.

38. Reuben Gold Thwaites (ed.), *The Jesuit Relations and Allied Documents*, LXVIII, 257–59. Whether or not these figures told of some event in tribal life is unknown, since none of the skins have been preserved. Early in the twentieth century, however, Dr. J. L. LaRue of Belva, Arkansas, reported that a Mr. Higgins, an English miner searching for a lost silver mine, found secreted in a cleft of the rocks on Pilot Mountain, located in Scott County, Arkansas, 212 slate tablets with

three pictures on each side. Before sending them to England, Higgins let Dr. LaRue copy the 1,272 pictures. When translated, the pictures told the story of Queen Singing Bird, the first Queen of the Quapaw Nation, and her husband, Silent Tongue, and reflected the "manners and customs of the Quapaws, their religion, and form of marriage." Documents that are supposedly translations of these pictures are on file in the Arkansas History Commission. See John Hugh Reynolds, "Aboriginal and Indian Remains," *Publications of the Arkansas Historical Association*, I, 274–76. Although he discounts the story as modern, one scholar has concluded: "There is no reason to believe that they [the Quapaws] could not have developed a mnemonic system for the keeping of records" such as that maintained by the Delaware in the Walam Olum. Paul Weer, "Passamaquoddy and Quapaw Mnemonic Records," *Proceedings of the Indiana Academy of Science*, Vol. LV, 29–32.

39. Joutel, *A Journal of the Last Voyage,* 156; Notes of Governor George Izard, Jan., 1827, Izard MSS, American Philosophical Society; Marquette, *Voyages,* 137.
40. Fletcher and La Flesche, *The Omaha Tribe,* 597; Bossu, *Travels in the Interior of North America,* 65; Dorsey, "Kwapa Folk-Lore," 130.
41. Dorsey, "Kwapa Folk-Lore," 130; Bossu, *Travels,* 63; Notes of Governor George Izard, Jan., 1827, Izard MSS, American Philosophical Society.
42. Ford, *Menard Site,* 156; Charlevoix, *Journal of a Voyage to North America,* II, 247; Nuttall, *A Journal,* 115–16, and 126.
43. Dorsey, "Kwapa Folk-Lore," 131; Bossu, *Travels,* 61–62. Dorsey in "A Study of Siouan Cults," B.A.E. *11 Ann. Rept.,* 393–94, lists the *Wapinan* societies as (1) those having superhuman communication with the Buffalo, (2) those having interviews with the Grizzley Bear, (3) those having interviews with the Panther, and (4) those having interviews with the Beaver.
44. Shea, *Early Voyages Up and Down the Mississippi,* 71–72 and 129–30.
45. Joutel, *A Journal of the Last Voyage,* 145–46 and 156; Thwaites, *The Jesuit Relations,* LXVIII, 251; Margry, *Discoveries,* I, 594–95.
46. Nuttall, *A Journal,* 135.
47. Joutel, *A Journal of the Last Voyage,* 159.
48. *Ibid.,* 158 and 160; Nuttall, *A Journal,* 290.
49. Bossu, *Travels,* 61.

Chapter II, A Century of Friendship, 1673–1763

1. Abraham P. Nasatir (ed.), *Before Lewis and Clark,* I, 53.
2. Marquette, *Voyages,* 153–61.
3. Shea, *Early Voyages Up and Down the Mississippi,* 172–73; Tonti,

Relation of Henri de Tonty, 73–74; French, *Historical Collections of Louisiana,* I, 60.

4. Margry, *Discoveries,* II, 190–93, 207, 212; Hennepin, *A Description of Louisiana,* 82.

5. French, *Historical Collections of Louisiana,* I, 47 and 60; Cox, *The Journeys of LaSalle,* I, 145; Jean Delanglez, "Tonti Letters," *Mid-America,* Vol. XXI (1939), 229n; Margry, *Discoveries,* II, 207.

6. Tonti, *Relation of Henri de Tonty,* 107.

7. John Francis Bannon, *The Spanish Borderlands Frontier, 1513–1821,* 96; Edmund R. Murphy, *Henry de Tonty, Fur Trader of the Mississippi,* 35–37; French, *Historical Collections of Louisiana,* I, 68.

8. Francis Parkman, *LaSalle and the Discovery of the Great West,* 428–29; Joutel, *A Journal of the Last Voyage,* 151.

9. Margry, *Discoveries,* III, 448; Joutel, *A Journal of the Last Voyage,* 154–56.

10. French, *Historical Collections of Louisiana,* I, 70–72 and 78.

11. Murphy, *Henry de Tonty,* 39; John G. Shea, *Catholic Missions Among the Indian Tribes of the United States,* 439.

12. Shea, *Early Voyages Up and Down the Mississippi,* 72–74 and 126–31. See also Delanglez, "Tonti Letters," 229.

13. Shea, *Early Voyages Up and Down the Mississippi,* 74 and 76; Shea, *Catholic Missions,* 442.

14. Verner W. Crane, "The Tennessee River as the Road to Carolina," *Mississippi Valley Historical Review,* Vol. III (June, 1916), 10–13.

15. Stanley Faye, "The Arkansas Post of Louisiana: French Domination," *The Louisiana Historical Quarterly,* Vol. XXVI (July, 1943), 646; Marcel Giraud, *A History of French Louisiana: The Reign of Louis XIV, 1698–1715* (trans. by Joseph C. Lambert), I, 84.

16. Bienville to Pontchartrain, Sept. 6, 1704, in Dunbar Rowland and A. G. Sanders (eds.), *Mississippi Provincial Archives, French Dominion,* III, 23.

17. Faye, "The Arkansas Post of Louisiana: French Domination," 669.

18. Verner Crane, *The Southern Frontier, 1670–1732,* 90; Bienville to Pontchartrain, Oct. 12, 1708, in Rowland and Sanders, *Mississippi Provincial Archives, French Dominion,* II, 39; W. David Baird, *The Chickasaw People,* 16–17.

19. For the British reaction to this activity see Westmoreland J. Chahaynd to the Lords Justices, Aug. 30, 1720, Vol. VIII, 94–100, British Public Record's Office MSS, South Carolina Archives.

20. [Bienville] Memoir on Louisiana, [1726], in Rowland and Sanders, *Mississippi Provincial Archives, French Dominion,* III, 513; Faye, "The Arkansas Post of Louisiana: French Domination," 662–67.

21. French, *Historical Collections of Louisiana,* III, 99–108.

22. Superior Council of Louisiana to the General Directors of the Company of the Indies, Feb. 27, 1725, in Rowland and Sanders, *Mississippi Provincial Archives, French Dominion*, II, 411; Thwaites, *Jesuit Relations*, LXVII, 259 and 261.

23. Thwaites, *Jesuit Relations*, LXVII, 249–55; Shea, *Catholic Missions*, 446–47.

24. Thwaites, *Jesuit Relations*, LXVIII, 68 and 217–19.

25. Perier to Maurepas, Apr. 10, 1730 and letter of Bienville, Aug. 25, 1733, in Rowland and Sanders, *Mississippi Provincial Archives, French Dominion*, I, 167–68 and 201–02.

26. *Ibid.*, 312–13; Walter B. Douglas, "The Sieurs de St. Ange," *Transactions of the Illinois State Historical Society, 1909*, 142.

27. Bienville to Maurepas, Feb. 16, 1737, Bienville and Salmon to Maurepas, Dec. 22, 1737, Bienville to Maurepas, May 5, 1739, and Salmon to Maurepas, May 4, 1740, in Rowland and Sanders, *Mississippi Provincial Archives, French Dominion*, I, 334, 357–59, 390, and 442; Faye, "The Arkansas Post of Louisiana: French Domination, 676.

28. John Francis McDermott (ed.), *Frenchmen and Frenchways in the Mississippi Valley*, 206–07; French, *Historical Collections of Louisiana*, II, 115–18; Faye, "The Arkansas Post of Louisiana: French Domination," 676–77.

29. Vaudreuil to Minister, Dec. 24, 1744 and Mar. 15, 1747, in N. M. Miller Surrey, *Calander of Manuscripts*, 1036 and 1077.

30. Faye, "The Arkansas Post of Louisiana: French Domination," 679.

31. Nasatir, *Before Lewis and Clark*, I, 27; Thwaites, *Jesuit Relations*, LXIX, 217; James Adair, *The History of the American Indians*, 320; Minister to Vaudreuil, Sept. 30, 1750, in Surrey, *Calander of Manuscripts*, 1160.

32. Faye, "The Arkansas Post of Louisiana: French Domination," 693; H. Morse Stephens and Herbert E. Bolton (eds.), *The Pacific Ocean in History*, 392–96.

33. Stephens and Bolton, *The Pacific Ocean in History*, 404; Faye, "The Arkansas Post of Louisiana: French Domination," 706–07.

34. Faye, "The Arkansas Post of Louisiana: French Domination," 708–12; Banishment of the Jesuits, July 9, 1763, in Clarence W. Alvord (ed.), *The Critical Period, 1763–1765*, 83.

35. Abbé de L'Isle Dieu to the Minister, Oct. 12, 1754, in Surrey, *Calander of Manuscripts*, 1255.

36. *Faye*, "The Arkansas Post of Louisiana: French Domination," 714–15.

37. Memo of Jerome Courtance, [1757–1760], in William L. McDowell, Jr. (ed.), *Documents Relating to Indian Affairs, 1754–1765*, 415.

38. Nasatir, *Before Lewis and Clark*, I, 53 and 55.

39. The Journal of M. Dabbadie, 1763–1764, in Alvord, *The Critical Period*, 162; Faye, "The Arkansas Post of Louisiana: French Domination," 721.

Chapter III, A Valuable Ally, 1763–1819

1. Lawrence Kinnaird (ed.), *Spain in the Mississippi Valley, 1765–1794*, in *Annual Report for the American Historical Association for 1945*, Pt. I, xv.

2. The Journal of M. Dabbadie, 1763–1764, in Alvord, *The Critical Period*, 333.

3. Aubry to Minister, Feb. 25, 1765, *ibid.*, 456.

4. Gage to Halifax, Nov. 9, 1764, *ibid.*, 352; and Gage to Johnson, Dec. 6, 1764, *ibid.*, 367.

5. The Journal of M. Dabbadie, 1763–1764, *ibid.*, 229 and 234–35.

6. Aubry to Johnstone, Feb. 7, 1765, in Dunbar Rowland (ed.), *Mississippi Provincial Archives, 1763–1766: English Dominion*, I, 275.

7. Campbell to Johnstone, Dec. 12, 1764, *ibid.*, 267; Stuart to de La Gauterais, Jan. 13, 1765, in Alvord, *The Critical Period*, 405–07.

8. John R. Alden, *John Stuart and the Southern Colonial Frontier*, 201–203.

9. Farmar to Gage, Dec. 12–19, 1765, in Clarence W. Alvord and Clarence E. Carter (eds.), *The New Regime, 1765–1767*, 133–34.

10. Farmar to Stuart, Dec. 16, 1765, *ibid.*, 127.

11. Alden, *John Stuart*, 238–39.

12. Statement of Payment for Indian Presents, Jan. 9, 1770, in Kinnaird, *Spain in the Mississippi Valley*, Pt. I, 154–55; Anna Lewis, *Along the Arkansas*, 143.

13. Lewis, *Along the Arkansas*, 135 and 145.

14. Marjorie O. Thomas, "The Arkansas Post of Louisiana, 1682–1783" (M.A. thesis, San Diego State College, 1948), 41 and 41n.

15. *Ibid.*, 55–56; Stanley Faye, "The Arkansas Post of Louisiana: Spanish Domination," *The Louisiana Historical Quarterly*, Vol. XXVII (July, 1944), 133–34.

16. Lewis, *Along the Arkansas*, 136.

17. Alden, *John Stuart*, 329.

18. Faye, "The Arkansas Post of Louisiana: Spanish Domination," 641–42, 648, and 649; Thomas, "Arkansas Post," 73.

19. The Journal of M. Dabbadie, Mar., 1764, in Alvord, *The Critical Period*, 174.

20. Thomas, "Arkansas Post," 69.

21. *Ibid.*, 70.

22. John Caughey, *Bernado de Galvez in Louisiana, 1776–1783*, 101; Clarence W. Alvord (ed.), *Kaskaskia Records, 1778–1790*, xix; Faye, "The Arkansas Post of Louisiana: Spanish Domination," 661.

23. Act of Possession, Nov. 22, 1780, in Kinnaird, *Spain in the Mississippi Valley*, Pt. I. 401; Thomas "Arkansas Post," 50.

24. De Villiers to Galvez, July 11, 1781, *ibid.*, 430–31.

25. Faye, "The Arkansas Post of Louisiana: Spanish Domination," 682.

26. Arrell M. Gibson, *The Chickasaws*, 73; Caughey, *Bernado de Galvez*, 231; Faye, "The Arkansas Post of Louisiana: Spanish Domination," 682; Thomas, "Arkansas Post," 87.

27. Faye, "The Arkansas Post of Louisiana: Spanish Domination," 684–86; Lewis, *Along the Arkansas*, 176–80.

28. *Ibid.*; Caughey, *Bernado de Galvez*, 240–41.

29. Faye, "The Arkansas Post of Louisiana: *Spanish Domination*," 680–81; Thomas, "Arkansas Post," 94.

30. Faye, "The Arkansas Post of Louisiana: Spanish Domination," 693–94.

31. Don Jacobo Du Breuil to Don Francisco Cruzat, Oct. 25, 1786, in Kinnaird, *Spain in the Mississippi Valley*, Pt. II, 187–88.

32. Miro to Du Breuil, Jan. 25, 1787, *ibid.*, 197–98.

33. Perez to Miro, Aug. 6, 1790, *ibid.*, 369.

34. Abraham P. Nasatir, *Spanish War Vessels on the Mississippi, 1792–1796*, 169.

35. W. David Baird, *The Osage People*, 23; Carondelet to Trudeau, May 6, 1793, in Kinnaird, *Spain in the Mississippi Valley*, Pt. III, 155.

36. Nasatir, *Before Lewis and Clark*, I, 214 and 321.

37. Abraham P. Nasatir and Ernest R. Liljegren, "Materials Relating to the History of the Mississippi Valley," *The Louisiana Historical Quarterly*, Vol. XXI (Jan., 1936), 35–36. See also Secret Orders to Don Carlos Howard, Nov. 26, 1795, Spanish Archives (translations), Manuscripts Division, University of Illinois Library.

38. Nasatir and Liljegren, "Materials Relating to the History of the Mississippi Valley," 45.

39. Carondelet to de las Casas, Nov. 24, 1794, in James A. Robertson (ed. and trans.), *Louisiana Under the Rule of Spain, France, and the United States, 1785–1807*, I, 308–309; Nasatir, *Spanish War Vessels*.

40. Annie H. Abel, "The History of the Events Resulting in Indian Consolidation West of the Mississippi," *Annual Report of the American Historical Association, 1906*, I, 241–454.

41. Clarence Edwin Carter (ed.), *The Territorial Papers of the United States*, XIII, 18n.

42. John B. Treat to the Sec. of War, Nov. 15, 1805, *ibid.*, 276–281; Donald Jackson, *The Journals of Zebulon Montgomery Pike*, II, 17; Eron Opha Rowland, *Life, Letters and Papers of William Dunbar*, 210–11; and A. Stewart to Sec. of War, July 20, 1807, Letters Received by the Sec. of War, Main Series, Records of the War Department, National Archives (hereinafter NA), Microcopy 221, Roll 12.

43. Sec. of War to Daniel Bissell, May 9, 1804, in Carter, *Territorial Papers*, XIII, 22.

44. Treat to William Davy, Apr. 15, 1806, Letterbook, Arkansas Trading

House, Records of the Superintendent of Indian Trade, NA, Microcopy 142; Jackson, *The Journals of Zebulon Montgomery Pike*, II, 18n.

45. John Mason to John Johnson, May 20, 1808, in Carter, *Territorial Papers*, XIV, 185–87.

46. Sec. of War to Treat, Mar. 15, 1805, Treat to Davy, Aug. 25, 1805, and Treat to John Shee, Apr. 25, 1807, Letterbook, Arkansas Trading House, Records of the Superintendent of Indian Trade, NA, Microcopy 142.

47. Treat to Shee, Mar. 23, 1807, *ibid.*; Treat to Sec. of War, Nov. 15, 1805, in Carter, *Territorial Papers*, XIII, 276–77; William Lovely to Clark, Aug. 9, 1814, *ibid.*, XV, 53–54; Treat to Sec. of War, Jan. 7, 1808, *ibid.*, XIV, 164–65.

48. Mason to J. B. Waterman, May 29, 1810, Letterbook, Arkansas Trading House, Records of the Superintendent of Indian Trade, NA, Microcopy 142.

49. Treat to Sec. of War, Mar. 27, 1806 and May 20, 1806, in Carter, *Territorial Papers*, XIII, 463–64 and 511–12.

50. Treat to Sec. of War, Jan. 7, 1808 and July 26, 1808, *ibid.*, XIV, 144–45 and 205–206.

51. James Wilkinson to Sec. of War, Sept. 22, 1805, and Treat to Sec. of War, May 20, 1806, *ibid.*, XIII, 227–30 and 511–12; Treat to Sec. of War, Apr. 1, 1807, Letterbook, Arkansas Trading House, Records of the Superintendent of Indian Trade, NA, Microcopy 142.

52. Memorial of the Grand Jury of Arkansas County, Oct. 4, 1815, in Carter, *Territorial Papers*, XV, 87–88.

53. *American State Papers: Indian Affairs*, II, 97.

54. Musick and Parker to Clark, Aug. 1, 1816, in Carter, *Territorial Papers*, XV, 180–82. See also St. Louis *Missouri Gazette*, Aug. 31, 1816.

55. Statement of the Former Spanish Commandant, June 5, 1816, in Carter, *Territorial Papers*, XV, 178–80; Names and numbers of tribes in Missouri Territory by William Clark Nov. 4, 1816, Indian Papers, Missouri Historical Society.

56. William Russell to Edward Hempstead, Nov. 1, 1813, in Carter, *Territorial Papers*, XIV, 720–21; Return Meigs to Sec. of War, Feb. 17, 1816, *ibid.*, XV, 121–23; *American State Papers: Indian Affairs*, II, 98.

57. Clark, et al., to Sec. of War, Dec. 7, 1816, William Clark MSS, Missouri Historical Society.

58. *Ibid.; American State Papers: Indian Affairs*, II, 97.

59. Petition of Inhabitants of Missouri Territory, [1816], in Carter, *Territorial Papers*, XV, 182–83.

60. Resolution of the Territorial Assembly, Jan. 2, 1817, *ibid.*, 224–25; *Missouri Gazette*, June 11, 1817.

61. Clark to Sir, Apr. 4, 1817, William Clark MSS, Missouri Historical Society.

62. 7 U.S. Stat., 156.
63. Stephen H. Long to Thomas A. Smith, Jan. 30, 1818, in Carter, *Territorial Papers*, XIX, 4–10.
64. *American State Papers: Indian Affairs*, II, 176 and 177; 7 U.S. Stat., 176; and Quapaw Treaty, Aug. 24, 1818, File No. 96, Ratified Indian Treaties, 1722–1865, General Records of the United States, NA, Microcopy 668, Roll 5.
65. Nuttall, *A Journal*, 132.

Chapter IV, Into the Wilderness, 1819–39

1. Petition to Congress by Inhabitants of Arkansas County, Nov. 2, 1818, in Carter, *Territorial Papers*, XIX, 1012.
2. *Ibid.*; Petition to the President by the Territorial Assembly, Feb. 11, 1820, *ibid.*, 143–45.
3. *Arkansas Gazette*, Feb. 11, 1820 and Dec. 29, 1821; Petition to the President, Feb. 11, 1820, and Robert Crittenden to John C. Calhoun, Sept. 28, 1823, in Carter, *Territorial Papers*, XIX, 143–45 and 546–50.
4. McKinney to Miller, Sept. 28, 1819, and Miller to Calhoun, Feb. 15, 1820, *ibid.*, 110–11 and 149–50.
5. *Ibid.*, 150n; 38th Cong., 1st sess., *House Ex. Doc. 57*, 3.
6. Calhoun to Henry W. Conway, Feb. 14, 1824, in Carter, *Territorial Papers*, XIX, 607–08.
7. Miller to Calhoun, Feb. 15, 1820, and Calhoun to Miller, June 20, 1820, *ibid.*, 149–50 and 199–200.
8. *Arkansas Gazette*, May 12, 1821; Crittenden to Calhoun, May 17, 1821, in Carter, *Territorial Papers*, XIX, 288–89.
9. Miller to Calhoun, Mar. 24, 1820, and Crittenden to Calhoun, July 7, 1821, *ibid.*, 153–55 and 299–300.
10. Quapaw Treaty of Aug. 24, 1818, File No. 96, Ratified Indian Treaties, 1722–1865, General Records of the United States, NA, Microcopy 668, Roll 5; *American State Papers: Indian Affairs*, II, 165.
11. William Rector to Josiah Meigs, Apr. 14, 1819, in Carter, *Territorial Papers*, XIX, 62–67.
12. Miller to Calhoun, Aug. 12, 1821, *ibid.*, 310–11; 7 U.S. Stat., 176.
13. *Arkansas Gazette*, Oct. 7, 1820 and Dec. 2, 1820.
14. John Trimble to Meigs, Jan. 3, 1822, and Conway to Edmund P. Gains, June 26, 1822, in Carter, *Territorial Papers*, XIX, 389 and 445–46.
15. Memorial to the Congress by the Territorial Assembly, Oct. 17, 1821, *ibid.*, 328.

16. *Arkansas Gazette*, Dec. 29, 1821.

17. Jedediah Morse, *A Report to the Secretary of War of the United States on Indian Affairs*, [1822], 236.

18. Conway to Gains, June 26, 1822, in Carter, *Territorial Papers*, XIX, 445–46.

19. Crittenden to Calhoun, Sept. 28, 1823, *ibid.*, 546–50.

20. Conway to Calhoun, Dec. 17, 1823, *ibid.*, 579–80.

21. Calhoun to Lewis McLane, Jan. 7, 1824, *ibid.*, 589–90; Calhoun to Crittenden, Apr. 28, 1824, Gully Collection, Arkansas History Commission.

22. 4 U.S. Stat., 41; Calhoun to Crittenden, June 26, 1824, in Carter, *Territorial Papers*, XIX, 681–82. The disposition of the $7,000 warrant became the source of considerable controversy. Conway turned over to Crittenden only $6,400 of the sum entrusted to him. Accused later of fraud, Conway challenged Crittenden to a duel in which he was mortally wounded on October 19, 1827. See McKinney to Conway, Jan. 8, 1825, Letters Sent (hereinafter LS), Office of Indian Affairs (hereinafter OIA), NA, Microcopy 21, Roll 1; *Arkansas Gazette*, May 22, 1827 and July 24, 1827.

23. *Arkansas Gazette*, May 4, 1824.

24. *Ibid.*, July 13, 1824.

25. *Ibid.*, July 27, 1824.

26. *Ibid.*, Nov. 11, 1824.

27. *Ibid.*

28. *Ibid.*

29. 7 U.S. Stat. 232.

30. *American State Papers: Indian Affairs*, II, 542–44. The Choctaw Treaty of Doaks Stand in 1820 required only a partial cession of their Mississippi domain, in return for which they secured title to all of what is now southern Oklahoma.

31. Crittenden to the people of Arkansas, *Arkansas Gazette*, Apr. 24, 1833.

32. *Ibid.*, June 28, 1825; Izard to Sec. of War, July 1, 1825, in Carter, *Territorial Papers*, XIX, 83–84; Ginger L. Ashcraft, "Antoine Barraque and His Involvement in Indian Affairs of Southwest Arkansas, 1816–1832," *The Arkansas Historical Quarterly*, Vol. XXXII (Autumn, 1973), 226.

33. Izard to James Barbour, Sept. 3, 1825, Letters Received (hereinafter LR), OIA, Arkansas Superintendency, NA, Microcopy 234, Roll 29; Gray to Sec. of War, Sept. 30, 1825, in Carter, *Territorial Papers*, XX, 119–20; Gray to Sec. of War, Oct. 1, 1825, in *American State Papers: Indian Affairs*, II, 706.

34. Barbour to Izard, July 8, 1825, and Izard to Sec. of War, Sept. 24, 1825, in Carter, *Territorial Papers*, XX, 87–89 and 112–13; John Clark to Izard,

Nov. 8, 1825, Gully Collection, Arkansas History Commission.

35. Receipt of Heckaton, et al., Dec. 14, 1825, *ibid;* Izard to Sec. of War, Apr. 29, 1826, in Carter, *Territorial Papers,* XX, 232–33.

36. Gray to Barbour, Apr. 6, 1826, *ibid.,* 225–27; Dallas T. Herndon, "When the Quapaws Went to Red River—A Translation," in *Publications of the Arkansas Historical Association,* IV, 326–331; Voyage des Quapaws, Jan. 14, 1826, Gully Collection, Arkansas History Commission.

37. Report of Antoine Barraque, Mar. 31, 1826, and Gray to Barbour, Apr. 30, 1826, in Carter, *Territorial Papers,* XX, 234–35 and 236–38.

38. Izard to Sec. of War, Apr. 24, 1826, *ibid.,* 232–33; 38th Cong. 1st sess., *House Ex. Doc. 57,* 4.

39. Sarasin, et al., to Great War Chief, Jan. 28, 1827, LR, OIA, Caddo Agency, NA, Microcopy 234, Roll 31; Richard Hannum to John Pope, [Dec., 1832], LR, OIA, Neosho Agency, NA, Microcopy 234, Roll 530.

40. Hannum to Sir, Mar. 17, 1832, *ibid.;* Sarasin, et al., to Great War Chief, Jan. 18, 1827, LR, OIA, Caddo Agency, NA, Microcopy 234, Roll 31; Gray to Barbour, May 15, 1827, in Carter, *Territorial Papers,* XX, 465–67.

41. Izard to Sec. of War, June 6, 1827, *ibid.,* 473–74; *Arkansas Gazette,* Sept. 5, 1826.

42. *Arkansas Gazette,* Feb. 13, 1827.

43. *Ibid.,* Sept. 5, 1826; McKinney to Barbour, Jan. 8, 1827, *American State Papers: Indian Affairs,* II, 704; McKinney to Gray, Feb. 27, 1827, in Carter, *Territorial Papers,* XX, 405–06.

44. Sarasin, et al., to Great War Chief, Jan. 28, 1827, LR, OIA, Caddo Agency, NA, Microcopy 234, Roll 31; McKinney to Gray, May 19, 1828, and Barbour to Sarasin, et al., Mar. 26, 1827, in Carter, *Territorial Papers,* XX, 684 and 433–34.

45. Gray to Barbour, Apr. 1, 1827, and Gray to Porter, Aug. 30, 1828, *ibid.,* 441–42 and 742–43; Gray to Barbour, June 30, 1828, LR, OIA, Red River Agency, NA, Microcopy 234, Roll 727.

46. Sarasin, et al., to Brother, Jan. 30, 1828, LR, OIA, Caddo Agency, NA, Microcopy 234, Roll 31; Wigton King to Sec. of War, Dec. 8, 1828, in Carter, *Territorial Papers,* XX, 807–808; Heckaton, et al., to Our Great Father, July 10, 1831, and Affidavit of Antoine Barraque, Sept. 28, 1831, LR, OIA, Neosho Agency, NA, Microcopy 234, Roll 530.

47. Izard to Sec. of War, June 29, 1827, in Carter, *Territorial Papers,* XX, 496–97; John Pope to Sec. of War, June 22, 1829, *ibid.,* XXI, 43–47.

48. Izard to Sec. of War, June 29, 1827, and McKinney to Gray, Aug. 18, 1828, *ibid.,* XX, 496–97 and 708n; McKinney to Sec. of War, Apr. 28, 1828, *ibid.,* XXI, 21.

49. Gray to Barbour, July 14, 1828, *ibid.,* XX, 702–708; Pope to Eaton, Mar.

15, 1830, and Jehiel Brooks to Eaton, Dec. 29, 1830, *ibid.*, XXI, 194–96 and 304–305.

50. Pope to Eaton, Sept. 9, 1830, *ibid.*, 269–71; S. S. Hamilton to Brooks, Sept. 24, 1830, LR, OIA, Red River Agency, NA, Microcopy 234, Roll 727.

51. Heckaton, et al., to Great War Chief, Oct. 15, 1831, LR, OIA, Neosho Agency, NA, Microcopy 234, Roll 530. See also Eaton to Heckaton, Jan. 4, 1831, LS, OIA, NA, Microcopy 21, Roll 7.

52. *Ibid.*; James Edington to Hugh L. White, Aug. 2, 1831, and Sevier to Lewis Cass, Dec. 16, 1831, in Carter, *Territorial Papers*, XXI, 352–57 and 439.

53. Heckaton, et al., to Our Great Father, July 10, 1831, LR, OIA, Neosho Agency, NA, Microcopy 234, Roll 530.

54. Rector to Sec. of War, June 16, 1831, and Heckaton to Col. Sevier, Sept. 26, 1831 and Oct. 5, 1831, *ibid.*; 38th Cong., 1st sess., *House Ex. Doc. 57*, 3–4.

55. Heckaton to Great War Chief, Oct. 15, 1831, LR, OIA, Neosho Agency, NA, Microcopy 234, Roll 530; Elbert Herring to Pope, Jan. 30, 1832, in Carter, *Territorial Papers*, XXI, 447–48.

56. Pope to Cass, Apr. 17, 1832, and Herring to Pope, Apr. 30, 1832, *ibid.*, 497–98 and 503–504.

57. Hannum to Herring, May 14, 1833, Hannum to Sir, Mar. 17, 1832, and Hannum to Respected Sir, May 13, 1832, LR, OIA, Neosho Agency, NA, Microcopy 234, Roll 530.

58. *Arkansas Gazette*, June 17, 1832.

59. *Ibid.*, May 15, 1833; Hannum to Respected Sir, May 13, 1833, LR, OIA, Neosho Agency, NA, Microcopy 234, Roll 530.

60. Minutes of a Council held with the Quapaw Indians at New Gascony, A.T., May 11 and 13, 1833, Documents Relating to Ratified and Un-ratified Treaties, Records of the Bureau of Indian Affairs, NA, T–494, Roll 3. For the printed version see 23rd Cong., 1st sess., *Senate Misc. Doc. 521*, IV, 724–26.

61. *Ibid.*

62. 7 U.S. Stat., 424–26

63. Hannum to W. L. Fulton, July 13, 1833, LR, OIA, Neosho Agency, NA, Microcopy 234, Roll 530.

64. *Ibid.*; Heckaton to President and Sec. of War, [1833], and Pope to Herring, Dec. 12, 1833, *ibid.*; D. Kurtz to Brooks, May 13, 1833, LS, OIA, NA, Microcopy 21, Roll 10; Schermerhorn to Herring, Mar. 1, 1834, LR, OIA, Western Superintendency, NA, Microcopy 234, Roll 92.

65. Brooks to Herring, July 10, 1833, and Tononzeka, et al., to Great War Chief, Aug. 31, 1833, LR, OIA, Caddo Agency, NA, Microcopy 234, Roll 31; Herring to Pope, Feb. 26, 1834, in Carter, *Territorial Papers*, XXI,

915; 38th Cong., 1st sess., *House Ex. Doc. 57*, 4.

66. Rector to Gibson, Sept. 16 and Nov. 10, 1834, and George Fletcher to Sir, Sept. 1, 1835, LR, Quapaw, Records of the Commissary General of Subsistence, Records of the Bureau of Indian Affairs, NA.

67. *Report of the Commissioner of Indian Affairs, 1839*, 473.

68. Herring to William Armstrong, Dec. 16, 1834, LS, OIA, NA, Microcopy 21, Roll 14.

69. Instructions for the government of John and Charles McClellan, Dec. 10, 1835, and Armstrong to Commissioner of Indian Affairs (hereinafter CIA), LR, OIA, Western Superintendency, NA, Microcopy 234, Roll 921; J. Brown to George Gibson, Dec. 26, 1835, LR, Quapaw, Records of the Commissary General of Subsistence, Records of the Bureau of Indian Affairs, NA. See also Records of the survey of 17 May 1836 by John and Charles McClellan, Case F, No. 129, Records of the General Land Office, NA.

70. *Report of the Commissioner of Indian Affairs, 1839*, 474; Thomas J. Farnham, *Travels in the Great Western Prairies*, 133.

71. *Ibid.*; Herring to Brooks, Feb. 13, 1834, LS, OIA, NA, Microcopy 21, Roll 12; Fletcher to Sir, Sept. 1, 1835, and Brown to Gibson, Dec. 26, 1835, LR, Quapaws, Records of the Commissary General of Subsistence, Records of the Bureau of Indian Affairs, NA; Mary Whatley Clarke, *Chief Bowles and the Texas Cherokees*, 63. That those Quapaws who remained in the vicinity of Red River represented one of the three traditional villages is deduced from an 1879 tribal roll in 41st Cong., 2nd sess., *House Ex. Doc. 127*, and from an 1873 roll that bears the date of April 12 and is filed in Quapaw-Quapaw Indians MSS, Indian Archives, Oklahoma Historical Society (hereinafter OHS).

72. J. M. Lucey, "The Catholic Church in Arkansas," in *Publications of the Arkansas Historical Association*, II, 432; Fred W. Allsopp, *Folklore of Romantic Arkansas*, I, 262–63 and 272–74.

Chapter V, The Dispossessed, 1839–65

1. Instructions for the government of John and Charles McClellan, Dec. 10, 1835, LR, OIA, Western Superintendency, NA, Microcopy 234, Roll 921.

2. *Report of the Commissioner of Indian Affairs, 1839*, 474; Heckaton, et al., to Great Father, Sept. 14, 1840, LR, OIA, Neosho Agency, NA, Microcopy 234, Roll 530.

3. Clarke, *Chief Bowles*, 60–61 and 63.

4. *Ibid.*, 94ff.

5. Grant Foreman, *Advancing the Frontier, 1830–1880*, 233.

6. Grant Foreman (ed.), *A Traveler in Indian Territory, The Journal of Ethan Allen Hitchcock, late Major-General in the United States Army,* 255–58.
7. Grant Foreman, *The Five Civilized Tribes,* 187, 122.
8. Grant Foreman (ed.), *A Pathfinder in the Southwest,* 51.
9. Muriel H. Wright and George Shirk, "Artist Möllhausen in Oklahoma—1853," *The Chronicles of Oklahoma,* Vol. XXXI (Winter, 1953–54), 417.
10. Grant Foreman (ed.), "The Journal of the Proceedings at Our First Treaty with the Wild Indians, 1835," *The Chronicles of Oklahoma,* Vol. XIV (Dec., 1936), 416.
11. Carolyn Thomas Foreman, "The Armstrongs of Indian Territory," *The Chronicles of Oklahoma,* Vol. XXXI (Winter, 1952–53), 427; A. M. Gibson, "An Indian Territory United Nations: The Creek Council of 1845," *The Chronicles of Oklahoma,* Vol. XXXIX (Winter, 1961–62), 400; Foreman, *The Five Civilized Tribes,* 289 and 298; Foreman, *Advancing the Frontier,* 201; and *Report of the Commissioner of Indian Affairs, 1843,* 422.
12. R. A. Callaway to William Armstrong, Feb. 6, 1840, LR, OIA, Neosho Agency, NA, Microcopy 234, Roll 530.
13. *Report of the Commissioner of Indian Affairs, 1840,* 315; James S. Raines to Sec. of War, Oct. 25, 1846, LR, OIA, Neosho Agency, NA, Microcopy 234, Roll 530.
14. *Report of the Commissioner of Indian Affairs, 1840,* 315, and *1851,* 403; John B. Luce to Armstrong, Sept. 30, 1842, LR, OIA, Neosho Agency, NA, Microcopy 234, Roll 530.
15. *Report of the Commissioner of Indian Affairs, 1845,* 527.
16. Petition of War te she, et al., Oct. 7, 1848, LR, OIA, Neosho Agency, NA, Microcopy 234, Roll 531.
17. Henry R. Schoolcraft, *History of the Indian Tribes of the United States,* I, 523ff.
18. Quapaw Annuity Role, Nov. 11, 1844, File No. 128, Special Files of the Office of Indian Affairs, NA, Microcopy 574, Roll 24.
19. *Ibid.*; Raines to Sec. of War, Oct. 25, 1846, LR, OIA, Neosho Agency, NA, Microcopy 234, Roll 530; *Report of the Commissioner of Indian Affairs, 1848,* 534; Schoolcraft, *History of the Indian Tribes,* I, 523; *Report of the Commissioner of Indian Affairs, 1852,* 395.
20. Office Memo [1842], LR, OIA, Neosho Agency, NA, Microcopy 234, Roll 530 (Frames 429–32) and Armstrong to T. H. Crawford, June 2, 1842, File No. 6, Special Files of the Office of Indian Affairs, NA, Microcopy 574, Roll 1.
21. *Report of the Commissioner of Indian Affairs, 1842,* 463; *1844,* 472; and *1845,* 528.

22. *Ibid.*, *1843*, 420; and *1846*, 277.

23. *Ibid.*, *1845*, 528.

24. *Ibid.*, *1842*, 463.

25. *Ibid.*, *1844*, 473.

26. See, for example, the Quapaw Annuity Roll, Nov. 11, 1844, File No. 128, Special Files of the Office of Indian Affairs, NA, Microcopy 574, Roll 24.

27. *Report of the Commissioner of Indian Affairs, 1848,* 534.

28. Schoolcraft, *History of the Indian Tribes,* I, 523ff.

29. Carolyn Thomas Foreman, "The Choctaw Academy," *The Chronicles of Oklahoma,* Vol. VIII (Mar., 1932), 81; Luce to Armstrong, Jan. 18, 1842, LR, OIA, Neosho Agency, NA, Microcopy 234, Roll 530.

30. Statement of Heckaton enclosed in Luce to Armstrong, Sept. 30, 1842, *ibid.*

31. *Ibid.*

32. *Report of the Commissioner of Indian Affairs, 1842,* 464.

33. D. B. Cummings to Sec. of War, Jan. 31, 1843, LR, OIA, Neosho Agency, NA, Microcopy 234, Roll 530.

34. Patterson to Barker, Sept. 18, 1843, *ibid.*

35. Barker to Crawford, Aug. 16, 1844, *ibid.*

36. Barker to Crawford, Oct. 2, 1844, *ibid.*

37. Crawford to Barker, Dec. 3, 1844, LS, OIA, NA, Microcopy 21, Roll 36.

38. Medill to Raines, May 26, 1847, *ibid.*, Roll 39.

39. Patterson to Raines, Apr. 13, 1847, LR, OIA, Schools, NA, Microcopy 234, Roll 783.

40. Patterson to Medill, Oct. 14, 1848, *ibid.*, Roll 784.

41. B. A. James to Medill, Sept. 27, 1848, LR, OIA, Neosho Agency, NA, Microcopy 234, Roll 531.

42. *Report of the Commissioner of Indian Affairs, 1848,* 536–37; and *1849,* 1117.

43. *Ibid.*, *1852*, 395.

44. Gilbert J. Garraghan, *The Jesuits of the Middle United States,* II, 568 and 568n; W. W. Graves, *Life and Letters of Rev. Father John Schoenmakers, S. J., Apostle to the Osages,* 154 and 187–88; and *Report of the Commissioner of Indian Affairs, 1853,* 378.

45. *Report of the Commissioner of Indian Affairs, 1853,* 380–81; and *1857,* 207–10.

46. Graves, *Life and Letters,* 250–51.

47. *Report of the Commissioner of Indian Affairs, 1857,* 206.

48. Dorn to Manypenny, Dec. 1, 1853, LR, OIA, Neosho Agency, NA, Microcopy 234, Roll 531.

49. Manypenny to Dorn, June 8, 1854, LS, OIA, NA, Microcopy 21, Roll 49; Dorn to Manypenny, Aug. 24, 1854, LR, OIA, Neosho Agency, NA,

Microcopy 234, Roll 531; and Treaty with the Quapaws at the Neosho Agency, Aug. 12, 1854, File No. 274–A, Ratified Indian Treaties, 1722–1869, NA, Microcopy 668, Roll 10.

50. R. M. McClellan to President, Dec. 20, 1854, LS, Records of the Indian Division, Office of the Secretary of the Interior, NA, Microcopy 606, Roll 2.

51. *Report of the Commissioner of Indian Affairs, 1855,* 174.

52. Dorn to G. W. Drennen, July 28, 1857, LR, OIA, Neosho Agency, NA, Microcopy 234, Roll 531.

53. A. B. Greenwood to Elias Rector, Nov. 17, 1859, LS, OIA, NA, Microcopy 21, Roll 62; and Dorn to Greenwood, Apr. 27, 1860, LR, OIA Neosho Agency, NA, Microcopy 234, Roll 531.

54. Dorn to Greenwood, Nov. 30, 1860, LR, OIA, Neosho Agency, NA, Microcopy 234, Roll 532.

55. Articles of Agreement, Jan. 21, 1861, *ibid.; Report of the Commissioner of Indian Affairs, 1860,* 120; and Greenwood to Dorn, Feb. 26, 1861, LS, OIA, NA, Microcopy 21, Roll 65.

56. Dorn to Greenwood, July 18, 1859, LR, OIA, Neosho Agency, NA, Microcopy 234, Roll 532.

57. W. David Baird, "Fort Smith and the Red Man," *The Arkansas Historical Quarterly,* Vol. XXX (Winter, 1971), 339–40.

58. Ohland Morton, "The Confederate States Government and the Five Civilized Tribes, Part II," *The Chronicles of Oklahoma,* Vol. XXXI (Autumn, 1953), 299 and 321.

59. Baird, "Fort Smith and the Red Man," 340–41.

60. Annie H. Abel, *The American Indian as Slaveholder and Secessionist,* 235.

61. The text of the treaty is found in *The War of Rebellion: A Compilation of the Official Records of the Union and Confederate Armies,* Series IV, Vol. I, 659–66. That War te she and Ki he cah te da signed the treaty instead of one chief identified as Wat-ti-shi nek Kat eh de is my own deduction. No such name appears in the record again, and it seems to be a corruption of the names of the two leaders then serving as chiefs.

62. Arrell M. Gibson, *Oklahoma: A History of Five Centuries,* 200–202.

63. *Report of the Commissioner of Indian Affairs, 1862,* 143; and W. G. Coffin to P. P. Elder, Aug. 1, 1862, LR, OIA, Neosho Agency, NA, Microcopy 234, Roll 533.

64. For a good account of the tragic situation in Kansas see Edmund J. Danziger, Jr., "The Office of Indian Affairs and the Problem of Civil War Indian Refugees in Kansas," *The Kansas Historical Quarterly,* Vol. XXXV (Autumn, 1969), 257–75.

65. *Ibid.,* 266–67; and Annie H. Abel, *The American Indian as a Participant in the Civil War,* 115.

66. Elder to Coffin, June 22, 1862, LR, OIA, Neosho Agency, NA, Microcopy 234, Roll 533.

67. *Ibid.; Report of the Commissioner of Indian Affairs, 1862,* 143; and Coffin to Elder, Aug. 1, 1862, LR, OIA, Neosho Agency, NA, Microcopy 234, Roll 533.

68. Elder to W. P. Dole, July 9, 1862, *ibid.*

69. *Report of the Commissioner of Indian Affairs, 1862,* 144.

70. B. B. Chapman, "An Interim Report on Site of the Battle of Round Mountain," *The Chronicles of Oklahoma,* Vol. XXVIII (Winter, 1950–51), 493.

71. Coffin to C. E. Mix, Sept. 19, 1863, LR, OIA, Neosho Agency, NA, Microcopy 234, Roll 533.

72. Elder to Dole, Aug. 10, 1863, *ibid.*

73. Fuller to Dole, Apr. 16, 1863, *ibid.*

74. 38th Cong., 1st sess., *House Ex. Doc. 57,* 2.

75. 38th Cong., 1st sess., *Senate Report 37.*

76. George C. Snow to D. N. Cooley, Dec. 11, 1865, LR, OIA, Neosho Agency, NA, Microcopy 234, Roll 533.

77. Dole to Coffin, Mar. 17, 1865, LS, OIA, NA, Microcopy 21, Roll 76.

78. *Report of the Commissioner of Indian Affairs, 1864,* 330–31.

79. C. C. Hutchinson to Snow, Apr. 12, 1865, LR, OIA, Neosho Agency, NA, Microcopy 234, Roll 533.

80. *Report of the Commissioners of Indian Affairs, 1865,* 292 and 294–95.

81. Ki he cah te da, et al., to Sec. of the Interior, Aug. 12 and Oct. 19, 1865, and James Harlan to Doctor, Sept. 4, 1865, LR, OIA, Neosho Agency, NA, Microcopy 234, Roll 533.

82. *Report of the Commissioner of Indian Affairs, 1865,* 481–83 and 497.

83. *Ibid.,* 485–87, 501, and 505–506.

84. *Ibid.,* 441.

Chapter VI, Peace and Accommodation, 1866–88

1. Edward E. Hill, *The Office of Indian Affairs, 1824–1880: Historical Sketches,* 145–46.

2. *Report of the Commissioner of Indian Affairs, 1867,* 324; Petition of the Quapaws, et al., Apr. 13, 1866, Snow to E. Sells, July 18, 1866, Snow to CIA, Nov. 30, 1866, and Mitchell to James Harlan, June 18, 1866, LR, OIA, Neosho Agency, NA, Microcopy 234, Roll 534.

3. Statement of Quapaw headmen, Jan. 10, 1867, and Snow to CIA, Feb. 21, 1867, *ibid.*

4. J. C. Blunt to N. G. Taylor, Dec. 15, 1868, *ibid.;* 41st Cong., 3rd sess., *House Report 39,* 51.

5. Treaty of Feb. 23, 1867, Documents Relating to Ratified and Unratified Treaties, Records of the Bureau of Indian Affairs (hereinafter RBIA), NA, T–494, Roll 7.
6. 15 U.S. Stat., 513–16. The specific areas ceded by the Quapaws, however, were not determined until sometime later.
7. *Ibid.*, 526–29; 41st Cong., 3rd sess., *House Report 39*, 52.
8. Taylor to J. H. Embry, Aug. 4, 1868, LS, OIA, NA, Microcopy 21, Roll 87; Petition of Delegates, Sept. 10, 1868, LR, OIA, Neosho Agency, NA. Microcopy 234, Roll 535.
9. Mitchell to James Worthan, Jan. 1, 1868, *ibid.*
10. Thomas Murphy to Taylor, Feb. 23, 1868, *ibid.; Report of the Commissioner of Indian Affairs, 1868*, 272.
11. Snow to Murphy, Mar. 17, 1869, LR, OIA, Neosho Agency, NA, Microcopy 234, Roll 535.
12. *Report of the Commissioner of Indian Affairs, 1869*, 380–82.
13. 42nd Cong., 2nd sess., *House Ex. Doc. 276*, 2; 17 U.S.Stat., 133.
14. *Report of the Commissioner of Indian Affairs, 1872*, 243; Cyrus Beede to H. W. Jones, Oct. 23, 1872, Quapaw-Quapaw Indians MSS, Indian Archives, OHS.
15. Blunt to Taylor, Jan. 19, 1869, LR, OIA Neosho Agency, NA, Microcopy 234, Roll 535.
16. Caldwell and Carter to J. D. Cox, Apr. 25, 1869, Claims of the Senecas, Shawnees, Mixed Seneca and Shawnee, and Quapaws Under the Treaty of Feb. [23], 1867, RBIA, NA.
17. 41st Cong., 3rd sess., *House Report 39*, 52 and vii.
18. William Nicholson, "A Tour of Indian Agencies in Kansas and the Indian Territory in 1870," *The Kansas Historical Quarterly*, Vol. III (Aug., 1934), 301–302; 41st Cong., 3rd sess., *House Report 39*, 51–55.
19. *Ibid.*, vi; Brunot to CIA, Oct. 24, 1870, LR, OIA, Neosho Agency, NA, Microcopy 234, Roll 536.
20. 41st Cong., 3rd sess., *House Report 39*, ix.
21. 41st Cong., 3rd sess., *Senate Ex. Doc. 26*, 21; *Report of the Commissioner of Indian Affairs, 1871*, 500; Muriel H. Wright, "A Report to the General Council of the Indian Territory Meeting at Okmulgee in 1873," *The Chronicles of Oklahoma*, Vol. XXXIV (Spring, 1956), 13; Journal of the 6th Annual Session, May 3–15, 1875, LR, OIA, Central Superintendency, NA, Microcopy 234, Roll 65.
22. E. P. Smith to Enoch Hoag, June 24, 1873, Quapaw-Quapaw Indian School MSS, Indian Archives, OHS.
23. Rayner Wickersham Kelsey, *Friends and the Indians, 1655–1917*, 202n; *Report of the Commissioner of Indian Affairs, 1872*, 243, and *1873*, 214; Lewis F. Hadley, "The Mystery of the Ponca Removal (in part at least) Explained," MSS dated Aug., 1882 (hereinafter "The Mystery of

the Ponca Removal"), Lewis F. Hadley Papers, National Anthropological Archives, Smithsonian Institution.

24. *Report of the Commissioner of Indian Affairs, 1874,* 299; Monthly
Report of the Quapaw Mission School, Jan., 1875, Quapaw-Quapaw
Indian School MSS, Indian Archives, OHS.

25. Jones to Hoag, Nov. 12, 1874, LR, OIA, Quapaw Agency, NA, Microcopy 234, Roll 704.

26. Monthly Report of the Quapaw Mission School, Jan., 1875, Quapaw-
Quapaw Indian School MSS, Indian Archives, OHS.

27. Monthly Report, Sept. 30, 1877, *ibid.*

28. James M. Hayworth to E. A. Hayt, Sept. 1, 1879, LR, OIA, Quapaw
Agency, NA, Microcopy 234, Roll 708.

29. Nicholson to J. Q. Smith, Oct. 19, 1876, *ibid.,* Roll 705.

30. W. H. Johnson to Maj. Doane, Feb. 23, 1895, Quapaw-Quapaw Indian
School MSS, Indian Archives, OHS; Avery, "The Social and Economic
History of the Quapaw Indians After 1833," 37.

31. For a listing of texts and supplies used by the school see Estimates for
school year, Sept. 1, 1881 to June 30, 1882, Box 437,719, Old Quapaw
(Seneca) Agency, Record Group 75, Federal Records Center, Fort Worth,
Texas (hereinafter FRC).

32. J. W. Powell, "Indian Linguistic Families of America North of Mexico,"
B.A.E. 7 *Ann. Report,* 112.

33. Monthly Report, Sept., 1887, Quapaw-Quapaw Indian School MSS, Indian Archives, OHS.

34. "The Mystery of the Ponca Removal," Lewis F. Hadley Papers, National
Anthropological Archives, Smithsonian Institution.

35. *Report of the Commissioner of Indian Affairs, 1873,* 214.

36. M. C. Wilkinson to E. P. Smith, Dec. 12, 1873, LR, OIA, Quapaw
Agency, NA, Microcopy 234, Roll 703; *Report of the Commissioner of
Indian Affairs, 1874,* 213 and 229.

37. *Ibid.,* 213 and 228.

38. John Hotel to CIA, Feb. 9, 1878, LR, OIA, Quapaw Agency, NA, Microcopy 234, Roll 705.

39. Hoag to Jones, Mar. 10, 1875, and Jones to Hoag, Mar. 13, 1875, *ibid.*;
Shanks to Smith, Mar. 20, 1875, and Hoag to Smith, Apr. 1, 1875, LR,
OIA, Central Superintendency, NA, Microcopy 234, Rolls 65 and 66.

40. Larrabee to CIA, Apr. 5, 1875, *ibid.,* Roll 66; *Report of the Commissioner of Indian Affairs, 1875,* 267.

41. See ledger containing copy of these contracts in Box 437,722, Old
Quapaw (Seneca) Agency, Record Group 75, FRC.

42. Shanks to Smith, July 10, 1875, LR, OIA, Central Superintendency, NA,
Microcopy 234, Roll 65. Shanks' 123 page final report to Commissioner
Smith is dated Aug. 5, 1875 and is found in *ibid.,* Roll 66.

43. Report of General Sheridan, Aug. 12, 1875, LR, OIA, Quapaw Agency, NA, Microcopy 234, Roll 704.
44. Larrabee to CIA, July 26, 1874, LR, OIA, Central Superintendency, NA, Microcopy 234, Roll 66; "The Mystery of the Ponca Removal," Lewis F. Hadley Papers, National Anthropological Archives, Smithsonian Institution.
45. *Report of the Commissioner of Indian Affairs, 1876*, 57.
46. See Chapter IV, note 71.
47. *Report of the Commissioner of Indian Affairs, 1876*, 57.
48. Hotel to CIA, Mar. 23, 1876, LR, OIA, Quapaw Agency, NA, Microcopy 234, Roll 704.
49. Smith to Hotel, June 3, 1876, LS, OIA, NA, Microcopy 21, Roll 130.
50. "The Mystery of the Ponca Removal," Lewis F. Hadley Papers, National Anthropological Archives, Smithsonian Institution.
51. Hotel, et al., to President, June 10, 1877, LR, OIA, Quapaw Agency, NA, Microcopy 234, Roll 706. See also *Report of the Commissioner of Indian Affairs, 1877*, 417–18.
52. Nicholson to Smith, Sept. 4, 1877, LR, OIA, Quapaw Agency, NA, Microcopy 234, Roll 705.
53. "The Mystery of the Ponca Removal," Lewis F. Hadley Papers, National Anthropological Archives, Smithsonian Institution.
54. Hotel, et al., to President, June 18, 1877, and Hotel to CIA, Aug. 3, 1877 and Feb. 9, 1878, LR, OIA, Quapaw Agency, NA, Microcopy 234, Roll 705.
55. *Report of the Commissioner of Indian Affairs, 1877*, 499.
56. "The Mystery of the Ponca Removal," Lewis F. Hadley Papers, National Anthropological Archives, Smithsonian Institution.
57. Hotel to CIA, Aug. 3, 1877 and Feb. 9, 1878, LR, OIA, Quapaw Agency, NA, Microcopy 234, Roll 705.
58. Nicholson to Smith, Sept. 4 and 27, 1877, *ibid.*
59. *Report of the Commissioner of Indian Affairs, 1878*, 64.
60. Jones to Hayt, Sept. 3, 1878, *ibid.*; Acting CIA to Jones, Sept. 19, 1878, Box 437,724, Old Quapaw (Seneca) Agency, Record Group 75, FRC.
61. E. J. Brooks to Laban Miles, Mar. 26, 1879, Quapaw-Quapaw Indians MSS, Indian Archives, OHS.
62. Proceedings of Council and Petition to CIA, July 11, 1882, *ibid.*
63. Henry M. Teller to CIA, Feb. 19, 1883, *ibid.*; B. B. Chapman, "Establishment of the Iowa Reservation," *The Chronicles of Oklahoma*, Vol. XXI (Dec., 1943), 374.
64. Minutes of the Quapaw Council, Oct. 17, 1889, Quapaw-Quapaw Indians MSS, Indian Archives, OHS.
65. Snow to Cooley, Dec. 11, 1865, LR, OIA, Neosho Agency, NA, Microcopy 234, Roll 533.

66. F. A. Walker to Hoag, Apr. 23, 1872, and Jones to Hayt, Apr. 1, 1879, LR, OIA, Quapaw Agency, NA, Microcopy 234, Roll 708; J.D.C. Atkins to J. V. Summers, Feb. 16, 1887, Quapaw-Quapaw Indians MSS, Indian Archives, OHS.

67. Towle to Asst. Adj. Gen., July 5, 1879, LR, OIA, Quapaw Agency, NA, Microcopy 234, Roll 710.

68. Report of the Commissioner of Indian Affairs, 1879, 181–82.

69. Hayworth to Hayt, May 10, 1879, LR, OIA, Quapaw Agency, NA, Microcopy 234, Roll 708; Report of the Commissioner of Indian Affairs, 1879, 184.

70. T. S. Kist to Hayt, Oct. 27, 1879 and Nov. 3, 1879, LR, OIA, Quapaw Agency, NA, Microcopy 234, Roll 709. For copies of agreement see Contract Ledger, Box 437,722, Old Quapaw (Seneca) Agency, Record Group 75, FRC.

71. Report of the Commissioner of Indian Affairs, 1881, 155.

72. Ibid., 1880, 210; B. D. Dyer to H. Price, May 23, 1881, Special Case No. 80, Land Division, RBIA, NA.

73. Dyer to Price, July 31, 1882, and Teller to CIA, Sept. 20, 1882, ibid.

74. Teller to CIA, Feb. 5, 1885, ibid.

75. Acting Sec. of the Interior to CIA, June 7, 1887, ibid.

76. Summers to Atkins, May 28, 1888, ibid. For a listing of permits issued in 1887 see Large Journal, Box 437,733, Old Quapaw (Seneca) Agency, Record Group 75, FRC.

77. Report of the Commissioner of Indian Affairs, 1868, 272.

78. J. E. McKeighan to Mitchell, Apr. 17, 1870, and A. C. Farnham to E. S. Parker, Nov. 11, 1870, LR, OIA, Neosho Agency, NA, Microcopy 234, Roll 536; Contract between Quapaw chiefs and MR Ft.S & G. RR, May 30, 1874, Quapaw-Quapaw Indians MSS, Indian Archives, OHS.

79. Mitchell to Hoag, July 5, 1870, and McKeighan to Mitchell, Sept. 7, 1870, LR, OIA, Neosho Agency, NA, Microcopy 234, Roll 536; Cady to Hoag, Sept. 23, 1870, LS, OIA, NA, Microcopy 21, Roll 98; Jones to Hoag, May 19, 1873, and Hoag to Jones, June 3, 1873, Quapaw-Quapaw Indians MSS, Indian Archives, OHS.

80. J. R. Hollowell to CIA, July 6, 1879, and Hayworth to Hayt, Sept. 20, 1879, LR, OIA, Quapaw Agency, NA, Microcopy 234, Roll 708.

81. Proclamation of Agent T. S. Kist, May 22, 1880, ibid., Roll 711.

82. Dyer to Trowbridge, Aug. 14, 1880, ibid.; Report of the Commissioner of Indian Affairs, 1882, 83.

83. Ibid., 81; E. J. Brooks to Kist, June 24, 1880, Quapaw-Quapaw Indians MSS, Indian Archives, OHS.

84. Various purchase orders, 1882, ibid.

85. Crowell to Dyer, Jan. 13, 1883, J. W. Preston to Dyer, 1883, and Quapaw payment roll, Aug. 14, 1883, ibid.

86. Statement of Crowell, [1884], *ibid.*
87. F. N. Moore to Teller, Mar. 18, 1884, L. C. Wilbur to Sec. of Interior, Mar. 28, 1884, and Richard Buck, et al., to Sec. of Interior, Apr. 3, 1884, Special Case No. 80, Land Division, RBIA, NA.
88. G. D. Williams to Price, Apr. 22, 1884, and W. M. Ridpath to Atkins, Oct. 3, 1885, *ibid.*
89. A. B. Upshaw to Summers, July 23, 1886, Quapaw-Quapaw Indians MSS, Indian Archives, OHS.
90. Upshaw to Summers, Nov. 30, 1887, and Atkins to Summers, Jan. 10, 1888, *ibid.*
91. L.C.Q. Lamar to CIA, May 16, 1885, *ibid.*
92. C. A. Diveley to CIA, Feb. 10, 1886, Special Case No. 80, Land Division, RBIA, NA.
93. *Report of the Commissioner of Indian Affairs, 1882,* 81.
94. *Ibid.,* 84.
95. *Ibid., 1883,* 80.
96. Upshaw to Summers, Aug. 24, 1888, Quapaw-Quapaw Indians MSS, Indian Archives, OHS.

Chapter VII, Accepting Allotment, 1888–96

1. Dyer to Trowbridge, May 22, 1880, LR, OIA, Quapaw Agency, NA, Microcopy 234, Roll 711; E. M. Marble to Dyer, Aug. 19, 1880, Quapaw-Quapaw Indians MSS, Indian Archives, OHS.
2. T. J. Morgan to Sec. of Interior, Apr. 19, 1890, Special Case 193, Land Division, RBIA, NA.
3. 7 U.S. Stat., 425.
4. Testimony of Alphonsus Vallier, Sept. 7, 1886, Quapaw-Quapaw Indians MSS, Indian Archives, OHS; Vallier Testimony, May 21, 1895 and A. Ray to Breckenridge, Apr. 20, 1887, Special Case 193, Land Division, RBIA, NA.
5. Frank Vallier to CIA, May, 1884, Special Case 80; Mathews, et al., adoption resolution, Jan. 1, 1885, Wade adoption resolution, July 20, 1886, W. C. Lykins to A. B. Upshaw, Oct. 16, 1886, and Testimony of John Smith, June 28, 1895, Special Case 193, Land Division, RBIA, NA.
6. Douthat, et al., adoption resolution, Apr. 12, 1887, and Summers to Atkins, Jan. 6, 1888, *ibid.*
7. Abner W. Abrams to George W. Lockwood, Mar. 4, 1889, *ibid.*
8. Acting CIA to T. J. Moore, Nov. 7, 1889, Quapaw-Quapaw Indians MSS, Indian Archives, OHS; Hedges adoption resolution, Oct. 11, 1887, Special File 193, Land Division, RBIA, NA.
9. Upshaw to Summers, Nov. 1, 1886, *ibid.*

10. Summers to Atkins, Dec. 10, 1887 and Jan. 6, 1888, *ibid.*

11. D. M. Browning to Sec. of Interior, Aug. 11, 1898, and Atkins to Summers, Mar. 27, 1888, *ibid.* See also Atkins to Summers, two letters of Mar. 27, 1888, Quapaw-Quapaw Indian MSS, Indian Archives, OHS.

12. Interview with Robert Whitebird, Quapaw, Oklahoma, Nov. 28–29, 1975.

13. Charley Quapaw, et al., to Sec. of Interior, June 9, 1888, and Alphonsus Vallier to Sec. of Interior, June 14, 1888, Special Case 193, Land Division, RBIA, NA.

14. Browning to George H. Lamar, Mar. 21, 1895, *ibid.* His support of the various parties is inferred from the Quapaw roll approved Mar. 15, 1889, and Summers to J. H. Oberly, Mar. 19, 1899, *ibid.*

15. *Ibid.*, and T. J. Morgan to Sec. of Interior, Nov. 19, 1890, *ibid.*

16. J. W. Noble to CIA, May 27, 1889, *ibid.* The Fishes were deleted, for example, but so too were four full bloods. On the other hand, Mrs. Abrams was added, although initially not listed because of an oversight.

17. Abrams to Lockwood, May 13, 1889, and Minutes of proceedings, Aug. 8, 1889, Records of the National Council, Robert Whitebird Collection, Quapaw, Oklahoma; Charley Quapaw and Alphonsus Vallier to R. B. Belt, June 29, 1889, Special Case 193, Land Division, RBIA, NA.

18. Abrams Testimony, Oct. 3, 1892, *ibid.*; 52nd Cong., 1st sess., *Senate Report 615*, 13 and 14.

19. Abrams and Lockwood, Mar. 4, 1889, Special Case 193, Land Division, RBIA, NA.

20. Quapaw and Vallier to Belt, June 29, 1889, and Morgan to Sec. of Interior, Apr. 19, 1890, *ibid.*

21. R. A. Gardner to CIA, Aug. 10, 1889, *ibid.*

22. Morgan to Sec. of Interior, Nov. 3, 1890, *ibid.*; Morgan to Moore, Oct. 30, 1889, Quapaw-Quapaw Indians MSS, Indian Archives, OHS. See also Appendix I.

23. Abrams, et al., to CIA, [Dec. 21, 1889], and Morgan to Sec. of Interior, Jan. 31, 1890 and Feb. 7, 1890, Special Case 193, Land Division, RBIA, NA.

24. 51st Cong., 1st sess., *House Report 559*, 1.

25. Morgan to Sec. of Interior, Jan. 31, 1890, Special Case 193, Land Division, RBIA, NA.

26. *Ibid.*; Morgan to Sec. of Interior, Feb. 7, 1890, Noble to CIA, Feb. 8, 1890, and Authorized Roll, Feb. 8, 1890, *ibid.* See Appendix II.

27. 51st Cong., 1st sess., *House Report 559*.

28. Minutes of proceedings, Mar. 25, 1890, Records of the National Council, Robert Whitebird Collection, Quapaw, Oklahoma.

29. 26 Stat. 998.

30. Minutes of proceedings, July 16, 1891, Records of the National Council,

Robert Whitebird Collection, Quapaw, Oklahoma.

31. *Report of the Commissioner of Indian Affairs, 1891,* 237.
32. Minutes of proceedings, Jan. 7, 1892, Records of the National Council, Robert Whitebird Collection, Quapaw, Oklahoma.
33. Council to Cooper, May 13, 1892, *ibid.*
34. Statement of funds remitted to T. J. Moore, Aug. 31, 1891, Quapaw-Quapaw Indians MSS, Indian Archives, OHS.
35. *Report of the Commissioner of Indian Affairs, 1891,* 237, and *1892,* 243.
36. See Morgan to Sec. of Interior, Apr. 9, 1890, and Browning to Sec. of Interior, Aug. 11, 1893, Special Case 193, Land Division, RBIA, NA.
37. Charley Quapaw, et al., to Belt, May 22, 1891, *ibid.;* Minutes of proceedings, June 22, 1891, Records of the National Council, Robert Whitebird Collection, Quapaw, Oklahoma.
38. Minutes of proceedings, June 8, 1892, *ibid.;* George Chandler to CIA, June 29, 1892, Special Case 193, Land Division, RBIA, NA.
39. Resolution of the Quapaw Council, July 19, 1892, *ibid.*
40. Gardner to Sir, Oct. 4, 1892, *ibid.*
41. Browning to Sec. of Interior, Aug. 11, 1893, *ibid.*
42. Testimony of A. W. Abrams, Oct. 3, 1892, *ibid.*
43. John M. Reynolds to CIA, Aug. 28, 1893, *ibid.*
44. John Charters to CIA, Mar. 10, 1890, *ibid.*
45. Testimony of Charters, Oct. 3, 1892, and Testimony of M. E. Douthat, [June, 1895], *ibid.*
46. Minutes of proceedings, Dec. 9, 1892, Records of the National Council, Robert Whitebird Collection, Quapaw, Oklahoma.
47. Receipts of Catherine Gordon, 1896, and M. E. Douthat, Dec. 26, 1894, *ibid.*
48. 24 U.S. Stat., 388–91.
49. 51st Cong., 2nd sess., *Congressional Record,* 2091; 51st Cong., 1st sess., *House Report 559;* and 51st Cong., 2nd sess., *House Report 3805.*
50. 52nd Cong., 1st sess., *Senate Report 615,* 16 and 24.
51. *Ibid.*
52. 52nd Cong., 1st sess., *House Report 2040.*
53. Abrams to Morgan, Jan. 9, 1893, SEN 52A–F13, Records of the United States Senate, NA.
54. Endorsement, *ibid.*
55. These fears were revealed in the hearings. See 52nd Cong., 1st sess., *Senate Report 615.*
56. 52nd Cong., 2nd sess., *House Report 2256.*
57. *Report of the Commissioner of Indian Affairs, 1892,* 243–44; 52nd Cong., 1st sess., *Senate Report 615,* 14 and 22.
58. Minutes of proceedings, Mar. 23 and 30, 1893, Records of the National Council, Robert Whitebird Collection, Quapaw, Oklahoma; Browning

to Sec. of Interior, Apr. 9, 1894, SEN 54A–F12, Records of the United States Senate, NA.

59. Abrams, et al., to CIA, Apr. 6, 1893, Special Case 193, Land Division, RBIA, NA.

60. *Report of the Commissioner of Indian Affairs, 1893*, 141.

61. See a copy of the plat of the Quapaw reservation in Robert Whitebird Collection, Quapaw, Oklahoma.

62. *Report of the Commissioner of Indian Affairs, 1893*, 141; John Medicine, et al., to Sec. of Interior, Sept. 25, 1893, Special Case 193, Land Division, RBIA, NA.

63. See Abrams' testimony in 52nd Cong., 1st sess., *Senate Report 615*.

64. Minutes of proceedings, Mar. 15, 1894, Records of the National Council, Robert Whitebird Collection, Quapaw, Oklahoma.

65. Browning to Doan, Feb. 23, 1897, Quapaw-Quapaw Indian MSS, Indian Archives, OHS.

66. Families comprising this group included the Duschissins, Crosses, Locias, Cousattes, Dardennes, Davises, Bonos, Blaneys, Lewises, Mitchells, Sanderses and Fosters. See Browning to Doan, Nov. 13, 1894, Special Case 193, Land Division, RBIA, NA.

67. *Ibid.*; Morgan to Moore, Mar. 8, 1892, Quapaw-Quapaw Indians MSS, Indian Archives, OHS.

68. Browning to Doane, Nov. 13, 1894, Special Case 193, Land Division, RBIA, NA.

69. See Minutes of proceedings, July 19, 1892, Records of the National Council, Robert Whitebird Collection, Quapaw, Oklahoma.

70. Transcript of council meeting, Jan. 7, 1895, Special Case 193, Land Division, RBIA, NA.

71. Action of General Council, Jan. 12, 1895, *ibid.*

72. Browning to Sec. of Interior, Apr. 4, 1894, SEN 54A–F12, Records of the United States Senate, NA.

73. 53rd Cong., 3rd sess., *Congressional Record*, 1233.

74. 28 U.S. Stat., 907.

75. 53rd Cong., 3rd sess., *Congressional Record*, 2491.

76. Minutes of proceedings, Mar. 1895, Records of the National Council, Robert Whitebird Collection, Quapaw, Oklahoma.

77. 28 U.S. Stat., 907.

78. Browning to F. M. Cockrell, Apr. 7, 1896, SEN 54A–F12, Records of the United States Senate, NA.

79. A. W. Able to CIA, July 8 and 18, 1895, Special Case 193, Land Division, RBIA, NA.

80. *Ibid.*; Affidavit of Alphonsus Vallier, Nov. 22, 1895, *ibid.*

81. Lamar to Hoke Smith, Dec. 27, 1895, *ibid.*

82. Affidavit of Alphonsus Vallier, Nov. 22, 1895, and Browning to Lamar, Nov. 14, 1895, *ibid.*

83. Browning to Sec. of Interior, Feb. 11, 1896, *ibid.*

84. Peter Clabber, et al., to CIA, July 22, 1895, Aug. 19, 1895, and Dec. 31, 1895, and Samuel Crawford to Sec. of Interior, Feb. 8, 1896, Mar. 2 and 16, 1896, *ibid.*

85. John M. Reynolds to CIA, Mar. 18, 1896, *ibid.*

86. Browning to Doane, Feb. 23, 1897, Quapaw-Quapaw Indians MSS, Indian Archives, OHS.

Chapter VIII, On the White Man's Road, 1896–1921

1. Arrell M. Gibson, *Wilderness Bonanza*, 32–37.

2. *Ibid.*, 39–40; Twelfth Annual Report, Miami Field Office, U. S. Geological Survey, June 30, 1935, 54242–1935–013, Quapaw Agency, Central Classified Files, 1907–39 (hereinafter CCF), RBIA, NA.

3. Thomas P. Smith to Doane, Oct. 7, 1895, 52960–1918–324, *ibid.*

4. Browning to Sec. of Interior, Dec. 18, 1896, *ibid.*

5. Abrams and Crawford, "Before the Honorable The Secretary of the Interior in the matter of the Allotment and Leasing of Lands in the Quapaw Agency," Washington, D.C., Nov. 30, 1896, H. 22–7, Hargrett Pamphlet Collection, Gilcrease Institute, Tulsa, Oklahoma.

6. 30 U.S. Stat., 72.

7. Smith to Doane, July 26, 1897, 52960–1918–324, Quapaw Agency, CCF, RBIA, NA.

8. Report of W. W. McConihe, May 15, 1909, 3889–1909–320, Seneca Agency, *ibid.*

9. Wm. Grimes to Paul Ewert, Jan. 23, 1909, 1776–1909–320, *ibid.*; Records of the Quapaw Mining and Milling Company, Small Ledger, Robert Whitebird Collection, Quapaw, Oklahoma.

10. See Large Ledger, n.d., *ibid.*

11. See the terms of Minnie Captain Quapaw lease, *ibid.*; Ira C. Deaver to CIA, Aug. 29, 1908, 53398–1908–311, Seneca Agency, CCF, RBIA, NA.

12. Ewert to Attorney General, Jan. 11, 1909, 1776–1909–320, *ibid.*

13. Ewert to Sec. of Interior, Feb. 8, 1917, and Asst. Sec. of Interior to Attorney General, Sept. 26, 1919, 46212–1915–322, *ibid.*

14. Ewert to Sec. of Interior, Feb. 8, 1917, *ibid.*

15. Ewert to Sec. of Interior, Mar. 30, 1910, 91127–1909–320, *ibid.*

16. *Ibid.*; E. B. Linnen to Sec. of Interior, Mar. 26, 1910, *ibid.*

17. Deaver to CIA, Mar. 29, 1908, 53398–1908–311, *ibid.*

18. Sec. of Interior to John H. Stephens, Apr. 12, 1912, 12610–1912–306,

and Ewert to Attorney General, Dec. 1, 1909, 97475–1909–032, *ibid.*

19. *Ibid.*

20. Rowsey to Springer, Jan. 12, 1900, William A. Springer MSS, Chicago Historical Society, Chicago, Illinois.

21. *Ibid.*, Feb. 6, 1900.

22. *Ibid.*, Feb. 12, 1900.

23. R. G. Valentine to CIA, May 16, 1907, 90827–1907–320, Seneca Agency, CCF, RBIA, NA.

24. Memo of J.R.W., [June, 1907], *ibid.*

25. H. B. Durant to J. G. Wright, Nov. 27, 1906, 52960–1918–324, Quapaw Agency, *ibid.*

26. C. F. Larrabee to Wright, Nov. 21, 1907, *ibid.*, and Peter Clabber to F. E. Leupp, Mar. 2, 1907, 90827–1907–320, Seneca Agency, *ibid.*

27. Memo of J.F.M., Apr. 7, 190[7], *ibid.*; Leupp to Sec. of Interior, Mar. 27, 1907, 52960–1918–324, Quapaw Agency, *ibid.* In Moore v. Girten (82 S.W. 848) the court declared: "There is no prohibition against the Quapaw Indians leasing their lands which they hold by patent."

28. Clabber to CIA, Mar. 2, 1907, 90827–1907–320, Seneca Agency, CCF, RBIA, NA.

29. See Quapaw Council to CIA, Mar. 8, 1907, *ibid.*

30. Horace B. Durant to CIA, May 10, 1907, *ibid.*

31. Memo of J.F.M., Apr. 7, 190[7], *ibid.*

32. Valentine to CIA, May 16, 1907, *ibid.*; Larrabee to Wright, Nov. 21, 1907, 52960–1918–324, Quapaw Agency, *ibid.*

33. *Ibid.*

34. Memo to J.R.W., [June, 1907], 90827–1907–320, Seneca Agency, *ibid.*

35. Deaver to CIA, Apr. 17, 1908, 26640–1908–352, *ibid.*

36. Larrabee to Sec. of Interior, May 6, 1908, 90827–1907–320, *ibid.*

37. Ewert to Attorney General, Dec. 1, 1909, 93457–1909–032, *ibid.*

38. Ewert to Goodrum, Mar. 26, 1909, 12656–1909–311, *ibid.*

39. See, for example, E. T. McCarthy to Joseph L. Bristow, Sept. 25, 1909, 40233–1909–311, *ibid.*

40. Ewert to Sec. of Interior, Mar. 30, 1910, 91127–1909–320, *ibid.*

41. 162 Fed. Reporter 817; Charles Bonaparte to Sec. of Interior, Oct. 5, 1908, 67948–1908–175.2, Seneca Agency, CCF, RBIA, NA.

42. Ewert to Attorney General, Jan. 5, 1909, 4172–1909–311, Ewert to CIA, Feb. 13, 1909, and Ewert to Goodrum, Mar. 26, 1909, 12656–1909–311, *ibid.*

43. Ewert to Sec. of Interior, Mar. 23, 1910, 91127–1909–320, *ibid.*

44. 181 Fed. Reporter 847; 114 C.C.A. 160.

45. 237 U.S. Reports 74–84.

46. Ewert to Sec. of Interior, Feb. 8, 1917, 46212–1915–322, pt. 1, Seneca Agency, CCF, RBIA, NA.

47. Cato Sells to Ewert, Mar. 13, 1917, *ibid.*
48. Asst. Sec. of Interior to Attorney General, Sept. 26, 1919, *ibid.* See also 261 Fed. Reporter 523, and 284 Fed. Reporter 86.
49. Ewert believed, for instance, that the Miami Royalty Company which had paid the royalties to Moore should have been sued as well. See Ewert to Sec. of Interior, Feb. 8, 1917, 46212–1915–322, pt. 1, Seneca Agency, CCF, RBIA, NA.
50. This particular law was known as the "non-competent act." See Acting CIA to J. J. Bulger, June 13, 1908, 38308–1908–311, *ibid.*, and 34 U.S. Stat., 1013–18.
51. As an example see the case of Sarah E. Gordon as reflected in Larrabee to Sec. of Interior, July 25, 1908, 37835–1908–311, Seneca Agency, CCF, RBIA, NA.
52. Garfield to Moses E. Clapp, Mar., 1908, 14577–1908–316, *ibid.* See also 60th Cong., 1st sess., *House Report 1229.*
53. 35 U.S. Stat., 751.
54. For the 1902 act see 32 U.S. Stat., 245–75; for an example of the sale of heirship lands consider "Indian Lands Listed For Sale," Nov. 4, 1909, 94883–1909–310, Seneca Agency, CCF, RBIA, NA.
55. "Regulations Governing Removal of Restrictions on Allotments on the Quapaw Agency, Oklahoma," Washington, D.C., Mar. 15, 1909, 25625–1910–013, *ibid.*
56. Ewert to CIA, Jan. 3, 1913, 24173–1911–127, *ibid.*
57. C. F. Hauke to J. F. Murphy, Aug. 9, 1910, 66735–1910–127, *ibid.*
58. C. L. Ellis, et al., to CIA, Jan. 20, 1911, 98602–1910–127, pt. 1, *ibid.*
59. For examples of those that did and the procedure followed see the case of Effie Imbeau Crane, 63579–1910–306, and that of Jessie May Cousatte Gilmore, 6939–1914–306, *ibid.*
60. Ewert to Sec. of Interior, Aug. 5, 1910, 66735–1910–127, *ibid.*
61. C. L. Ellis to CIA, Jan. 17, 1911, 5210–1911–306, *ibid.*
62. Hauke to Ewert, Feb. 28, 1913, 24683–1913–350, *ibid.* For the act of Congress see 36 Stat. 855.
63. Sec. of Interior to Robert J. Gamble, Apr. 25, 1912, 18410–1912–013, and Hauke to Clabber, Apr. 18, 1912, 34383–1912–306, Seneca Agency, CCF, RBIA, NA.
64. 37 U.S. Stat., 678.
65. 224 U.S. Reports 665.
66. Franklin K. Lane to Henry F. Ashurst, Feb. 1, 1916, 98898–1911–313, Seneca Agency, CCF, RBIA, NA.
67. S. Lyman Tyler, *A History of Indian Policy*, 109–10.
68. For examples of two who did see the cases of Samuel A. Douthit, 42917–1910–306, Seneca Agency, CCF, RBIA, NA, and of Ira W. Cousatte as reflected in Hauke to Sec. of Interior, May 24, 1916, 5–1,

Part 5, Land Sales Allotted, Quapaw Agency, CCF, Office of the Secretary, Records of the Department of the Interior, NA. Both Douthit
and Cousatte were of little Indian blood and the lands involved were
not inherited.

69. Sells to Carl F. Mayer, Aug. 19, 1919, 48177–1919–312, Seneca
Agency, CCF, RBIA, NA.

70. Mayer to Sells, May 12, 1920, and J. R. Wise and Mayer to CIA, Feb. 8,
1921, 41545–1917–013, *ibid.*

71. Mayer to Carl F. Hayden, May 16, 1920, *ibid.*

72. Synopsis of Report by Messrs. E. B. Linnen and J. W. Howell, [Jan.,
1918], and Affidavit of Charles Goodeagle, Jan. 30,ᵇ 1918, 11530–
1917–320, pt. 2, and Deaver to CIA, Jan. 16, 1918, and Sells to Sec. of
Interior, May 27, 1918, 6332–1918–127, pt. 1, *ibid.*

73. Report of Inspector H. G. Wilson, Aug. 5, 1916, 90314–1916–320, *ibid.*

74. See, for example, the cases of Jessie Daylight, a minor, in 52770–
1916–127, and Joseph Greenback, a full blood, in 109509–1916–320,
ibid.

75. Mayer to CIA, Oct. 31, 1919, and E. B. Meritt to Mayer, June 17, 1920,
99493–1919–312, *ibid.* On the other hand, Leroy Redeagle, a full
blood, was issued a certificate of competency even though his allotment was in the mining district. See the records in this case in
113704–1917–127, *ibid.*

76. Joseph W. Howell to Sells, June 18, 1919, 5271–1918–324, and Charles
Burke to Ray McNaughton, Dec. 19, 1925, 5808–1918–127, pt. 6, *ibid.*

77. Burke to Sec. of Interior, Aug. 15, 1923, 5271–1918–324, pt. 9, *ibid.*
There are ten linear feet of material in this file.

78. S. G. Hopkins to Attorney General, Mar. 19, 1918, 5808–1918–127, pt.
1, and Ewert to Sec. of Interior, Feb. 8, 1917, 46212–1915–322, pt. 1,
ibid.

79. Burke to Sec. of Interior, Jan. 25, 1922, 81432–1920–324, pt. 1, *ibid.*

80. Meritt to Charles P. Lusk, July 30, 1914, 93818–1914–350, and Meritt
to Deaver, Sept. 15, 1914, 59224–1919–350, *ibid.*

81. 36 U.S. Stat., 855, and 37 Stat., 678.

82. Mayer to CIA, May 20, 1919, 32105–1919–353, Seneca Agency, CCF,
RBIA, NA.

83. Mayer to CIA, Sept. 4, 1919, 41545–1917–013, *ibid.*

84. Sells to R. L. Owens, Sept. 16, 1919, 75558–1919–154, *ibid.* See also
Sells to Sec. of Interior, July 18, 1919, 32105–1919–353, *ibid.,* and
Annual Narrative Report, 1921, Quapaw Agency, RBIA, NA.

85. Sells to Sec. of Interior, May 27, 1918, 6332–1918–127, pt. 1, Seneca
Agency, CCF, RBIA, NA.

86. For a copy of the bill see *ibid.,* pt. 6.

87. Memoranda of Decision... , June 17, 1922, *ibid.*, pt. 7.
88. Leslie Lyons to Attorney General, Oct. 8, 1923, *ibid.;* and 292 Fed. Report 935.
89. Asst. Attorney General to Sec. of Interior, Dec. 10, 1923 and Feb. 14, 1924, 6332–1918–127, pt. 1, Seneca Agency, CCF, RBIA, NA.
90. See page 167.
91. Sells to Sec. of Interior, Aug. 10, 1918, 5808–1918–127, pt. 1, Seneca Agency, CCF, RBIA, NA; Decree in the case of Apple and Harris v. Robinson, et al., May 22, 1920, and Howell to Sells, May 24, 1920, *ibid.*, pt. 2.
92. See page 167.
93. Vern E. Thompson to CIA, July 16, 1923, 5271–1918–234, pt. 18, Seneca Agency, CCF, RBIA, NA.
94. Burke to Sec. of Interior, Aug. 15, 1923, *ibid.*
95. 22 Fed. Reporter (2nd) 81.
96. 226 U.S. Reports 623.
97. Howell to C. J. Rhoads, Aug. 14, 1929, 5271–1918–324, pt.15, Seneca Agency, CCF, RBIA, NA.
98. Howell to Sells, June 18, 1919, 5271–1918–324, *ibid.*
99. Sells to Snyder, May 10, 1920, 41545–1917–013, *ibid.*
100. Mayer to Sells, May 12, 1920, *ibid.*
101. Wise and Mayer to CIA, Jan. 8, 1921, *ibid.*
102. Hauke to Clabber, Apr. 18, 1912, 34333–1912–306, *ibid.*
103. Clabber, et al., to CIA, May 3, 1917, 62392–1917–313, *ibid.*
104. Act of the Council, Mar. 18, 1919, 41545–1917–013, *ibid.*
105. Mayer to CIA, June 18, 1920, *ibid.*
106. Mayer to Sells, May 12, 1920, *ibid.*
107. Mayer to CIA, Nov. 18, 1920, *ibid.*
108. See enclosure in Mayer to CIA, June 18, 1920, *ibid.*
109. *Ibid.*
110. 66th Cong., 3rd sess., House of Representatives, *Allotments of the Quapaw Indians: Hearings before the Committee on Indian Affairs on H.R. 15780*, Jan. 22, 1921, 4–5.
111. *Ibid.*, 13.
112. 66th Cong., 3rd sess., *House Report 1225.*
113. 41 U.S. Stat., 1225–1249.

Chapter IX, The Poor Rich Quapaws

1. Gertrude C. Bonnin, et al., *Oklahoma's Poor Rich Indians;* and 68th Cong., 1st sess., House of Representatives, *Investigation of the Ad-*

ministration of Indian Affairs in Oklahoma: Hearings before a Sub-committee of the Committee on Indian Affairs on H. Res. 348, Nov. to Dec., 1924.

2. Joe C. Jackson, "Schools Among the Minor Tribes in Indian Territory," *The Chronicles of Oklahoma*, Vol. XXXII (Spring, 1954), 65 and 65n; Samuel J. Crawford, *Before the Department of Justice In Re Sale of Quapaw Lands to Walter T. Apple: Brief and Argument*, 10–11.

3. Ketcham to J. C. Grogan, Feb. 20, 1913, St. Mary's MSS, Bureau of Catholic Missions, Washington, D.C.; *Report of the Commissioner of Indian Affairs, 1894*, 139; Sister Mary Urban Kehoe, "The Educational Activities of Distinguished Catholic Missionaries Among the Five Civilized Tribes," *The Chronicles of Oklahoma*, Vol. XXIV (Summer, 1946), 174.

4. Velma Nieberding, "St. Mary's of the Quapaws," *The Chronicles of Oklahoma*, Vol. XXXI (Spring, 1953), 7 and 9; "The Quapaws," *The Indian Sentinel* (1904–1905), 47.

5. *Ibid.*, 48; Report of the Catholic Indian Schools, Sept. 16, 1902 to Feb. 9, 1903; Dannis to Ketcham, Dec. 10, 1903, Nov. 3, 1903, and Sept. 18, 1904, St. Mary's MSS, Bureau of Catholic Missions, Washington, D.C.

6. Report of Edgar A. Allen, Mar. 19, 1910, 24056–1910–816.2, Seneca Agency, CCF, RBIA, NA.

7. Nieberding, "St. Mary's of the Quapaws," 12–13.

8. Dannis to Ketcham, Sept. 7, 1904, St. Mary's MSS, Bureau of Catholic Missions, Washington, D.C.

9. See, for example, Resolution of the Council, May 27, 1920, 47695–1920–803, Seneca Agency, CCF, RBIA, NA.

10. J. L. Suffecool to CIA, June 10, 1927, 19888–1926–803, Quapaw Agency, *ibid.*

11. George G. Kamp to William Hughes, May 30, 1927, St. Mary's MSS, Bureau of Catholic Missions, Washington, D.C.

12. Avery, "The Social and Economic History of the Quapaw Indians after 1833," 47.

13. Nieberding, "St. Mary's of the Quapaws," 5; "The Quapaws," *The Indian Sentinel* (1904–1905), 45.

14. "The Quapaws," *The Indian Sentinel* (1904–1905), 47.

15. *Ibid.*

16. *Report of the Commissioner of Indian Affairs, 1894*, 139.

17. Father Wagner to Hughes, Jan. 12, 1926, St. Mary's MSS, Bureau of Catholic Missions, Washington, D.C.

18. As quoted in Avery, "The Social and Economic History of the Quapaw Indians after 1833," 42.

19. John Joseph Mathews, *The Osages, Children of the Middle Waters*,

744; Weston La Barre, *The Peyote Cult, Yale University Publications in Anthropology, No. 19,* 155–56.

20. *Ibid.,* plate 2 notes and 157–58.
21. Wilcomb E. Washburn, *The Indian in America,* 225.
22. List of Quapaws Receiving Money from KC Ft.S & M RR, May 29, 1896, Robert Whitebird Collection, Quapaw, Oklahoma.
23. 31 U.S. Stat., 1067; 32 U.S. Stat., 997.
24. These debts apparently stemmed from fees due Samuel J. Crawford. At any rate, the 240 acres ended up in his name. Personal interview with Robert Whitebird, Nov. 29, 1975.
25. Crawford, *Before the Department of Justice;* Larrabee to Sec. of Interior, June 5, 1908, General, Per Capita Payment, Quapaw Agency, CCF, 1907–36, Records of the Office of the Sec. of the Interior, NA; Quapaw Payment Roll, May 24, 1908, Box 351,868, Quapaw Indian Sub-Agency, Record Group 75, FRC.
26. Program of the Quapaw Agency for 1944, Box 351,090, *ibid.;* Twelfth Annual Report, Miami, Oklahoma, Field Office, Geological Survey, July 20, 1935, 54247–1935–031, Quapaw Agency, CCF, RBIA, NA.
27. *Ibid.;* Annual Narrative Report, 1925, Quapaw Agency, RBIA, NA.
28. Report of R. L. Spalsbury, Sept. 15, 1926, 43647–1926–150, Quapaw Agency, CCF, RBIA, NA.
29. Individual Indian Account Ledgers, 1918–25, 28–5–25 and 28–25–27, Quapaw Indian Agency Records, and Andrews to CIA, July 30, 1941, Individual Indian Money File, Box 414,000, Miami Agency Records, Record Group 75, FRC.
30. Report of Charles H. Berry, Sept. 27, 1932, 47305–1932–150, Quapaw Agency, CCF, RBIA, NA.
31. Spalsbury to CIA, Nov. 27, 1927, 51109–1927–150, and Mayer to CIA, Mar. 28, 1921 and Apr. 8, 1921, 25725–1921–314, *ibid.*
32. E. B. Meritt to Burke, May 24, 1921, and Burke to Mayer, July 30, 1921, *ibid.*
33. Flanery Memo, Dec. 1, 1925, 11625–1911–311, Seneca Agency, *ibid.;* Burke to Suffecool, July 19, 1927, Quapaw-Individual Moneys, 5–1, pt. 1, Quapaw Agency, CCF, 1907–36, Records of the Office of the Sec. of Interior, NA.
34. Andrews to CIA, Mar. 14, 1934, 44068–1938–225, and Apr. 10, 1930, 19778–1930–225, Quapaw Agency, CCF, RBIA, NA.
35. Suffecool to CIA, July 18, 1927, 35684–1927–225, *ibid.*
36. Budget Proposals, Dec. 15, 1927, 5601–1926–044, pt. 1, 33380–1925–225, pt. 1, and 1451–1925–225, *ibid.*
37. Budget Proposals, Dec. 15, 1927, 4490–1927–225 and 11338–1927–225, *ibid.*

38. Digest of Report of Messrs. Gillman and Smith, Oct. 25, 1929, 60709–1928–155, pt. 4, *ibid.*
39. Budget Proposal, Dec. 15, 1927, 46625–1927–225, pt. 1, and H. M. Gillman and Charles Smith to Burlew, Aug. 29, 1929, 60709–1928–155, pt. 1, *ibid.*
40. Andrews to CIA, Jan. 10, 1939, 62641–1928–225, *ibid.*
41. As an example of the latter, Mrs. Agnes Hoffman, the widow of Benjamin Quapaw, was permitted to use $30,000 to acquire a music store. See Budget Proposal, Dec. 15, 1927, 15892–1927–225 and file 51494–1927–225, *ibid.*
42. Berry to CIA, Sept. 27, 1932, 47305–1932–150, and Smith to Burlew, June 25, 1929, 60709–1928–155, pt. 2, *ibid.*
43. Smith to CIA, Apr. 2, 1929, *ibid.*, pt. 1.
44. See the blueprints and cost estimate for the tombstone of Benjamin Quapaw, Box 351,876, Quapaw Indian Sub-Agency, Record Group 75, FRC.
45. Andrews to CIA, Jan. 10, 1939, 62641–1928–225, Quapaw Agency, CCF, RBIA, NA.
46. Gillman and Smith to Burlew, Aug. 29, 1929, 60709–1928–155, pt. 1, *ibid.*
47. Budget Proposal, Dec. 15, 1927, 46625–1927–225, pt. 1, *ibid.*
48. Budget Proposal, Dec. 15, 1927, 5601–1926–044, pt. 1, *ibid.*
49. Digest of Report of Messrs. Gillman and Smith, Oct. 25, 1929, 66709–1928–155, pt. 4, *ibid.*
50. *Ibid.*; C. J. Rhodes to Suffecool, Aug. 21, 1930, *ibid.*
51. Suffecool to CIA, Dec. 4, 1929, 46625–1927–225, pt. 1–4, *ibid.*
52. Chandler to CIA, Nov. 11, 1922, 27152–1923–100, *ibid.*
53. Meritt to Suffecool, Dec. 2, 1927, Quapaw-Individual Moneys, 5–1, pt. 1, CCF, 1907–36, Records of the Office of the Sec. of the Interior, NA.
54. Griffin, et al., to John Collier, Aug. 28, 1933, and Collier to Andrews, Feb. 20, 1934, 40457–1933–253, Quapaw Agency, CCF, RBIA, NA.
55. Collier to Miami, Oklahoma, Chamber of Commerce, Feb. 27, 1942, *ibid.* For a list of unauthorized debts incurred in 1943 see Box 414,009, Miami Agency, Record Group 75, FRC.
56. W. H. Zimmerman to Andrews, Dec. 12, 1938, 54624–1933–225, Quapaw Agency, CCF, RBIA, NA.
57. Andrews to CIA, Jan. 23, 1939 and May 11, 1939, *ibid.*
58. Andrews to CIA, Dec. 22, 1938, *ibid.* See copies of these statements in Box 414,047, Miami Agency, Record Group 75, FRC.
59. Budgets were required of those who had accounts at the agency until after 1961, for example. A. C. Bidwell to T. J. Perry, Sept. 6, 1961, Mary Wilson file, Box 414,000, *ibid.*
60. Andrews could disburse $500 at one time but no more than $2,000

during any one year from a single account. Rhodes to Andrews, Dec. 20, 1932, Quapaw-Individual Moneys, 5–1, pt. 2, CCF, 1907–36, Records of the Office of the Sec. of the Interior, NA.

61. Harry Crawfish file, Box 414,047, Miami Agency, Record Group 75, FRC.

62. Andrews to CIA, Jan. 10, 1939, 62641–1929–225, Quapaw Agency, CCF, RBIA, NA.

63. Tabulation of individual accounts, Sept., 1963, Box 414,036, Miami Agency, Record Group 75, FRC.

64. Avery, "The Social and Economic History of the Quapaw Indians after 1833," 72–78; Suffecool to CIA, Nov. 9, 1926, 1451–1925–225, Quapaw Agency, CCF, RBIA, NA.

65. See General File on Divorces, Box 351,910, Quapaw Indian Sub-Agency, Record Group 75, FRC.

66. Sells to Sec. of Interior Oct. 13, 1920, 60165–1920–130, M. van Siclen to R. V. Ageton, July 9, 1923, 29863–1921–324, Smith to Burke, Nov. 29 to Dec. 2, 1928, 2971–1929–150, Walter S. Stevens Report, Jan. 9–13, 1936, 4088–1936–150, Charles H. Berry Report, Sept. 27, 1932, 47305–1932–150, and Miriam E. Keenan Report, July 11, 1942, 62641–1928–225, Quapaw Agency, CCF, RBIA, NA.

67. Mayer to CIA, Feb. 18, 1921, 7849–1921–324, pt. 1, *ibid.*

68. Burke to Sec. of Interior, May 20, 1921, *ibid.*

69. A. C. Wallace to Meritt, June 22, 1921, *ibid.*

70. Chandler to CIA, Feb. 27, 1922, *ibid.*, pt. 2.

71. Statement of decision of Commissioner of Indian Affairs, Mar. 4, 1922, and Burke to Sec. of Interior, Mar. 20, 1922, *ibid.*

72. Transcript of testimony before the Quapaw Leasing Commission, May 26, 1922, *ibid.*, pt. 13.

73. Albert B. Fall to CIA, June 19, 1922, Quapaw Leases, General, 5–1, pt. 1, CCF, 1907–36, Records of the Office of the Sec. of the Interior, NA.

74. Comparison of bids, July 22, 1922, 7849–1921–324, pt. 16, Quapaw Agency, CCF, RBIA, NA.

75. Burke to Sec. of Interior, July 27, 1922, *ibid.*, pt. 19.

76. Wallace to Burke, Aug. 19, 1922, *ibid.*, pt. 18.

77. Harry Crawfish, et al., to Sec. of Interior, Aug. 17, 1922, and Hastings and Durant to Sec. of Interior, Aug. 23, 1922, *ibid.*, pt. 19.

78. Chandler to CIA, Aug. 19, 1922, and Fall to CIA, Sept. 6, 1922, *ibid.*

79. 68th Cong., 2nd sess., *House Report 1422.*

80. Suffecool to Burke, Aug. 6, 1927, 82002–1922–225, Quapaw Agency, CCF, RBIA, NA.

81. Suffecool to CIA, Sept. 28, 1926, and C. B. Ames to The President, Mar. 11, 1927, 7849–1921–324, pt. 24, *ibid.*

82. 28 Fed. Reporter (2nd) 200; 40 Fed. Reporter (2nd) 479; and 282 U.S.

Reports 844. Ironically, Eagle-Picher, without admitting any liability, settled three similar suits out of court for $65,000. See Andrews to CIA, Nov. 19, 1931, 7849–1921–324, pt. 31, Quapaw Agency, CCF, RBIA, NA.

83. Memorandum Respecting Audit by Merton H. Cooper & Co., no date, *ibid.*, pt. 35; 71st Cong., 3rd sess., Senate, *Survey of Conditions of the Indians in the United States: Hearings Before a Subcommittee of the Committee on Indian Affairs Pursuant to S. Res. 79 and 308 (70th Cong.) and S. Res. 263 and 416 (71st Cong.)*, pt. 24, Nov. 17, 1930–Dec. 19, 1930, 1280ff.

84. Collier to Andrews, Aug. 18, 1933, 7849–1921–324, pt. 34, Quapaw Agency, CCF, RBIA, NA.

85. Clay C. Rogers to Harold L. Ickes, Dec. 29, 1933, *ibid.*; Memorandum of Nathan R. Margold, Aug. 21, 1934, 5271–1918–324, pt. 34, Seneca Agency, *ibid.*

86. Homer Cummings to Ickes, Jan. 26, 1935, 7849–1921–324, pt. 35, Quapaw Agency, *ibid.*

87. Memorandum of Zimmerman, May 25, 1936, *ibid.*

88. [Spurrier] to CIA, Sept. 2, 1936, *ibid.*

89. See copy of the printed petition filed with the court in *ibid.*, pt. 37.

90. George W. Potter to Ickes, Aug. 5, 1939, *ibid.*, pt. 38.

91. Andrews to CIA, Oct. 7, 1939 and Nov. 15, 1939, Lowery to Zimmerman, Nov. 28, 1939, and Andrews to Zimmerman, Dec. 5, 1939, *ibid.*, pt. 38.

92. Oscar L. Chapman to The Eagle-Picher Lead Company, Nov. 21, 1939, and Attorney General to Ickes, Feb. 12, 1940, *ibid.*

93. Memorandum to F. L. Kirgis to Sec. of Interior, Apr. 19, 1940, *ibid.*

94. Lowery to Taft, et al., Apr. 10, 1940, *ibid.*

95. Collier Memo to Sec. Ickes, Nov. 13, 1941, *ibid.*, pt. 39.

96. Zimmerman to Andrews, Sept. 30, 1942, *ibid.*, pt. 40.

97. Suffecool to CIA, Mar. 1, 1926, 5808–1918–127, pt. 6, Seneca Agency, *ibid.* The practice was continued through the 1940's as well. See Box 414,068, Miami Agency, Record Group 75, FRC.

98. E. C. Finney to Sec. of Interior, May 7, 1923, Andrew W. Mellon to Sec. of Interior, May 21, 1923, Edwin Goodwin to Sec. of Interior, July 30, 1923, Finney to Attorney General, June 11, 1924, and Attorney General to Sec. of Interior, Mar. 20, 1925, 51988–1921–302, pt. 1, Quapaw Agency, CCF, RBIA, NA.

99. Andrews to CIA, Mar. 7, 1931 and Oct. 23, 1932, Chandler to Rhoads, July 6, 1932, *ibid.*, pt. 2.

100. Andrews to CIA, Apr. 14, 1934, 11949–1934–302, *ibid.*

101. For the decisions in the case of Superintendent of the Five Civilized Tribes v. The Commissioner of Internal Revenue see 75 Fed. Reporter (2nd) 183, and 295 U.S. Reports, 418. See also Chapman to Guy T. Hel-

vering, Jan. 15, 1940, and Helvering to Chapman, May 17, 1940, 11949–1934–302, Quapaw Agency, CCF, RBIA, NA.

102. See Landman v. Commissioner of Internal Revenue in 123 Fed. Reporter (2nd) 787, and 315 U.S. Reports 310.

103. Andrews to CIA, Apr. 13, 1939, 72959–1938–302, pt. 1, Quapaw Agency, CCF, RBIA, NA; Margold to Sec. of Interior, Dec. 23, 1940, and Houston Thompson to Andrews, May 24, 1940, *ibid.*, pt. 2. See also individual tabulations of taxes saved and attorney fees due, [1940], 29213–1917–302, 82021–1927–302, 82026–1927–302, and 82093–1939–302, *ibid.*

104. A. S. J. Shaw to Suffecool, Aug. 15, 1927, and Burke to Elmer Thomas, Mar. 21, 1928, 40292–1927–302, *ibid.*

105. H. L. McCracken to Andrews, Aug. 19, 1935, and Zimmerman to Andrews, Oct. 24, 1935, *ibid.*

106. 75th Cong., 1st sess., House of Representatives, *Tax Upon Lead and Zinc on Quapaw Indian Lands in the State of Oklahoma: Hearings Before the Committee on Indian Affairs on H.R. 5559*, Mar. 17, 1937.

107. 50 U.S. Stat., 68; J. C. Carmichael to Andrews, Oct. 8, 1941, and A. Francis Porta to N. A. Gray, June 22, 1942, 40292–1927–302, Quapaw Agency, CCF, RBIA, NA. Thompson received a fee of $2,500 for his assistance in getting the legislation passed. See Andrews to CIA, Nov. 30, 1937, 7679–1936–013, *ibid.*

108. In Beaver, et al., v. Short, the United States District Court for the Eastern District of Oklahoma ruled in July, 1924, that the inheritance laws of Oklahoma were inapplicable because the estates had accrued from income derived from restricted Indian land. See 300 Fed. Reporter 113. For the Supreme Court decision see 270 U.S. Reports 555.

109. See the case of Oklahoma Tax Commission v. United States in 131 Fed. Reporter (2nd) 635, and 319 U.S. Reports 598. Mr. Justice Murphy strongly dissented from the majority opinion written by Mr. Justice Black. He was joined by Justices Reed, Frankfurter, and Stone.

110. See copy of the decree, May 1, 1939, 22336–1938–302, Quapaw Agency, CCF, RBIA, NA.

111. Mayer to CIA, May 16, 1918, 57907–1918–310, Seneca Agency, *ibid.*

112. 66th Cong., 1st sess., *Senate Report 285* and *House Report 267*; 41 Stat. 355.

113. Quapaw Townsite Commission to CIA, May 27, 1920, 57907–1918–310, Seneca Agency, CCF, RBIA, NA.

114. Smith to Burke, Nov. 29–Dec. 2, 1928, 2971–1929–150, Quapaw Agency, *ibid.*

115. G. C. C. Lindquist to Samuel A. Elliot, Jan. 31, 1933, 9130–1933–150, *ibid.*

116. Andrews to CIA, Mar. 25, 1936, 32560–1924–150, pt. 1, *ibid.*

117. Whit Y. Mauzy to Attorney General, Dec. 1, 1937, and Resolution of the Quapaw Council, May 18, 1937, *ibid.*; Andrews to CIA, July 12, 1939, *ibid.*, pt. 2; and Andrews to CIA, Jan. 19, 1938, 31946–1925–175.5, *ibid.*

118. Andrews to CIA, Sept. 10, 1942, and Charles B. Wilson to CIA, Feb. 17, 1943, *ibid.*

119. See Kenneth R. Philp, "The Failure to Create a Red Atlantis: John Collier and the Controversy over the Wheeler-Howard Bill of 1934," *Indian-White Relations: A Persistent Paradox* (ed. by Jane F. Smith and Robert M. Kvasnicka), 171–200.

120. 73rd Cong., 2nd sess., House Representatives, *Readjustment of Indian Affairs: Hearings Before the Committee on Indian Affairs on H. R. 7902*, pt. 5, 1934, 157 (hereinafter *Hearings on H.R. 7902*).

121. *Muskogee Daily Phoenix*, Mar. 18, 1934.

122. *Ibid.*, Mar. 15, 1934.

123. For Thompson's testimony see 73rd Cong., 2nd sess., *Hearings on H. R. 7902*, pt. 5, 1934, 165.

124. *Miami Daily News-Record*, Mar. 25, 1934; Minutes of Meeting Held at Miami, Oklahoma, Mar. 24, 1934, Quapaw Agency Records, Record Group 75, FRC.

125. For Thompson's Apr. 9, 1934 testimony see 73rd Cong., 2nd sess., *Hearings on H. R. 7902*, pt. 5, 1934, 167–72. See also Thompson to Burton K. Wheeler, Apr 6, 1934, in 73rd Cong., 2nd sess., Senate, *To Grant to Indians Living Under Federal Tutelage the Freedom to Organize for Purposes of Local Self-Government and Economic Enterprises: Hearings Before the Committee on Indian Affairs on S. 2755 and S. 3645*, pt. 2, 1934, 533–34.

126. *Tulsa Tribune*, Mar. 3, 1934 and Mar. 27, 1934. See also *Muskogee Daily Phoenix*, Mar 25, 1934.

127. See my commentary in *Indian-White Relations*, 215–21.

128. 71st Cong., 3rd sess., Senate, *Survey of Conditions of the Indians in the United States: Hearings Before a Subcommittee of the Committee on Indian Affairs*, pt. 37, Oct. 14, 1937–May 12, 1939, 21356.

129. Status of Tribal Organizations in Oklahoma... , [1940], 19699–1936–259, Quapaw Agency, CCF, RBIA, NA.

130. See file 19737–1933–417, pts. 1 and 2, *ibid.*

131. Narrative Reports, 1934–41, Quapaw Agency, RBIA, NA.

132. B. L. Little to CIA, Oct. 28, 1939, 32068–1936–225, and Andrews to CIA, Mar. 1, 1943, 19699–1936–259, Quapaw Agency, CCF, RBIA, NA.

133. Zimmerman to Sec. of Interior, May 18, 1937, and Stewart to Daiker, July 22, 1937, 18958–1937–310, pt. 1, *ibid.*

134. Andrews to CIA, June 30, 1938, 41630–1938–310, *ibid.*

135. Cummings to Ickes, May 26, 1933, 51988–1921–302, pt. 3, *ibid.*

136. Griffin to CIA, Nov. 21, 1931, 65673–1931–306. *ibid.*

137. 76th Cong., 1st sess., Senate, *Extending Restrictions on Quapaw Indian Lands: Hearings Before the Committee on Indian Affairs on H. R. 3796,* June 19, 1939.

138. 76th Cong., 1st sess., *House Report 427;* 53 Stat. 7127.

Chapter X, The Last Three Decades

1. Petition of Protest, May 1, 1947, Quapaw Papers, Robert Whitebird Collection, Quapaw, Oklahoma; Thompson, et al., Application for Allowance of Attorney Fees, [1954], Box 32, Docket 14, Records of the Indian Claims Commission, NA.

2. Original Petition, filed Nov. 3, 1947, *ibid.* In calculating the area ceded in 1824, Thompson used the boundaries described in the published version of the Treaty of 1818 rather than in its manuscript form. Had he used the latter, the size of the ceded tract would have been considerably larger, as would have been the final judgment.

3. 128 Court of Claims Repts. 45.

4. Lloyd E. Roberts to J. A. Langston, Apr. 12, 1954, Box 32, Docket 14, Records of the Indian Claims Commission, NA.

5. *Annual Report of the Indian Claims Commission, 1969,* appendix 2.

6. 68 Stat. 801; 86th Cong., 1st sess., *House Report 593.*

7. Report of Meeting of Quapaw Tribe of Indians Held at Northeastern A. & M. College, Miami, Oklahoma, Aug. 19, 1956, Box 414,001, Miami Agency, Record Group 75, FRC. It was not true, however, that no written record existed of how the traditional chiefs were selected, nor was it true that Victor Griffin owed his position to two old women. Griffin had been elected on April 3, 1929, defeating Antoine Greenback for the office. See file labeled "Tribal Councilmen and Committees, Various Tribes," Box 351,868, Quapaw Indian Sub-Agency, *ibid.*

8. Report of Meeting of Quapaw Tribe of Indians Held at Northeastern A. & M. College, Miami, Oklahoma, Aug. 25, 1957, Box 414,001, Miami Agency, *ibid.*

9. *Ibid.,* Aug. 30, 1959; 86th Cong., 1st sess., *House Report 593* and *Senate Report 335;* 73 U.S. Stat., 221.

10. Report of Meeting of Quapaw Tribe of Indians Held at Northeastern A. & M. College, Miami, Oklahoma, July 30, 1960, Box 414,001, Miami Agency, Record Group 75, FRC.

11. Annual Report of the U.S. Geological Survey, Miami, Oklahoma, Office, 1960, *ibid.*

12. Statistical Reports, 1930, Quapaw Agency, RBIA, NA, and Annual Statistical Report, 1943, Box 414,010, Miami Agency, Record Group 75, FRC. In 1975 of an estimated population of 1,600, only 324 were one-fourth Quapaw blood or more. Of this number, forty-nine were one-half blood or more; only five were full bloods. Personal interview with Lloyd Buffalo, Quapaw, Oklahoma, Dec. 26, 1974.

13. Report of Meeting of Quapaw Tribe of Indians Held at Northeastern A. & M. College, Miami, Oklahoma, Aug. 30, 1959, Box 414,001, Miami Agency, Record Group 74, FRC.

14. *Ibid.*, Aug. 19, 1956.

15. Personal interview with Robert Whitebird, Quapaw, Oklahoma, Nov. 28–29, 1975. See also 84th Cong., 1st sess., House of Representatives, *Muskogee and Anadarko Area Indian Tribes, Oklahoma: Hearings Before the Subcommittee on Indian Affairs of the Committee on Interior and Insular Affairs pursuant to H. Res. 30*, Aug. 25 and 26, 1955, 47.

16. 91st Cong., 2nd sess., *House Report 91–1154*; 84 U.S. Stat., 325.

17. Report of Meeting of Quapaw Tribe of Indians Held at Northeastern A. & M. College, Miami, Oklahoma, Aug. 10, 1958, Box 414,001, Miami Agency, Record Group 75, FRC.

18. *Ibid.*; *Tulsa World*, June 28, 1970.

19. Mrs. Supernaw died in 1972, and with her death the naming ceremony ceased. She bequeathed her father's sacred eagle feather fan to Robert Whitebird, who since retiring from the tribal chairmanship in 1968 has become the Quapaw spiritual leader.

Appendix I

1. Special Case 193, 11815–1896, encl. 81–132, Land Division, Records of the Bureau of Indian Affairs, National Archives.

2. Added later by virtue of "Auth. 21191."

3. Name deleted by virtue of "Auth. 21191."

4. The four names comprising the Newman family were later added by virtue of "Auth. 21191."

5. Name originally deleted but then returned to the roll by virtue of "Auth. 21191."

6. *Ibid.*

7. *Ibid.*

8. *Ibid.*

9. Added later by virtue of "Auth. 20125."

10. Name deleted from roll by virtue of "Auth. 20125."
11. Name stricken from the roll, with no reference as to why.
12. Name added to the roll by virtue of "Auth. 20125."
13. Name stricken from the roll, with no reference as to why.

Appendix II

1. Special Case 193, Land Division, Records of the Bureau of Indian Affairs, National Archives.

BIBLIOGRAPHY

Manuscript Collections

Chicago, Illinois

Chicago Historical Society
  William M. Springer MSS

Columbia, South Carolina

South Carolina State Archives
  British Public Records Office Collection

Fort Worth, Texas

Federal Records Center (National Archives and Records Service)
  Record Group 75
    Miami Agency
    Old Quapaw Agency, Records of Indian Agents, 1871–99
    Old Quapaw (Seneca) Agency
    Quapaw Indian Agency
    Quapaw Indian Sub-Agency
    Seneca Indian School

Little Rock, Arkansas

Arkansas History Commission
  Gully Collection
  Izard Papers
  McAlmont-Vaughn Collection

Oklahoma City, Oklahoma

Oklahoma Historical Society, Indian Archives

Quapaw-Quapaw Indians MSS
Quapaw-Quapaw Indian Schools MSS

Philadelphia, Pennsylvania

American Philosophical Society, Manuscript Division
    Izard MSS

Quapaw, Oklahoma

Robert Whitebird
    Quapaw Indian Papers (Personal Collection)

St. Louis, Missouri

Missouri Historical Society, Manuscript Division
    Chouteau Papers
    William Clark MSS
    Forts Papers
    Indians Papers
    Sibley Papers
    Stewart MSS

Tulsa, Oklahoma

Gilcrease Institute of Art and American History, Library
    Hargrett Pamphlet Collection

Washington, D.C.

Bureau of Catholic Missions
    St. Mary's of the Quapaws MSS
National Archives
    Cartographic Archives Division
    General Records of the United States (Record Group 11)
        Ratified Indian Treaties, 1722–1865 (Microcopy 668)
    Records of the General Land Office (Record Group 49)
    Records of the Bureau of Indian Affairs (Record Group 75)
        Board of Indian Commissioners, Special Reports
        Claims of the Senecas, Shawnees, Mixed Senecas and Shawnees and
            Quapaws Under the Treaty of Feb. [23], 1867
        Documents Relating to the Negotiation of Ratified and Unratified
            Treaties with Various Tribes of Indians (Microcopy T–494)
        General Correspondence, 1907–39, Classified Files
            Quapaw Agency
            Seneca Agency

Inspector Reports, Special Files
Letters Received, 1824–81 (Microcopy 234)
  Arkansas Superintendency
  Caddo Agency
  Central Superintendency
  Cherokee Agency, West
  Choctaw Agency
  Neosho Agency
  Quapaw Agency
  Red River Agency
  Southern Superintendency
  Schools
  Western Superintendency
Letters Sent, 1824–81 (Microcopy 21)
Narrative Reports
  Quapaw Agency
  Seneca Agency
Records of the Land Division
  Ancient and Miscellaneous Surveys
  Bound Field Notes
  Reservations
  Special Cases
Special Files, 1807–1904 (Microcopy 574)
Special Series A
Statistical Reports, Quapaw Agency, 1923–30
Records of the Office of Indian Trade
  Arkansas Trading House, 1805–10
    Daybook
    Invoice Book
    Letterbook (Microcopy 142)
Records of the Commissary General of Subsistence
  Letters Received, Quapaw
Records of the Secretary of War Relating to Indian Affairs
  Letters Received, 1800–23 (Microcopy 271)
  Letters Sent, 1800–24 (Microcopy 15)
Records of the Indian Claims Commission (Record Group 279)
Records of the Office of the Secretary of the Interior (Record Group 48)
  Central Classified Files, 1907–36
    Quapaw Agency
    Seneca Agency
  Central Classified Files, 1937–53
    Quapaw Agency
Records of the United States Senate (Record Group 46)

Records of the War Department (Record Group 107)
  Letters Received by the Secretary of War, Main Series, 1801–1807
  (Microcopy 221)
Smithsonian Institution, National Anthropological Archives
  Lewis F. Hadley Papers

Urbana, Illinois

University of Illinois Library, Manuscript Division
  Spanish Archives (Translations)

Government Documents

Congressional

Congressional Record.
U.S. Congress, House Executive Documents:
  38th Cong., 1st sess., *No. 57.*
  40th Cong., 2nd sess., *No. 122.*
  41st Cong., 2nd sess., *No. 127.*
  42nd Cong., 2nd sess., *No. 276.*
  76th Cong., 1st sess., *No. 71.*
U.S. Congress, House Hearings:
  66th Cong., 3rd sess., *Allotments of the Quapaw Indians: Hearings Before the Committee on Indian Affairs on H. R. 15780.* Jan. 22, 1921.
  68th Cong., 1st sess., *Investigation of the Administration of Indian Affairs in Oklahoma: Hearings Before a Subcommittee of the Committee on Indian Affairs on H. Res. 348.* Nov. 11, 1924–Dec. 12, 1924.
  73rd Cong., 2nd sess., *Readjustment of Indian Affairs: Hearings Before the Committee on Indian Affairs on H. R. 7902.* 9 parts. 1934.
  74th Cong., 1st sess., *To Promote the General Welfare of the Indians of Oklahoma: Hearings Before the Committee on Indian Affairs on S. 2047.* Apr. 8–11, 1935.
  75th Cong., 1st sess., *Tax Upon Lead and Zinc on Quapaw Lands in the State of Oklahoma: Hearings Before the Committee on Indian Affairs on H. R. 5559.* Mar. 17, 1937.
  84th Cong., 1st sess., *Muskogee and Anadarko Area Indian Tribes, Oklahoma: Hearings Before the Subcommittee on Indian Affairs of the Committee on Interior and Insular Affairs pursuant to H. Res. 30.* Aug. 25 and 26, 1955.
U.S. Congress, House Miscellaneous Documents:
  52nd Cong., 1st sess., *No. 340, pt. 15.*

U.S. Congress, House Reports:
41st Cong., 3rd sess., *No. 39.*
42nd Cong., 3rd sess., *No. 98.*
51st Cong., 1st sess., *No. 559.*
51st Cong., 2nd sess., *No. 3805.*
52nd Cong., 1st sess., *No. 2040.*
52nd Cong., 2nd sess., *No. 2256.*
60th Cong., 1st sess., *No. 1229.*
66th Cong., 1st sess., *No. 267.*
66th Cong., 3rd sess., *No. 1225.*
68th Cong., 2nd sess., *No. 1422.*
76th Cong., 1st sess., *No. 427.*
82nd Cong., 2nd sess., *No. 2503.*
86th Cong., 1st sess., *No. 593.*
91st Cong., 2nd sess., *No. 91–1154.*

U.S. Congress, Senate Executive Documents:
32nd Cong., 2nd sess., *No. 54.*
41st Cong., 3rd sess., *No. 26.*

U. S. Congress, Senate Hearings:
71st Cong., 3rd sess., *Survey of Conditions of the Indians in the United States: Hearings Before a Subcommittee of the Committee on Indian Affairs pursuant to S. Res. 79 and 308 (70th Cong.) and S. Res. 263 and 416 (71st Cong.),* Part 24. Nov. 17, 1930–Dec. 19, 1930.

73rd Cong., 2nd sess., *To Grant to Indians Living Under Federal Tutelage the Freedom to Organize for Purposes of Local Self-Government and Economic Enterprises: Hearings Before the Committee on Indian Affairs on S. 2755 and S. 3645.* 2 parts. Feb. 27, 1934 and Apr. 26–May 17, 1934.

76th Cong., 1st sess., *Extending Restrictions on Quapaw Indian Lands: Hearings Before a Subcommittee of the Committee on Indian Affairs on H. R. 3796.* June 19, 1939.

76th Cong., 1st and 2nd sess., *Survey of Conditions of the Indians in the United States: Hearings Before a Subcommittee of the Committee on Indian Affairs pursuant to S. Res. 79 and 308 (70th Cong.) and subsequent Continuing Resolutions until the end of the Regular Session of the 76th Congress.* Part 37. Oct. 14, 1937–May 12, 1939.

U. S. Congress, Senate Miscellaneous Documents:
23rd Cong., 1st sess., *No. 512.*

U.S. Congress, Senate Reports:
52nd Cong., 1st sess., *No. 615.*
59th Cong., 2nd sess., *No. 5013,* Vol. I and II.
66th Cong., 1st sess., *No. 285.*
86th Cong., 1st sess., *No. 335.*

Other

American State Papers: Indian Affairs. Vol. II. Washington, 1834.
Carter, Clarence E., comp. and ed. *Territorial Papers of the United States.* Washington, 1936–54.
  The Territory of Arkansas, 1819–1836. Vols. XIX, XX, and XXI. 1953–54.
  The Territory of Louisiana–Missouri, 1803–1821. Vols. XIII, XIV, and XV. 1948–51.
Federal Reporter. First and Second Series.
Kappler, Charles J., comp. and ed. *Indian Affairs: Laws and Treaties.* 3 vols. Washington, 1904.
Report of the Commissioner of Indian Affairs, 1836–1906.
Report of the Indian Claims Commission, 1969.
United States Circuit Courts of Appeals Reports.
United States Court of Claims Reports.
United States Reports.
United States Statutes at Large.
War of Rebellion: A Compilation of the Official Records of the Union and Confederate Armies. Series IV, Vol. I. Washington, 1880–1900.

Special Sources

Buffalo, Lloyd, Interview. Quapaw, Oklahoma, Dec. 26, 1974.
Whitebird, Robert, Interview. Quapaw, Oklahoma, Nov. 28 and 29, 1975.

Newspapers and Periodicals

Arkansas Gazette (Little Rock)
Miami (Oklahoma) *Daily News–Record*
Missouri Gazette (St. Louis)
Muskogee (Oklahoma) *Daily Phoenix*
Niles Register
Tulsa (Oklahoma) *Tribune*
Tulsa (Oklahoma) *World*

Theses

Avery, Essie J. "The Social and Economic History of the Quapaw Indians after 1833." M.A. Thesis, Oklahoma State University, 1940.
Buford, Dora E. "A History of the Indians Under the Quapaw Agency." M.A. Thesis, University of Oklahoma, 1932.

Thomas, Marjorie. "Arkansas Post of Louisiana, 1682–1783." M.A. Thesis, San Diego State College, 1943.

Books

Abel, Annie H. *The American Indian as Slaveholder and Secessionist.* Cleveland, 1915.
———. *The American Indian as a Participant in the Civil War.* Cleveland, 1919.
———. *The American Indian Under Reconstruction.* Cleveland, 1925.
Adair, James. *The History of the American Indians.* Reprint. New York, 1966.
Alden, John R. *John Stuart and the Southern Colonial Frontier.* New York, 1966.
Allsopp, Fred W. *Folklore of Romantic Arkansas.* Vol. I. New York, 1931.
Alvord, Clarence W., ed. *Kaskaskia Records, 1778–1790.* Springfield, 1909.
———. *The Critical Period, 1763–1765.* Springfield, 1915.
———, and Clarence E. Carter, eds. *The New Regime, 1765–1767.* Springfield, 1916.
Baird, W. David. *The Chickasaw People.* Phoenix, 1974.
———. *The Osage People,* Phoenix, 1972.
Bannon, John Francis. *The Spanish Borderlands Frontier, 1513–1821.* New York, 1970.
Berlandier, Jean Louis. *The Indians of Texas in 1830.* Ed. and intro. by John C. Ewers. Washington, 1969.
Bonnin, Gertrude, C., et al. *Oklahoma's Poor Rich Indians.* Philadelphia, 1924.
Bossu, Jean–Bernard. *Travels in the Interior of North America, 1751–1762.* Trans. and ed. by Seymour Feiler. Norman, 1962.
Bushnell, David I., Jr. *Burials of the Algonquins, Siouan, and Caddoan Tribes West of the Mississippi.* Bureau of American Ethnology *Bulletin 83.* Washington, 1927.
———. *Native Villages and Village Sites East of the Mississippi.* Bureau of American Ethnology *Bulletin 69.* Washington, 1919.
———. *Villages of the Algonquian, Siouan, and Caddoan Tribes West of the Mississippi.* Bureau of American Ethnology *Bulletin 77.* Washington, 1922.
Caldwell, Joseph R. and Robert L. Hall, eds. *Hopewellian Studies, Illinois State Museum Scientific Papers.* Vol. XII. Springfield, 1964.
Caughey, John. *Bernado de Galvez in Louisiana, 1776–1783.* Berkeley, 1934.
[Champigny, Jean Chevalier de]. *The Present State of the Country and*

inhabitants, Europeans and Indians, of Louisiana, on the north continent of America. London, 1744.

Charlevoix, Pierre de. *Journal of a Voyage to North America.* Vol. II. Reprint, Ann Arbor, 1966.

Clarke, Mary Whatley. *Chief Bowles and the Texas Cherokees.* Norman, 1972.

Cohen, Felix. *Handbook of Federal Indian Law.* Washington, 1942.

Collot, Victor, *A Journey in North America.* Vols. I and II. Paris, 1826.

Cox, Isaac Joslin, ed. *The Journeys of Rene Robert Cavelier Sieur de LaSalle*, Vols. I and II. New York, 1905–1906.

Crane, Verner. *The Southern Frontier, 1670–1732.* Philadelphia, 1929.

Crawford, Samuel J. *Before the Department of Justice in Re Sale of Quapaw lands to Walter T. Apple: Brief and Argument.* Washington, 1906.

Debo, Angie. *And Still the Waters Run: The Betrayal of the Five Civilized Tribes.* 2nd ed. Princeton, 1972.

———. *The Road to Disappearance.* Norman, 1941.

Du Pratz, Le Page. *The History of Louisiana.* Reprint. New Orleans, 1947.

Farnham, Thomas J. *Travels in the Great Western Prairies.* Vol. XXVIII in R. G. Thwaites, *Early Western Travels (q.v.).*

Fletcher, Alice C. and Francis La Flesche. *The Omaha Tribe.* Bureau of American Ethnology *Twenty–seventh Annual Report, 1905–06.* Washington, 1911.

Ford, James A. *Menard Site: The Quapaw Village of Osotouy on the Arkansas River, Anthropological Papers of the American Museum of Natural History,* Vol. XLVIII, Pt. 2, New York, 1961.

Foreman, Grant, ed. *A Pathfinder in the Southwest.* Norman, 1941.

———, ed. *A Traveler in Indian Territory, The Journal of Ethan Allen Hitchcock, late Major–General in the United States Army.* Cedar Rapids, 1930.

———. *Advancing the Frontier, 1830–1880.* Norman, 1933.

———, ed. *Adventure on Red River.* Norman, 1937.

———. *Indians and Pioneers: The Story of the American Southwest before 1830.* New Haven, 1930.

———. *The Five Civilized Tribes.* Norman, 1934.

———. *The Last Trek of the Indians.* Chicago, 1946.

French, Benjamin, ed. *Historical Collections of Louisiana.* Vols. I, II, and III. New York, 1846.

Galpin, S. A. *Report upon the Conditions and Management of Certain Indian Agencies in the Indian Territory now under the Supervision of the Orthodox Friends.* Washington, 1877.

Garraghan, Gilvert J. *The Jesuits of the Middle United States.* Vol. II. New York, 1938.

Gibson, Arrell M. *Oklahoma: A History of Five Centuries.* Norman, 1965.
———. *The Chickasaws.* Norman, 1971.
———. *Wilderness Bonanza: The Tri-State District of Missouri, Kansas, and Oklahoma.* Norman, 1972.
Giraud, Marcel, *A History of French Louisiana: The Reign of Louis XIV, 1698–1715.* Trans. by Joseph C. Lambert. Baton Rouge, 1974.
Gorenstein, Shirley, ed. *North America.* New York, 1975.
Graves, W. W. *Life and Letters of Rev. Father John Schoenmakers, S. J., Apostle to the Osages.* Parsons, Kansas, 1928.
Hennepin, Father Louis. *A Description of Louisiana.* Trans. by John G. Shea. Reprint. Ann Arbor, 1966.
Hill, Edward E. *The Office of Indian Affairs, 1824–1880: Historical Sketches.* New York, 1974.
Hodge, F. W. *Handbook of American Indians North of Mexico.* Vol. II. Bureau of American Ethnology *Bulletin 30.* Washington, 1910.
Hyde, George E. *Indians of the Woodlands: From Prehistoric Times to 1725.* Norman, 1962.
———. *The Pawnee Indians.* 2nd ed. Norman, 1973.
Imlay, Gilbert. *A Topographical Description of the Western Territory of North America.* Reprint of 3rd ed. [1797]. New York, 1969.
Jackson, Donald. *The Journals of Zebulon Montgomery Pike.* Vol. II. Norman, 1966.
Joutel, Henri. *A Journal of the Last Voyage Perform'd by Monsr. de la Salle.* Reprint. New York, [1969].
Kellogg, Louise Phelps, ed. *Early Narratives of the Northwest, 1634–99.* New York, 1917.
Kelsey, Rayner Wickersham. *Friend and the Indians, 1655–1917.* Philadelphia, 1917.
Kinnaird, Lawrence, ed. *Spain in the Mississippi Valley, 1765–1794, Annual Report for the American Historical Association for 1945.* Vols. I, II, and III. Washington, 1946.
LaBarre, Weston. *The Peyote Cult, Yale University Publications in Anthropology, No. 19.* New Haven, 1938.
Lewis, Anna. *Along the Arkansas.* Dallas, 1932.
Lowery, Woodbury. *The Spanish Settlements Within the Present Limits of the United States. 1513–1561.* New York, 1901.
McDermott, John Francis, ed. *Frenchmen and Frenchways in the Mississippi Valley.* Urbana, 1969.
———, ed. *The Western Journals of Dr. George Hunter, 1796–1805, Transactions of the American Philosophical Society.* Vol. LIII, Pt. 4. Philadelphia, 1963.

McDowell, William L., ed. *Documents Relating to Indian Affairs, 1754–1765.* Columbia, South Carolina, 1970.

Margry, Pierre. *Discoveries and Settlements of the French in Western and Southern North America, 1614–1754.* Vols. I, II and III. Unpublished trans. in Burton Historical Collection, Detroit Public Library.

Marquette, Jacques. *Voyages of Marquette, in The Jesuit Relations, 59.* Ann Arbor, 1966.

Mathews, John Joseph. *The Osages, Children of the Middle Waters.* Norman, 1961.

Miner, H. Craig. *The Corporation and the Indian: Tribal Sovereignty and Industrial Civilization in Indian Territory, 1865–1907.* Columbia, Missouri, 1976.

Monette, John W. *History and the Discovery and Settlement of the Valley of the Mississippi.* Vols. I and II. New York, 1846.

Morse, Jedediah. *A Report to the Secretary of War of the United States on Indian Affairs,* [1822]. Reprint. New York, 1970.

Murphy, Edmund R. *Henry de Tonty, Fur Trader of the Mississippi.* Baltimore, 1941.

Nasatir, Abraham P., ed. *Before Lewis and Clark,* Vols. I and II. St. Louis, 1952.

———. *Spanish War Vessels on the Mississippi, 1792–1796.* New Haven, 1968.

Nuttall, Thomas. *A Journal of Travels into the Arkansas Territory.* Vol. XIII in R. G. Thwaites, *Early Western Travels (q.v.).*

Parkman, Francis. *LaSalle and the Discovery of the Great West.* Boston, 1903.

Peckham, Howard H. *Pontiac and the Indian Uprising.* Princeton, 1947.

Phillips, Philip, et al. *Archaelogical Survey in the Lower Mississippi Alluvial Valley, 1904–1947, Papers of the Peabody Museum of American Archaeology and Ethnology.* Vol. XXV. Cambridge, 1951.

Pittman, Philip. *Present State of European Settlements on the Mississippi.* Reprint. Cleveland, 1906.

Pope, John. *A Tour Through the Southern and Western Territories of the United States.* Richmond, 1792.

Riggs, Stephen R. *Dakota Grammar, Texts, and Ethnography, Contributions to North American Ethnology.* Vol. IX. Ed. by J. Owen Dorsey. Washington, 1893.

Robertson, James A., ed. and trans. *Louisiana Under the Rule of Spain, France, and the United States, 1785–1807.* Vols. I and II. Cleveland, 1911.

Romans, Bernard. *A Concise Natural History of East and West Florida.* Vol. I. New York, 1975.

Rowland, Dunbar, ed. *Mississippi Provincial Archives, 1763–1766: English Dominion.* Vol. I. Nashville, 1911.

————, and Albert G. Sanders, eds. *Mississippi Provincial Archives, French Dominion.* Vols. I, II, and III. Jackson, Mississippi, 1927–32.

Rowland, Eron Opha. *Life, Letters and Papers of William Dunbar.* Jackson, Mississippi, 1930.

Schoolcraft, Henry R. *History of the Indian Tribes of the United States.* Vol. I. Philadelphia, 1857.

Shea, John G. *A History of the Catholic Church in the United States.* Vol. I of 4 vols. New York, 1886–92.

————. *Catholic Missions Among the Indian Tribes of the United States.* Reprint. New York, 1969.

————, ed. *Discovery and Exploration of the Mississippi Valley.* 2nd ed. Albany, 1903.

————, ed. *Early Voyages Up and Down The Mississippi.* Albany, 1861.

Smith, Jane F., and Robert M. Kvasnicka, eds. *Indian-White Relations: A Persistent Paradox.* Washington, 1976.

Stephens, H. M., and Herbert E. Bolton, eds. *The Pacific Ocean in History.* New York, 1917.

Stoddard, Amos. *Sketches, historical and descriptive, of Louisiana.* Philadelphia, 1812.

Surrey, N. M. Miller, *Calendar of Manuscripts in Paris Archives and Libraries Relating to the History of the Mississippi Valley to 1803.* Vols. I and II. Washington, 1926–28.

Swanton, John R. *Indian Tribes of the Lower Mississippi Valley and Adjacent Coast of the Gulf of Mexico.* Bureau of American Ethnology *Bulletin 43.* Washington, 1911.

————. *Source Material on the History and Ethnology of the Caddo Indians.* Bureau of American Ethnology *Bulletin 132.* Washington, 1942.

————. *The Indian Tribes of North America.* Bureau of American Ethnology *Bulletin 145.* Washington, 1952.

————. *The Indians of the Southeastern United States.* Bureau of American Ethnology *Bulletin 137.* Washington, 1946.

Thompson, Vern E. *Brief History of the Quapaw Tribe of Indians.* Joplin, Missouri, 1937.

Thwaites, Reuben Gold, ed. *Early Western Travels, 1748–1846.* . . . 32 vols. Cleveland, 1904–1907.

————, ed. *The Jesuit Relations and Allied Documents.* 73 vols. Cleveland, 1896–1901.

Tonti, Henri de. *Relation of Henri de Tonty Concerning the Explorations of LaSalle from 1678 to 1683.* Trans. by Melville B. Anderson. Chicago, 1898.

Tyler, S. Lyman. *A History of Indian Policy.* Washington, 1973.

Washburn, Wilcomb E. *The Indian in America.* New York, 1975.

Whitaker, Arthur P. *The Spanish–American Frontier, 1783–1795*. Boston, 1927.

Wilson, Charles Banks, ed. *Quapaw Agency Indians*. Miami, Oklahoma, 1947.

Wright, Muriel H. *A Guide to the Indian Tribes of Oklahoma*. Norman, 1951.

Articles

Abel, Annie H. "The History of Events Resulting in Indian Consolidation West of the Mississippi," American Historical Association, *Annual Report, 1906*, 1908.

Ashcraft, Ginger L. "Antoine Barraque and His Involvement in Indian Affairs of Southeast Arkansas, 1816–1832," *The Arkansas Historical Quarterly*, Vol. XXXII (Autumn, 1973), 226–40.

Baird, W. David. "Fort Smith and the Red Man," *The Arkansas Historical Quarterly*, Vol. XXX (Winter, 1971), 337–48.

——. "The Reduction of a People: The Quapaw Removal, 1824–1834," *Red River Valley Historical Review*, Vol. I (Spring, 1974), 21–36.

Barnes, Lela, ed. "An Editor Looks at Early–Day Kansas: The Letters of Charles Monroe Chase—Concluded," *The Kansas Historical Quarterly*, Vol. XXVI (Autumn, 1960), 267–301.

Chapman, B. B. "An Interim Report on Site of the Battle of Round Mountain," *The Chronicles of Oklahoma*, Vol. XXVIII (Winter, 1950–51), 492–94.

——. "Establishment of the Iowa Reservation," *The Chronicles of Oklahoma*, Vol. XXI (Dec., 1943), 366–77.

Corbitt, D. C. and Roberta Corbitt, eds. "Papers from the Spanish Archives Relating to Tennessee and the Old Southwest, 1783–1800," *East Tennessee Historical Society Publications*, Vol. IX (1937), 111–42, and Vol. X (1938), 128–55.

Crane, Verner W. "The Tennessee River as the Road to Carolina," *Mississippi Valley Historical Review*, Vol. III (June, 1916), 3–18.

Danziger, Edmund J., Jr. "The Office of Indian Affairs and the Problem of Civil War Indian Refugees in Kansas," *The Kansas Historical Quarterly*, Vol. XXXV (Autumn, 1969), 257–75.

Delanglez, Jean. "M. LeMaire on Louisiana," *Mid-America*, Vol. XIX (April, 1937), 124–52.

——. "Tonti Letters," *Mid-America*, Vol. XXI (1939), 209–38.

Dorsey, James Owen, "A Study of Siouan Cults," Bureau of American Ethnology *Eleventh Annual Report, 1889–1890* (1894), 351–544.

———. "Camping Circles of Siouan Tribes," *American Anthropologist,* Vol. II, o.s. (April, 1889), 175–77.

———. "Kwapa Folk Lore," *The Journal of American Folk Lore,* Vol. VIII (Jan.–Mar., 1895), 130–31.

———. "Migrations of Siouan Tribes," *The American Naturalist,* Vol. XX (Mar., 1886), 211–22.

———. "Siouan Sociology," Bureau of American Ethnology *Fifteenth Annual Report, 1893–94* (1897), 205–44.

Douglas, Walter B. "The Sieurs de St. Ange," *Transactions of the Illinois State Historical Society, 1909* (1910), 135–53.

Falconer, W. A. "Arkansas and the Jesuits in 1727—A Translation," *Publications of the Arkansas Historical Association,* Vol. IV (1917), 351–78.

Faye, Stanley. "The Arkansas Post of Louisiana: French Domination," *The Louisiana Historical Quarterly,* Vol. XXVI (July, 1943), 633–721.

———. "The Arkansas Post of Louisiana: Spanish Domination," *The Louisiana Historical Quarterly,* Vol. XXVII (July, 1944), 629–716.

Foreman, Carolyn Thomas. "Education Among the Quapaws, 1829–1875," *The Chronicles of Oklahoma,* Vol. XXV (Spring, 1947), 15–29.

———. "Lewis Francis Hadley: The Long Haired Sign Talker," *The Chronicles of Oklahoma,* Vol. XXVII (Spring, 1949), 41–55.

———. "The Armstrongs of Indian Territory," *The Chronicles of Oklahoma,* Vol. XXXI (Autumn, 1952), 292–308, and (Winter, 1952–53), 420–53.

———. "The Choctaw Academy," *The·Chronicles of Oklahoma,* Vol. VIII (March, 1932), 77–114.

Foreman, Grant, ed. "The Journal of the Proceedings at Our First Treaty with the Wild Indians, 1835," *The Chronicles of Oklahoma,* Vol. XIV (Dec., 1936), 393–418.

Gibson, A. M. "An Indian Territory United Nations: The Creek Council of 1845," *The Chronicles of Oklahoma,* Vol. XXXIX (Winter, 1961–62), 398–413.

———. "Leasing of Quapaw Mineral Lands," *The Chronicles of Oklahoma,* Vol. XXXV (Autumn, 1957), 338–47.

Glover, W. B. "A History of the Caddo Indians," *The Louisiana Historical Quarterly,* Vol. XVIII (Oct., 1935), 872–946.

Hardin, J. Fair. "An Outline of Shreveport and Caddo Parrish History," *The Louisiana Historical Quarterly,* Vol. XVIII (Oct., 1935), 759–871.

Harris, Frank H. "Neosho Agency, 1838–1871,' *The Chronicles of Oklahoma,* Vol. XLIII (Spring, 1965), 35–57.

———. "Seneca Sub-Agency, 1832–1838," *The Chronicles of Oklahoma,* Vol. XLII (Summer, 1964), 75–94.

Herndon, Dallas T. "When the Quapaws Went to Red River—A Translation," *Publications of the Arkansas Historical Association*, Vol. IV (1917), 326–31.

Hoffman, Michael P. "The Kinkead–Mainard Site, 3PU2: A Late Prehistoric Quapaw Phase Site Near Little Rock, Arkansas," *The Arkansas Archeologist*, Vols. XVI, XVII, XVIII (1975–76–77), 1–41.

Jackson, Joe C. "Schools Among the Minor Tribes in Indian Territory," *The Chronicles of Oklahoma*, Vol. XXXII (Spring, 1954), 58–69.

Kehoe, Sister Mary Urban. "The Educational Activities of Distinguished Catholic Missionaries among the Five Civilized Tribes," *The Chronicles of Oklahoma*, Vol. XXIV (Summer, 1946), 166–82.

Kelley, E. H. "The Trail in Ottawa County," *The Chronicles of Oklahoma*, Vol. XXXI (Autumn, 1953), 324–31.

La Flesche, Francis. "Omaha and Osage Traditions of Separation," *Proceedings of the Nineteenth International Congress of Americanists* (1917), 459–62.

Lewis, Anna, ed. "Fort Charles, III, Arkansas: Reports for the Year 1783," *Mississippi Valley Historical Review*, Vol. XX (Mar. 1934), 537–49.

Lucey, J. M. "The Catholic Church in Arkansas," *Publications of the Arkansas Historical Association*, Vol. II (1908), 424–61.

Lyon, Owen. "The Trail of the Quapaw," *The Arkansas Historical Quarterly*, Vol. IX (Autumn, 1950), 205–13.

McGee, W. J. "The Siouan Indians: A Preliminary Sketch," Bureau of American Ethnology *Fifteenth Annual Report, 1893–94* (1897), 157–204.

Morris, Wayne, "Traders and Factories on the Arkansas Frontier, 1805–1822," *The Arkansas Historical Quarterly*, Vol. XXVIII (Spring, 1969), 28–48.

Morton, Ohland. "The Confederate States Government and the Five Civilized Tribes, Part II," *The Chronicles of Oklahoma*, Vol. XXXI (Autumn, 1953), 299–322.

Nasatir, A. P. and Ernest R. Liljegren. "Material Relating to the History of the Mississippi Valley," *The Louisiana Historical Quarterly*, Vol. XXI (Jan., 1936), 5–75.

Nicholson, William. "A Tour of Indian Agencies in Kansas and the Indian Territory in 1870," *The Kansas Historical Quarterly*, Vol. III (Aug., 1934), 289–384.

Nieberding, Velma, ed. "A Trip to Quapaw in 1903," *The Chronicles of Oklahoma*, Vol. XXXI (Summer, 1953), 142–67.

———. "St. Mary's of the Quapaws," *The Chronicles of Oklahoma*, Vol. XXXI (Spring, 1953), 2–14.

———. "The Strange Power of Peyote," *The West*, Vol. II (Feb., 1965), 30–33 and 69–70.

"Official Correspondence of Governor Izard, 1825–26," *Publications of the Arkansas Historical Association*, Vol. I (1906), 423–54.

Plaisance, Aloysius. "The Arkansas Factory, 1805–1810," *The Arkansas Historical Quarterly*, Vol. XI (Autumn, 1952), 184–200.

Powell, John W. "Indian Linguistic Families of America North of Mexico," Bureau of American Ethnology *Seventh Annual Report, 1885–86* (1891), 1–142.

Reynolds, John Hugh. "Aboriginal and Indian Remains," *Publications of the Arkansas Historical Association*, Vol. I (1906), 274–77.

Russell, Orpha. "EKVN-HV'LWUCE: Site of Oklahoma's First Civil War Battle," *The Chronicles of Oklahoma*, Vol. XXIX (Winter, 1951–52), 401–407.

Snyder, John P. "Captain John Baptiste Saucier," *Transactions of the Illinois State Historical Society, 1919* (1920), 216–63.

Stewart, Martha. "The Indian Mission Conference of Oklahoma," *The Chronicles of Oklahoma*, Vol. XL (Winter, 1962–63), 330–36.

"The Quapaws," *The Indian Sentinel* (1904–1905), 40–48.

Thompson, Vern E. "A History of the Quapaws," *The Chronicles of Oklahoma*, Vol. XXXIII (Autumn, 1955), 360–83.

Tracy, Valerie. "The Indian in Transition: The Neosho Agency, 1850–1861," *The Chronicles of Oklahoma*, Vol. XLVIII (Summer, 1970), 164–83.

Vaughn, Myra McAlmont. "Habitat of the Quapaw Indians," *Publications of the Arkansas History Association*, Vol. II (1908), 521–30.

Weer, Paul, "Passamaquoddy and Quapaw Mnemonic Records," *Proceedings of the Indiana Academy of Science*, Vol. LV (1945), 29–32.

Wright, Muriel H. "A Report to the General Council of the Indian Territory Meeting at Okmulgee in 1873," *The Chronicles of Oklahoma*, Vol. XXXIV (Spring, 1956), 7–16.

———, and George Shirk. "Artist Möllhausen in Oklahoma—1853," *The Chronicles of Oklahoma*, Vol. XXXI (Winter, 1953–54), 392–441.

———. "The Journal of Lieutenant A. W. Whipple," *The Chronicles of Oklahoma*, Vol. XXVIII (Autumn, 1950), 235–83.

INDEX